COMPARING THE SOCIAL POLICY EXPERIENCE OF BRITAIN AND TAIWAN

T0384823

Comparing the Social Policy Experience of Britain and Taiwan

Edited by
CATHERINE JONES FINER

Routledge
Taylor & Francis Group

LONDON AND NEW YORK

First published 2001 by Ashgate Publishing

Reissued 2018 by Routledge
2 Park Square, Milton Park, Abingdon, Oxon OX14 4RN
711 Third Avenue, New York, NY 10017, USA

Routledge is an imprint of the Taylor & Francis Group, an informa business

Publisher's Note
The publisher has gone to great lengths to ensure the quality of this reprint but points out that some imperfections in the original copies may be apparent.

Disclaimer
The publisher has made every effort to trace copyright holders and welcomes correspondence from those they have been unable to contact.

A Library of Congress record exists under LC control number: 00109867

ISBN 13: 978-1-138-63694-1 (hbk)
ISBN 13: 978-1-138-63696-5 (pbk)
ISBN 13: 978-1-315-20542-7 (ebk)

Contents

vii

List of Figures

List of Tables

x

List of Contributors

Pete Alcock is Professor of Social Policy and Head of the Department of Social Policy and Social Work at the University of Birmingham.

Ann Davis is Professor and Head of Social Work Studies at the University of Birmingham.

John Doling is Professor of Housing Studies at the University of Birmingham.

Hsiu-Hui Chen is Senior Specialist at the Department of Social Affairs, Ministry of the Interior, Taiwan.

Hsiao-Hung Nancy Chen is Professor and Dean of the Department of Sociology and College of Social Sciences, National Chengchi University, Taipei, Taiwan.

Catherine Jones Finer is Reader in Comparative Social Policy at the University of Birmingham.

Susan Hanley is Assistant Chief Probation Officer, West Midlands Probation Service, UK.

Yuan-shie Hwang is Associate Professor in the Department of Social Policy and Social Work, National Chi Nan University, Taiwan.

Yeun-wen Ku is Associate Professor in the Department of Social Policy and Social Work, National Chi Nan University, Taiwan.

Nick Le Mesurier is Research Associate at the Medical School, University of Birmingham.

Tony Maltby is Lecturer in Social Policy in the Department of Social Policy and Social Work, University of Birmingham.

Robert N. Matthews is a research student at the University of Birmingham.

Kate Morris is Lecturer in Social Work at the University of Birmingham.

Mike Nellis is Lecturer in the Department of Social Policy and Social Work, University of Birmingham.

Peter W. Preston is Professor of Politics at Birmingham University.

George Cheng Wang is Doctor and Professor at the National Chung-Cheng University, Taiwan.

Lih-Rong Wang is Associate Professor in the Department of Sociology, National Taiwan University.

Betty Y. Weng is Associate Professor in the Department of Youth and Child Welfare, Providence University, Taiwan.

Acknowledgements

So many people have contributed to this enterprise, it stands as a demonstration in itself of the virtues - and demands - of team effort.

Particular thanks are due to the individual contributors, for their willingness to deliver after the original conference (see below and Chapter 1) and thence revise, mostly under pressure. In this context, indeed, more than particular thanks are due to contributors from Taiwan, who contrived to keep in touch and respond to editorial queries, notwithstanding the trying, testing circumstances in which they found themselves, in the wake of the earthquake of September 1999. (Its epicentre was so close to the new National Chi Nan University as to require the evacuation of its students and staff to Taipei (some 150 kilometres to the north) for teaching purposes, in between weekends spent on reconstruction work back at the university.) The determination of those so affected to 'deliver regardless', is as much testimony to their academic commitment, as it is a humbling example to others.

We are grateful to the University of Birmingham - the Department of Social Policy and Social Work, and the School of Social Sciences - for helping to fund and organise the initial Birmingham - Taiwan Social Policy Conference, whose success inspired the preparation of this volume. In particular, Mary Knox's enterprise, patience and managerial skills in this connection proved invaluable and were much appreciated by this editor-to-be.

Finally we come to the 'book preparation team' *per se* which, on this as on previous occasions, has effectively meant Sue Gilbert - otherwise a key secretary in the Department of Social Policy and Social Work - wearing another hat. In the world of camera-ready copy it is impossible to overstate the importance and relief of being able to draw on such knowledge, experience and efficiency. Heartfelt thanks to Sue for helping to ensure this book actually 'went to market'.

INTRODUCTION

1 Editorial Introduction

CATHERINE JONES FINER

Beginnings

The immediate starting point for this book was the occasion of a Taiwan-Birmingham Social Policy and Social Work Conference, held at Birmingham University in April 1999. The novelty and success of this event generated the enthusiasm and commitment necessary for organising a publication to do justice to the papers presented and, it is hoped, to set a precedent for more such publications in the future. As far as possible, the papers have been grouped according to broad topic areas, but there has been no editorial interference with individual contributors' styles of approach or of course with their policy perspectives. Each has been free to identify a topic and thence to formulate the questions they wish to see asked and answered. As such, therefore, this collection constitutes an original contribution, in both methodological and substantive terms, to the study of comparative social policy.

Comparative social policy *per se* has been slow to develop as a truly international subject. Some of the reasons for this have been glaringly practical - difficulties of language, differences over definitions of terms and concepts, variability as to the sorts of data likely to be available, being foremost amongst them. More fundamental, however, have been problems intrinsic to the very idea of comparing social policies on other than a normative basis. 'How well are we doing, by comparison with those with whom we would wish to be compared, *according to the standards we have set for ourselves*' has certainly been the stance characteristic of social policy academics in the welfare state heartlands of Europe. To suggest that comparative social policy should be based on something other or additional to this, is in effect to strike at the very notion of social policy as embodying not merely a moral stance but - in principle, in the eyes of many champions - a moral stance of universal applicability. 'Relativism' for comparative purposes - whether in relation to specific social policy objectives or to notions of the good society *per se* - can in this context seem like a denial of values and an abnegation of concern.

3

Yet, without some measure of relativism, it is difficult to see much of a future for comparative social policy at this time, when the need for cross-national exchange - not merely with regard to the conduct of business and labour markets, but to the social support systems underpinning these - is being ever more widely appreciated. So far, the main line of response to this problem - as epitomised by Doyal and Gough's *A Theory of Human Need* (1991) - has been to try to render basic, would-be universal human values nonetheless relative to time and place for the purposes of cross-national evaluation. Ramesh Mishra's idea of universally applicable yet gradeable 'social standards' (e.g. Mishra, 1999, pp.115-131), represents another style of response to essentially the same issue. Far more taxing philosophically - though not necessarily in conflict with such attempts at baseline standard setting - is to acknowledge that, over and above respect for basic human values, notions of what constitutes 'the good society' can and will still differ, between societies of comparable economic and political sophistication. It is this latter (should-be) truism which the present collection is well placed to demonstrate, by virtue of its pairing of Britain with Taiwan.

Evolution of comparative social policy

Even amongst western nations, in the so called heydays (1950s/1960s) of the post-World War II welfare state, it was taken for granted that each country's social policy arrangements were so much an expression of its own preferences - based on national experience, collective sentiment and capacity - with regard to the nature of the good society and how best this was to be brought about, that they were not to be compared with those of any other place - and not to be thought of as readily transferable to any other place. Certainly Britain, the first to adopt the expression 'welfare state' in respect of itself, was protected by both ignorance and lack of interest from undue concern about what might be going on by way of 'social policy' in the rest of postwar western Europe (e.g. Finer 1999, pp.18-22).

Such developments in comparative social policy discourse as did begin to take place from the latter 1960s were primarily between 'friendly nations' which, in the British case - not least for linguistic and cultural reasons - meant primarily between Britain and North America (Canada as well as the USA). All were by then established as relatively low 'social spenders', and presumed to be of a relatively 'liberal' (i.e. 'hands-off') socio-moral persuasion, by continental European governmental standards. A genuinely European-based dialogue (inclusive of Britain) was slow to develop, being an eventual response to the faltering, belated attempts of the EU to develop a 'human face' and, more concretely, to pressures on other academics to find ways of communicating internationally in English.

Meanwhile, it happened that the USA and Britain were also the two western countries exercising the most direct postwar influence on the shaping of emergent and resurgent societies in post-World War II Asia Pacific: the USA as a spin-off from its military interests (in respect of Japan, Taiwan and South Korea) and Britain, by contrast, as a result of legacies of colonialism still operational in the cases of Hong Kong and Singapore, let alone Australasia (see below, Chapter 16). In other words, it has been the Anglophone, 'liberal', developed world which, for a combination of reasons, from the most accidental and pragmatic to the most deeply philosophical, seems to have contributed most, for all its own limitations, to the international recognition of East-West inter-regional relations as a key to further social policy development. It is within this scenario that the relationship between Britain and Taiwan is to be appreciated.

Britain and Taiwan as comparators

There are numerous stark contrasts to be drawn between the UK and Taiwan, historically, culturally and geo-politically. Nevertheless these two have key features in common, not least for the purposes of comparative social policy analysis. These latter characteristics have become ever more evident in their bearing upon UK-Taiwan relations in recent years. Hence the timeliness of this present exercise in mutual reflection and comparative review.

Both the UK and Taiwan can be described not merely as liberal market democracies, but as each of them offshore islands on the fringe of perceived contrasting continental notions and systems of governance. To be sure, the analogy is scarcely exact. EU Europe is supposed, by definition, to be 'liberal democratic' throughout. Nevertheless the UK remains famously 'in' Europe but not 'of' it, not least because prevailing styles of governance on the Continent are perceived as being alien to British liberal (not to say nationalistic) tradition. Indeed there are mounting voices on the right of British politics who wish to renegotiate (i.e. down-grade) even the terms and scale of the country's so far involvement in the EU.

By comparison, Taiwan has long been geographically a disputed and disputable part of China, and politically - from 1949 - a potential break-away bloc. Taiwan's main, centre-left, party of opposition (the Democratic Progressive Party) has been committed to securing formal independence for Taiwan from the communist mainland, for all that its latest election success (March 2000) is being deliberately played down with regard to its implications for relations with the Mainland.

Be all this as it may, no matter how realistic, risk-laden or otherwise may be the scenarios for 'go-it-alone' politics in each case, the mere fact of their reiteration in domestic political discourse gives the UK and Taiwan a key characteristic in common, over and above their shared, declared commitments to liberal, market values and (of late, in Taiwan's case) to democratic human rights. Not least, *both* sets of politicians and administrators have had every incentive to stress the importance and achievability of self-sustaining socio-economic-political development: which Britain's Prime Minister Blair has envisioned as a 'Stakeholder Society' (e.g. Finer, 1997, pp.305-308) and what Taiwan's officially revered mentor Sun Yat-sen had long before summed up as 'The Three Principles of the People' - namely Nationalism, Democracy and Livelihood (Sun, 1996). Of course there are and will remain glaring differences in social policy and practice between the two countries: the products not merely of historical experience and cultural background, but of present expectations and outlook, both internal and external. But such differences need not and should not preclude dialogue.

Respective patterns of development

Britain has long seen itself as the founder of the modern welfare state idea, complete with its own more particular 1940s 'wartime halo'. The British Welfare State, as legislated for from 1945, was a reward to the people for a job (World War II) well done, as well as an honouring of promises already made during the war about a better Britain to come. In such a heady climate the case for postwar *economic* reconstruction allegedly took a back seat. It was only after 20 years of so-called consensual welfare state politics and in eventual, belated, response to Britain's lack lustre economic performance and especially to the oil crisis-led economic doldrums of the 1970s, that both Britain's Conservative and especially its Labour political parties were involved in a fundamental rethinking of their positions.

Margaret Thatcher took over the leadership of the Conservative Party from Edward Heath in 1975 and then won the 1979 Election on a promise, inter alia, to roll back the burden of the welfare state - along with freeing the labour market from trades union domination and encouraging 'self-help and self respect' amongst the general population. Whatever Thatcher's actual achievements in these respects over her period in office, it took nearly twenty years for the Labour Party - *the* hitherto party of the so-called big-spending, big bureaucracy welfare state - to escape being marooned in opposition by rendering itself electable under the new, post-Thatcherite, order of the day. In effect - just as had the Conservative Party in respect of the Welfare State in 1951 - New Labour's successful claim (at last) was that 'we can run the new Britain better than you can' (e.g. Finer, 1997, p.304).

Taiwan has been moving, over the same period, from an opposite starting point, yet possibly, ultimately, in a converging social policy direction. The 1949 'settlement' of the KMT in Taiwan, under the leadership of Chiang Kai-shek, was not intended to be a permanent arrangement and was certainly not a 'victory' arrangement. Interestingly, there was not clear ideological water between the then KMT and the youthful, post Long March, Communist Party - both of which had been run along Leninist party lines - so much as a conflict of persons and personalities between Mao Tse-tung and Chiang Kai-shek. Nevertheless, the emphasis in post-1949 'occupied Taiwan' was upon, first, military-political consolidation in preparation for the supposed return of the KMT to resume control of the mainland and, second, economic regeneration geared, with the help of American aid, initially to Taiwanese agricultural self-sufficiency but subsequently (from the 1960s) to export-led economic growth, itself a high-risk proposition. The prime social policy/social welfare developments over this period concerned social insurance, in respect of those categories of people deemed vital to the survival of the system: the military, the professionals (including teachers) and essential workers in industry.

During the 1970s, however, key developments took place which bore upon Taiwan way over and above the worldwide effects of the oil price shocks. The US decided (1970) to switch its recognition of China from the government based in Taipei to the government based in Beijing. Likewise, the UN decided (1971) to have Communist China replace The Republic of China (Taiwan) as a permanent member of its Security Council. In 1975 Chiang Kai-shek died, just one year before Mao Tse-tung's death.

Altogether the world was a new place for Taiwan. Significantly, however, it was in the wake of such upheaval that the society embarked on the political and thence social policy developments which have since rendered its quality of life - not least in the eyes of its own citizens - so increasingly at odds with the lack of international recognition.

The layout of this book

As already remarked, the object has been as far as possible to pair contributions from Taiwan and from Birmingham on related topic areas, without in any way interfering with the content of their treatment.

The initial four overview chapters (two from Birmingham, two from Taiwan) offer between them such contrasting, illuminating insights into where we should be heading and how we should be getting there, as to be worthy of publication almost in their own right. Alcock's synoptic review of the development of the welfare state in Britain is nicely matched by Ku's series of rhetorical questions as to whether or not Taiwan should consider itself – or aim to be considered – as a welfare state at all. Likewise Davis' deliberately downbeat review of recent trends in social welfare service provision in Britain is followed by Chen's revelations on the attempts to 'privatise' social welfare services (from a starting point of mostly *non-existing* public provision) in Taipei city.

Following this, the paired presentations in respect of pensions and health care, respectively, are again to be welcomed precisely for their different angles and styles of approach to the topic areas in question. On the whole, the Taiwanese interest - as maybe befits a recently fast-developed society - is focused more on the economics of pension provision (Ku and Chen) and selective health insurance (Wang) than on the niceties of 'thinking the unthinkable' with regard to *existing* pensions provision (Maltby) or on the operational dilemmas facing an *existing*, ageing NHS (Matthews).

After which, the section 'Family and community care and control' covers a multitude of topics and points of interest, precisely because priorities in this area were freely nominated rather than specified in advance. Nevertheless there are interestingly paired papers dealing with different aspects of family policy (Weng and Morris); and three (Wang, Hwang and Le Mesurier) dealing with key issues relating to care in the community for elderly people. After which, again, we have a British contribution on the treatment of young offenders in the community

(Hanley and Nellis) which could conceivably offer ideas to Taiwan with regard to a problem as yet 'under-experienced' on its own account.

The collection concludes with a British pair of papers (Doling and Finer, and Preston) reflecting, from different disciplinary perspectives, on the shifting state of West-East and East-West social scientists' understanding with particular reference to social welfare. Herein, it is to be hoped, may lie some strategic pointers for the future.

References

Doyal, L. and Gough I. (1991), *A Theory of Human Need,* Macmillan, Basingstoke.

Finer, C. Jones (1999), 'Trends and Developments in Welfare States' in Jochen Clasen (ed) *Comparative Social Policy: Concepts, Theories and Methods*, Blackwell, Oxford.

Finer, C. Jones (1997), 'Social Policy' in Patrick Dunleavy, Andrew Gamble, Ian Holliday, Gillian Peele (eds) *Developments in British Politics, 5*, Macmillan, Basingstoke.

Mishra R. (1999), *Globalization and the Welfare State*, Edward Elgar, Cheltenham, UK.

Sun, Yat-sen (2nd edition) (1996), *San Min Chu I: The Three Principles of the People; with two supplementary chapters by Chiang Kai-shek*, Government Information Office, Taipei.

PART I
OVERVIEW OF TRENDS IN SOCIAL POLICY AND SOCIAL SERVICES DELIVERY

2 The development of the British welfare state

PETE ALCOCK

Overview

The first point to understand, for an international audience, about welfare policy in the United Kingdom is that the UK is, in practice, made up of four 'subnations' with varying degrees of autonomy over policy development and delivery. This is particularly true of Northern Ireland (part of the UK, but not of Britain) which has separate administration of many aspects of policy and is currently undergoing significant political changes to restructure the nature of that autonomy. But it is also true of Scotland (which has a separate legal system, and many different institutions and policy initiatives) and Wales (which has less autonomy, but is also administered through a separate government office), both of which are developing new national assemblies which will have a number of devolved powers.

When writing about national policy developments, therefore, one has to be careful to be clear how far such developments extend across all four subnations. In the welfare field, however, much policy is common - for instance, in health, education and social security - and this is especially the case within mainland Britain. For the most part, therefore, we will be discussing policy development within Britain (meaning England, Wales and Scotland), although by and large similar arrangements also apply in Northern Ireland.

A century of change

Welfare policy in Britain can be traced back to the early years of the nineteenth century, and indeed beyond that to the onset of industrialisation and capitalist economic relations in the seventeenth century. We cannot explore such a distant and detailed history here. However, we can set an understanding of current, and prospective, welfare policies within the context of the key political, economic and ideological developments of the twentieth century. This historical context can be divided loosely into six broad stages of development:

- *Early reform:* during the first two decades of the twentieth century a new role for the state in providing welfare services for a wider range of citizens was introduced in a number of key areas. These included: social security through state insurance for pensions, unemployment and sickness; primary education (up to 12) in local state schools; the establishment of a ministry of health; and the beginning of the building of public sector housing to rent.
- *Responding to recession:* between the two world wars Britain, in common with most other western industrial nations, experienced severe economic recession. Although there was some piecemeal growth in welfare services during this period, the pressure of social need meant that in many areas limited public provision could not meet expected public demand, leading to some cuts (for instance, in social security benefits in 1930) and much suffering.
- *The post-war welfare state:* in the late 1940s, following the end of the Second World War, the new Labour government in Britain engaged in the most significant and rapid period of welfare reform in the century. During this period, as we shall discuss below, public services providing near universal coverage for most welfare needs were introduced with widespread popular and political support. The period is often credited as having established a 'welfare state' within Britain.
- *Incremental growth:* throughout the 1950s and 1960s a political consensus over the desirability of state welfare was allied to long a period of economic boom, and this resulted in gradual growth in welfare provision and welfare expenditure within the services established by the post-war reforms. Between 1951 and 1976 welfare spending on education, health and social security grew as a proportion of gross domestic product (GDP) from 11 to 22 per cent.
- *Containment and retrenchment:* in the mid-1970s the long post-war boom came to an end and economic and political priorities altered sharply in Britain. In the 1980s a Conservative government openly hostile to the collective values of state welfare provision was in power, the proportionate rise in welfare spending was halted and significant reforms were introduced to privatise and marketise welfare provision.
- *The new welfare mix:* at the end of the twentieth century state welfare

provision remains significant and widespread, despite the cutbacks of the 1980s. Nevertheless other private, voluntary and informal forms of welfare provision have been openly encouraged and major changes have been introduced into public welfare provision, leading to a new mix of welfare services; and this more eclectic approach has been embraced by the new Labour government elected in 1997, which has championed a 'third way' between state monopoly welfare and private market provision.

The changes outlined here are discussed in more detail in books examining the history of welfare development in Britain, in particular Glennerster (1995), Thane (1996), and Page and Silburn (1999). Despite the shifts in both policy and ideology, however, there are significant continuities within British welfare policy, especially when compared with policy developments in other countries throughout the developed world. Britain does provide a paradigm case of the Anglo-Saxon welfare model, sometimes also referred to as the 'Beveridgean welfare state'.

From this perspective British welfare provision is associated most closely with the major national reforms of the late 1940s and the establishment of universal, redistributive, national welfare services. The clearest exposition of the rationale behind these reforms was provided by the Beveridge Report of 1942. In his report Beveridge outlined a plan for a peculiarly British social insurance scheme for social security, but he also talked about the need for comprehensive health and education services and for state support for full employment (for men). His ideas were largely taken up by the post-war Labour government; and, despite the reforms which have been made since then, the basic structure of much of the Beveridge vision remains in place in the country.

The British welfare state

The British welfare reforms of the 1940s were based upon both policy and political alliances. In policy terms the creation of the welfare state involved significant changes to both economic and social policy. Beveridge's report on social insurance envisaged a commitment to social policy provision through the state in order to guarantee that key welfare needs were met for all citizens. He characterised this graphically as the combating of five great social 'evils' - want, disease, ignorance, squalor and idleness. These were to be removed from post-war society through new policy initiatives - comprehensive social security protection, free state education, a national health service, public housing for all who wanted it, and employment for working-age men.

The social policy changes needed to deliver on these promises, and more, were introduced by the post-war Labour government. However, the last promise, in particular, involved a change also in economic policy, to utilise state involvement and state investment to boost economic activity and ensure full employment. This broad strategy of 'demand management' had been advocated by a contemporary of Beveridge's, the economist Keynes. The marrying of such strategies for economic growth with the public provision of social welfare was referred to by some as the Keynes/Beveridge approach (see Cutler et al, 1986). Of course, welfare reform also supported economic growth, for instance, providing a healthier and better educated workforce for the growing manufacturing industries. It was a virtuous circle which seemed over the next two decades to have produced the success of well-being for all within a broadly capitalist economy; and, although it was not without its critics, even socialist commentators pointed to the ways in which welfare policy could co-exist with capitalist economic growth (Gough, 1979).

It is perhaps not surprising, therefore, that this joint policy approach attracted ideological and practical support across a wide spectrum of political opinion. In particular the Keynes/Beveridge approach was supported by both the major parties of government - indeed it even attracted a pseudonym, *Butskellism*, based on an amalgam of the names of the Labour chancellor of the exchequer, Gaitskell, and his Conservative successor in 1951, Butler. Butskellism within the political sphere meant that social policy development would continue along similar lines to cement welfare policy within the British social order in the latter half of the twentieth century. And over the next few decades from the 1950s to the mid-1970s welfare provision continued to grow and develop in Britain, within the organisational structures established in the post-war welfare state.

Containment and retrenchment

The steady growth in welfare provision and social expenditure in the decades following the post-war reforms in Britain were accompanied, as they were in all developed countries, by a period of sustained economic boom. In a growing economy, meeting increased demands for welfare from expanding public services was a relatively painless process; and expenditure grew dramatically over three decades in both absolute and relative terms.

In the mid-1970s, however, the long boom came to an abrupt end, precipitated by the oil price rise of 1973. This had significant consequences for social policy throughout the world, as the other chapters in this collection reveal. In Britain, however, its consequences were particularly far-reaching, especially as they were accompanied at the end of the 1970s by the election to power of a right-wing Conservative government, which openly rejected the Butskellite consensus on welfare and argued that the response to the crisis required a change in direction for social policy. In essence, therefore, Britain became a paradigm example of changing welfare policy.

The problems caused for social policy by the economic crisis of the mid-1970s have been analysed by a wide range of welfare theorists. In Britain, however, it was a 'New Right' analysis which seemed to hold sway, especially amongst the leading members of the Thatcher governments of the 1980s. Their view was encapsulated in the 'overload thesis' developed by Bacon and Eltis (1976), which in simple terms argued that welfare needs would exert an ever-upward pressure on social expenditure and that at times of economic stagnation this would crowd out capital investment leading to an ever-worsening crisis in growth. The response to this, the New Right argued, was to cut welfare expenditure in order to provide resources for capital investment to grow; and such cuts in planned expenditure were forced on the UK government in the 1970s by the International Monetary Fund (IMF).

In the 1980s the overload thesis was given a political and ideological legitimacy by the Thatcher governments. These justified attempts to cut social spending by arguing that in any event public provision of welfare was too extensive, encouraging dependency on the state and restricting choice and diversity in the delivery of services. It was this political and ideological assault on state welfare which made the British experience of reform and retrenchment so dramatic. In Britain, it might be argued, social policy changed direction after the crisis of the 1970s with reforms of state welfare that went beyond the mere curtailment of costs - although in practice reductions in costs were not really achieved, and the reforms led to changes in the structure and operation of state welfare services rather than the wholesale abandonment of them.

The Thatcher governments of the 1980s pursued a number of policy goals aimed both at reducing the scope of state welfare and at reforming its internal structures. Key themes here included elements of privatisation of services, centralisation of control over resources and policy-planning, and encouragement of inequality as a means of promoting economic growth (see Johnson, 1990). In particular after the third election victory in 1987 the government sought to import market mechanisms into state services themselves. This involved the restructuring of health, education and social services to introduce *quasi-markets*, which were intended to make the allocation of resources responsive to consumer preferences and demands (Le Grand and Bartlett, 1993). These reforms changed welfare services; and, although they did not reduce absolute social spending, they did lead to a steadying of expenditure levels against overall GDP, which remained at 22 per cent between 1981 and 1991.

Under the Major government, which followed Thatcher's fall from the Conservative leadership in 1990, the proportion of expenditure began gradually to rise again. More generally, although Major inherited – and continued – a large part of the Thatcher legacy of welfare restructuring, he sought to restore some political faith in public services and public welfare planning. This could be seen, for instance, in his championing of 'Citizen's Charters' as a means of promoting accountable public services. Thus the Major governments were not simply a continuation of Thatcherite retrenchment (see Alcock, 1997); and to some extent they began to set the scene for the new period of welfare reform, which was to follow the 1997 election.

New Labour and the new welfare mix

Nevertheless, for most people in Britain, supporters and critics alike, the election of the new Labour government in May 1997 suggested a change in direction for welfare policy within the country, although the debate over Labour's new direction for welfare policy is a complex one, and should be seen within a broader historical and geographical context. The rethinking was begun in earnest after the 1992 election by the Social Justice Commission set up by the late John Smith (Borrie, 1994). By this time it was also clear that the pressures on welfare policy were affecting all developed capitalist societies. Esping-Andersen's (1996) analysis revealed that by the beginning of the 1990s all welfare states were 'in transition', with all welfare commitments under review. In this wider international context Britain in fact emerged as a low-welfare country in European terms, although not when compared to North America and the Far East (see table 2.1).

Table 2.1 Public social security and health expenditure as a percentage of gross GDP in 1990

Sweden	33.1	Canada	18.8
Denmark	27.8	New Zealand*	17.9
France	26.5	United States	14.6
Germany	23.5	Japan*	12.2
United Kingdom	22.3	Australia*	9.2
* 1986			

Source: Adapted from Esping-Andersen, 1996, table 1.1.

As a result of this, welfare policy was a key political priority for New Labour in their election manifesto, and they made a range of high-profile promises to improve on the service delivery targets achieved by the past Conservative governments. In fact, however, the detailed election promises did not drive the policy agenda, even in the early years of office; and the commitments to such things as cutting class sizes and waiting lists proved to be controversial to measure and difficult to achieve. Indeed it was the new government's commitments to pursue prudence in economic and fiscal policy and to undertake a longer term review of welfare policy and public spending, which actually dominated political and policy debate - and, in particular, the extent to which this represented the development of a third way for welfare reform.

The third way

The idea that Labour policy on welfare is based on a third way, between the alternatives of state socialism and the free market which dominated policy development over the past century, is one associated directly with the new prime minister (see Blair, 1998). However, it is in part, at least, also a direct descendant of the Social Justice Commission's review of social policy after the 1992 election (Borrie, 1994). In their report the Commission sought to characterise approaches under three broad groupings:

- *Levellers:* the old Labour left, concerned to use public services and benefits to redistribute from rich to poor;
- *Deregulators:* the New Right advocates of the free market and private protection;

- *Investors:* using public resources to invest in opportunities for all in order to improve economic competitiveness.

The Commission endorsed the third approach, and it is a broadly similar distinction which New Labour has since sought to capture in distancing itself from the welfare statism of old Labour and the free marketeering of the Thatcherite Conservatives. To some extent this is an endorsement of the need for social policy and social spending to be developed within the context of an economic policy geared to ensure economic growth within the new competitive global market - summed in one word, *prudence*, by the chancellor, Gordon Brown. However, it is also informed by a new, and perhaps distinctive, ideology of welfare – 'prudence for a purpose'.

Labour's purpose in welfare reform, and the third way which it is claimed this represents, can be identified by both positive and negative characteristics. The positive characteristics of the third way are the endorsement of a mixed economy of welfare services and the partnership in policy planning and delivery that is implicit in this, the active promotion of equality of opportunity, and the belief in the broader values of welfare spending as an investment in 'social capital'. The negative characteristics are to do with what the third way is not. It is not a return to old Labour policies of tax and spend, redistribution to achieve (spurious) equality and producer-dominated monopoly public services; and it is not the New Right credo of free market deregulation, privatisation, contracting-out and individual self-protection.

Endorsement of a mixed economy of welfare providers is at one level merely recognition of the real diversity in social provision which exists within Britain's 'welfare state'. Public services were developed and have always co-existed alongside the private, voluntary and informal sectors. Thatcherism may have altered the balance slightly between these; but it was a shifting balance in any case, which Labour is merely adjusting more openly. An important feature of the new balance which Labour is seeking to achieve can be found in their promotion of partnership. What is being promoted here is a revitalisation of the old notion of 'civil society', within which all partners, and all citizens, have mutual interests and obligations in securing local social and economic progress.

Linked to this is Labour's approach to the problem of inequality. They eschew the egalitarian ideals of redistributive policies aimed at equality of outcome, in favour of a more dynamic model of equality of opportunity. However, the dynamism in the model recognises the barriers which some may face in competing equally for the opportunities on offer, especially where these operate cumulatively over time to reduce individual, or whole community, life chances. Investment in social capital to promote equality of opportunity is also not a new idea, of course. Welfare spending on areas such as education, health and social security to support economic growth has been a central feature of recent analysis of the role of welfare spending in buttressing competitiveness in welfare capitalist economies (see Pfaller et al, 1991; Esping-Andersen, 1996). What Labour has now done is incorporate these dual values of welfare - individual protection and collective growth - into a virtuous circle, which contrasts starkly with the contradictory tension exemplified by the New Right fears of public welfare crowding out private initiative.

There are, however, in reality an extensive range of alternatives to both old Labour statism and New Right neo-liberalism. Partnership, social investment, equality of opportunity, mixed economies and so on can be pursued in different forms and with different investment and outcome priorities. To lump all of these together as a third way can disguise as much as it reveals. Thus Labour's new third way for welfare is really the beginning of a process of policy analysis and development rather than the culmination of one.

The ideological framework

In just two years of office Labour produced a wide range of policy reviews and official statements. These included a plethora of Green and White Papers on social security, pensions, education, health, childcare, families, local government, and more; a Royal Commission report on long-term care; and the work of a new unit to tackle social exclusion. Much has also been written by journalists, think-tank specialists and academics about the New Labour project and its policy implications (see Oppenheim, 1998; and Powell, 1999). There have also been the commentaries on the third way by Blair himself (1998), and by one of his leading policy gurus (Giddens, 1998). In all of this writing a number of new (or revitalised) concepts appear and re-appear; and these provide a guide to the ideological framework behind the government's new welfare policies.

For a start there is the use of the term *welfare* itself to describe social, and in particular social security, policy. Welfare is an ambiguous term. It has positive connotations of meeting people's basic human needs - providing for their welfare. However, it also has negative connotations inherited especially from American concerns about welfare dependence and the growing cost of public expenditure. The Blair government's close association with the Clinton programme of reform and renewal in the United States (see Jordan, 1998) has resulted in an increasing tendency to use the term in this narrower, more pejorative, sense - although its dual meaning also reveals a potential contradiction at the heart of the New Labour project between the commitment to provide for welfare for all and the determination to promote self-improvement and self-protection through the labour market.

This duality can be found in another key element of the third way, the link between rights and responsibilities. The right to welfare was a core principle of the post-war welfare state in Britain, captured famously by Marshall (1950) in his claim that such rights were the defining feature of twentieth-century social citizenship. Such a paternalistic approach is now challenged by Labour, however, in favour of a more contractual model within which citizens have duties to fulfil in order to secure their rights to social protection. This can be seen most clearly in the policy initiatives surrounding Labour's key concept of 'welfare to work', within which welfare provision is set against the obligation to seek self-protection through paid employment. Implied in this is a new model of *citizenship* based upon the twin expectations (or promises) of participation and obligation.

The link between citizenship and welfare has always been a central feature of welfare provision in modern societies - it was Marshall's (1950) key concept in the 1940s. It is therefore not a new idea. It is quite distinct, however, from New Right notions of private contracting within a free market. Labour see a continuing role for the public provision of welfare and have moved away from the privatisation agenda of the 1980s. This is most clearly revealed in their promotion of a new approach to the improvement of services, symbolised by the notion of *Best Value*, and discussed as a project of *modernisation* of public services. Labour see themselves as the modernisers of welfare services; and they have included the term in their early papers on reform of local government (DETR, 1998) and social services (DoH, 1998). The claim to modernity might appear to be a curious one, at a time when so many pundits are writing about the Western world having entered the 'post-modern' era, although the quest for modernisation addresses rather similar issues to those raised in many debates about post-modernity - and post-modernisers is not such a catchy buzz-word.

In general modernisation is simply a plea for recognition that the world has changed since the post war period, as recognised by Esping-Andersen (1996) and others. Giddens' (1998) analysis of the third way situates these in the context of the different risks and uncertainties which citizens now face in planning for their lives. These new risks require a new relationship between citizens and service providers, within which the need to promote the obligation to participate through paid work must be balanced against the challenge of combating the social exclusion which prevents so many citizens from participating.

A new social policy?

Challenging social exclusion and promoting welfare to work are key elements in the development of a new social policy under Labour at the beginning of the twenty-first century. Both draw on policy initiatives begun under the Conservatives, and have echoes of some of the ideas supported by past Labour administrations. However, the third way is a slippery concept, to which many shades of political opinion could in practice happily subscribe; it is far from clear that the rhetoric of modernisation has indeed been followed by Labour in the establishment of a genuinely new direction for social policy, to follow the earlier phases of twentieth-century policy development. However, there are some signs that a change in direction may be easier to detect a few years into the new millennium, if current trends are continued.

First, there are the continuing influences which will continue to be brought to bear by Britain's membership of the European Union. Labour have embraced many EU social policy initiatives, such as the Social Charter and the working time directive. If, as seems likely, they eventually take the country into the EU monetary union, then economic and social pressures for policy convergence will grow ever stronger. The EU has always been primarily an economic and trading union; but, at the turn of the century, it is dominated by new Social Democratic governments concerned to marry economic with social development. Such a context could strengthen the case for third-way policies in all member nations.

Second, there is the government's own policy agenda. Whatever the weight of the Thatcher legacy, New Labour are not the New Right - far from it. For Blair the securing of genuine equality of opportunity is an over-riding moral imperative; and for his chancellor, Gordon Brown, achieving some measure of social justice is an economic, as well as a social, policy objective. Both are strong supporters of social markets and welfare capitalism. These require changes in the direction of political debate and policy development; and in the 1999 Budget there was some evidence that such changes were taking place. The financial year 1999-2000 was the first year of the increased spending commitments outlined in the 1998 Comprehensive Spending Review. It was also the year in which major policy changes such as the minimum wage and Working Families' Tax Credit began to take effect. The Budget statement also revealed increases in benefits and tax relief for children (including a big hike in Child Benefit itself), for maternity and for pensioners, and an extension of the provisions to support welfare to work. These were a significant change in the direction of tax and benefit policy - described by some pundits as 'redistribution by stealth'. The pursuit of redistribution by stealth may seem a rather understated way to underpin a new phase in welfare policy development for Britain at the beginning of the twenty-first century; but its practical consequences may yet prove to be more enduring than its rather partial rhetoric.

References

Alcock, P. (1997), 'Consolidation or Stagnation? Social Policy under the Major Governments', in M. May, E. Brunsden and G. Craig (eds), *Social Policy Review 9*, Social Policy Association, London.

Bacon, R. and Eltis, W. (1976), *Britain's Economic Problem: Too Few Producers*, Macmillan, Basingstoke.

Beveridge, Sir W. (1942), *Social Insurance and Allied Services*, HMSO, Cmd 6404, London.

Blair, T. (1998), *The Third Way*, Fabian Society, London.

Borrie, Sir G. (1994), *Social Justice: Strategies for National Renewal. The Report of the Commission on Social Justice*, Vintage Books, London.

Cutler, T., Williams, K. and Williams, J. (1986), *Keynes, Beveridge and Beyond*, Routledge Kegan Paul, London.

Department of Environment, Transport and the Regions (DETR) (1998), *Modernising Local Government: Improving Local Services through Best Value*, DETR, London.

Department of Health (DoH) (1998a), *Modernising Social Services: Promoting Independence, Improving Protection, Raising Standards*, Cm 4169, The Stationery Office, London.

Esping Andersen, G. (ed) (1996), *Welfare States in Transition: National Adaptations in Global Economics*, Sage, London.

Giddens, A. (1998), *The Third Way*, Polity Press, Cambridge.

Glennerster, H. (1995), *British Social Policy Since 1945*, Macmillan, Basingstoke.

Gough, I. (1979), *The Political Economy of the Welfare State*, Macmillan, Basingstoke.

Johnson, N. (1990), *Reconstructing the Welfare State: A decade of change 1980-1990*, Harvester/Wheatsheaf, London.

Jordan, W. (1998), *The New Politics of Welfare: Social Justice in a Global Context*, Sage, London.

Le Grand, J. and Bartlett, W. (eds) (1993), *Quasi-Markets and Social Policy*, Macmillan, Basingstoke.

Marshall, T.H. (1950), *Citizenship and Social Class*, Cambridge University Press, Cambridge.

Oppenhein, C. (ed) (1998), *An Inclusive Society: Strategies for Tackling Poverty*, IPPR, London.

Page, R. and Silburn, R. (eds) (1999), *British Social Welfare in the Twentieth Century*, Macmillan, Basingstoke.

Pfaller, A., Gough, I. and Therborn, G. (1991), *Can the Welfare State Compete?*, Macmillan, Basingstoke.

Powell, M. (ed) (1999), *New Labour, New Welfare State? The third way in British social policy*, Policy Press, Bristol.

Thane, P. (1996), *The Foundations of the Welfare State,* 2nd Edition, Longman, Harlow.

3 To be or not to be a Taiwanese welfare state: Lessons from recent experience

YEUN-WEN KU

Introduction

This is an age of crisis and upheaval, particularly for East Asian countries after many decades of so-called 'economic miracle'. As growth is slowing down, the state of the economy is no longer only an economic issue. So we see the collapse of Suharto's power in Indonesia and the spread of violence. 'Mobs attack people and property for any reason – political, religious, ethnic or merely criminal', according to *The Economist* (30 January 1999).

Under such a situation, the Asia-Pacific Economic Cooperation forum (APEC) for the first time goes beyond its nature as an economic organization. In November 1998, APEC's 21 economic leaders gathered in Kuala Lumpur for two days of talks. The joint declaration, read out by Malaysian prime minister Mahathir Mohamad, said: 'For the APEC economies most affected by the crisis, it is important to continue and accelerate structural reforms within a framework of prudent, growth-oriented macro-economic policies.' He resolved to take measures to restore capital flows into the region, contain financial contagion and strengthen the social safety net (*South China Morning Post*, 19 November 1998).

After many years pursuing rapid economic growth, APEC members have learned the importance of social development as a concrete foundation for a real economic miracle, though this comes from a very bitter experience in the case of Indonesia. A further problem emerges: what kind of social safety net do APEC members need? We find no answer in the joint declaration and this leaves a lot of room for discussion.

Unfortunately, the necessity for a social safety net seems not to have attracted much attention or positive response from Taiwanese politicians, probably because the economy has proved relatively strong against the crisis. In a public speech just one month after the APEC declaration, Taiwanese vice-president Lien Chan clearly argued that Taiwan would not be moving towards the European style of welfare states, in order to avoid problems of low investment and heavy burdens upon governmental finance. He proposed a welfare model in which private enterprises and voluntary agencies, separate from the state, should be the two major providers of welfare services (*United Daily News*, 30 December 1998).

Even such high-ranking politicians as the vice-president of Taiwan still have a mistakenly hostile attitude to the welfare state, we shall argue. They always blame state welfare for slowing down economic growth and eroding the financial health of the government. Another significant example is Hsueh Chi, the deputy minister for the Council of Economic Planning and Development (CEPD). He exaggerated Sachs and Warner's study (1996), and said that a large element of state welfare would result in an inflexible labour market and high governmental expenditure; and that these in turn would induce high unemployment and low economic growth (Hsueh, 1997). Such a viewpoint is typical amongst Taiwanese economic policy makers.

Can the Taiwanese State really escape from welfare responsibility? How are the politicians and people in Taiwan to arrive at a more positive view on the welfare state? This study figures out the lessons we should learn.

Lesson 1: The expansion of state welfare is a fact

Although politicians do not favour the welfare state ideologically, the government introduced quite a lot of welfare provisions throughout the 1990s. In principle, the Constitution of 1949 had already imposed a wide range of welfare responsibilities on the state. In Articles 152 to 157, the Constitution reads that the state should maintain full employment, guarantee working conditions, harmonise industrial relations, establish a social security system, protect maternal welfare, and realise a national health system (Ku, 1997a, pp.32-33). Furthermore, the revision of the Constitution in 1997 declared for more specific welfare measures such as National Health Insurance (NHI), and protections for women, the handicapped, and minorities. These all lay down a basic legal context for social policy and legislation in Taiwan.

Social security in Taiwan consists of social insurance and social assistance, of which the former has expanded its coverage significantly.

The first legislation on social insurance was the Military Servicemen's Insurance Law of 1953. Labour insurance was first initiated in 1950 as an experimental programme and later became a statute in 1958. By 1980, three major systems of social insurance had been established for military servicemen, civil servants, and labourers, to cover the risks of maternity, injury and sickness, medical care, disability, old age, death, and funeral expenses (Ku, 1995). The benefit for medical care has now been transferred to the NHI. Of the three major systems, labour insurance is the largest, covering a workforce of 7.5 million, equivalent to 34.5 per cent of the total population (DGBAS, 1998, table 90). A national pension insurance (NPI) is also due to be introduced by 2000 (see Chapter 6 below).

For the poor, social assistance is the way to get cash benefit. The first act in this field was the Social Relief Law of 1943, helping those who were in poverty because of age, youth, pregnancy, disability, or disaster. It was replaced by the Social Assistance Law of 1980, which took the more progressive stance of adopting 'income', rather than cause of poverty, as the key criterion. But the 1980 Act contained no article to regulate the definition of poverty, leaving great power in the hands of government officials to determine the level of the poverty line according to their wishes rather than the needs of the poor. An incredibly low poverty line was set up, under which only 0.5 per cent of the total population qualified for it (Ku, 1995). This became the first target for improvement when the Government proposed the Social Assistance Law of 1997. The new Act specified the poverty line as being 60 per cent of per capita consumption expenditure in the previous year. Some scholars estimate that around 5 per cent of the total population should now benefit (e.g. C. Chen, 1996).

Apart from social assistance, there are some kinds of allowance specifically for the aged with insufficient incomes. Since 1994 the Living Allowance for Middle-Low Income Elderly People, and since 1995 the Welfare Allowance for Aged Farmers, have been set up by the Government and have together benefited around 583,024 people (the figure for 1997). In addition, some local authorities controlled by the opposition, the Democratic Progressive Party (DPP), would like to provide cash benefits to the aged.

In health care, the NHI is the first universal welfare system with a target to cover all of the population in Taiwan. It did not exist until the National Health Insurance Act was finally passed in 1994 and put in practice in 1995. The Act defines the Department of Health (DoH) as the department of central government with direct responsibility for policy making and supervision of the NHI. The Bureau of National Health Insurance (BNHI), which is also an official agency under the DoH, is the designated insurer to run the system. This makes it clear that the NHI is a state-run and centralised system. By the end of 1997, the number of the insured under the NHI was 20.5 million, around 96.3 per cent of the total population at that time (DGBAS, 1998, table 92). This figure is far higher than that before the NHI was enforced, when the proportion of population covered by at least one kind of social insurance programmes was only 59.7 per cent (BNHI, 1996, p.8).

The Child Welfare Law of 1973 was the first Act in the field of personal social services in favour of a particular disadvantaged group of people. Then came the Aged Welfare Law and the Handicapped Welfare Law in 1980, and the Youth Welfare Law in 1989. Nearly all of these Acts - except for the - except for Youth Welfare - were revised in the 1990s to improve and enhance service capacity. Furthermore, in the 1990s four brand-new Acts were passed in response to rising social concern over cases of abuse and violence, especially on children and women. These included the Regulation Against Child and Adolescent Prostitution (1995), the Act Against Sexual Violation (1997), the Act Against Domestic Violence (1998), in addition to the Act on Social Worker Qualification (1997) which established a professional social work system to deal with above problems as well as to guarantee quality of service. In short, we may say that the personal social services in Taiwan have gradually shifted focus from issues of general welfare to more specific cases of need.

At the beginning of 1999, the Government was concerned by increasing unemployment, which had risen to 3.05 per cent in August 1998, the highest level of the past. three decades. The Labour Council declared this 'the Year of Employment Security', in order to establish a more consistent employment security system. From 1 January 1999, Labour Insurance was going to include unemployment benefit, particularly for those laid off. It also signalled the integration of employment services and ensured retraining to help workers back into the labour market as fast as possible.

The main reason for such measures may be competition from the DPP, as well as demands from social movements (for detailed discussion please refer to Ku, 1998a; 1998b). Nevertheless these developments in welfare serve to strengthen the possibility of an eventual Taiwanese welfare state.

Lesson 2: The welfare state is not by definition a killer of economic growth

There is not enough evidence, internationally, to show that the welfare state is the killer of economic growth. To be sure, some on the New Right do argue the negative impacts of welfare. A significant example is the disputable argument made by David Marsland (1996, xvii):

> State welfare is causing grave damage in the United Kingdom, in the United States, and elsewhere throughout the free world. It is impeding the dynamism of global economic competition, and thus slowing world economic growth. Through the bureaucratic centralization and the underclass dependency which it inevitably creates, it poses a serious long-term threat to liberty and to the stability of democracy.

But, if this is really so, we would surely not have seen the violence in Indonesia and the coming of APEC declaration. Other scholars have reminded us of the positive function of state welfare for sustaining long-term accumulation and reproduction (e.g. Gough, 1979). Also, Gordon et al. have identified diverse institutions in the accumulation process, which cannot be created by any single capitalist, but which require state effort, such as education and health (1994). 'Without a stable and favourable external environment, capital investment in production will not proceed', they argue (Gordon et al, 1994, p.14).

Ku 1997b) has summed up the positive impacts made by state welfare, including:

1. Contributing to the formation of human capital - as with education and health - which is fundamental to the export-oriented development strategy in East Asia;
2. Enhancing social integration and therefore stabilizing productive relationships in favour of economic growth;
3. Maintaining domestic consumption power as a policy tool to manage supply-demand at macro-economic level;
4. Public purchases favouring domestic production and therefore contributing to economic growth;
5. Increasing employment opportunities, especially in public-sector and related service providers, both profit-making and non-profit.

In Taiwanese experience, the growth of social security expenditure in the 1990s was significant: from 4.5 per cent GDP in 1991 to 6.1 per cent in 1997, while the rate of growth of GDP was declining from 11.7 per cent to 8.7 per cent. This might seem to be evidence that welfare is indeed the killer of economic growth. However, the sharpest decline in economic growth was between 1991 and 1994, from 11.7 per cent to 8.6 per cent, over a period when social security expenditure remained stable at around 4.4 per cent - 4.5 per cent GDP. Whereas, from 1994 to 1997, social security expenditure jumped to 6.1 per cent, while the rate of growth of GDP was floating around 8.5 per cent, without any significant decline (Ku et al, 1999, p.33).

The relationship between welfare and economic performance is not a clear-cut trade-off in our view. Blaming welfare for slowing down economic growth is too arbitrary to believe. It oversimplifies the complicated interaction between welfare and economy and can merely be an excuse for irresponsibility and for the inability of the state to meet people's needs.

Lesson 3: Globalization is a restraint

It is true that capitalist globalization has significantly constrained the capacity of a national welfare state. It has meant sharper international economic competition and this in turn may change the balance of power between capital and labour (Wilding, 1997).

In a global economy, the flow of capital is far faster than the flow of labour, especially since the right to work is still under the strict control of every national state. Capital can easily move to profitable areas elsewhere, while the labour force is left to lose its jobs. Workers are forced to compete with each other not only at domestic but also at international level. A crude example - which led to a strike by French seamen - was when a cross-channel ferry company based in Britain employed Polish crews in February 1995. The average salary of the French seamen was 10,000 francs per month; that of Polish seamen was 2,500 francs, they worked much longer shifts, and had no social security cover (Jordan, 1996, p.121).

A similar situation occurred in Taiwan as labour-intensive industries moved to low labour-cost areas, such as South-east Asia and China. This raised the unemployment rate and in turn increased pressures on state welfare. If the Government pours more public resources into state welfare as a result, then the shortage of money for economic development could be critical and inflict even greater damage on profit-making enterprises. Yet if the Government is unwilling to expand its welfare efforts, it could forfeit its position as the ruling power in the next election. A great difficulty looms (Ku, 1997b).

> In the process of globalization, local labourers are not only competing with other labourers in the country, but also competing with foreign labourers for limited job opportunities. The having or not having jobs and the levels of wages will influence employees' subsistence and enterprises' profits directly. However, wage levels are very difficult to raise because of global competition. If the Government should raise wages through social programmes and statutes, they risk reducing job opportunities. Both high unemployment and low wages will greatly damage the legitimacy of the state economic crisis will transform into a political crisis...

Although the possibility of a supranational social policy or inter-national social development strategy has been advocated (e.g. Wilding, 1997; Midgley, 1997), developments in this direction lag far behind the process of globalization. For the time being the national state must still strive to keep capital and jobs in its own territory, but without pushing down wages and working conditions. Is there a way out of this dilemma? A lot of new ideas have been introduced into welfare provisions, though none of them are perfect. We shall consider privatisation first.

Lesson 4: Privatisation offers one way, but not an all-purpose solution

One impact of the welfare reforms in Western welfare states should not be neglected. Since the publication of Norman Johnson's book on welfare pluralism (1987), the idea that social and health care may be obtained from four different sectors, namely the statutory, the voluntary, the commercial and the informal, has been widely acclaimed in Taiwan. So have been the concepts of privatisation, decentralisation, managerialism, mixed economy of welfare, quasi-market, non-profit organizations and community care. All of these imply a less dominant role for the state in the collective provision of social welfare.

A sizeable literature and studies relating to these theories have been appearing in Taiwan, particularly focused on the privatisation of social welfare. Also, official reports published by the Department of Social Affairs clearly demonstrate a policy preference for welfare developments drawing on service providers from the private sector: from family and community, from the voluntary sector, and even from profit-making organizations (W. Chen, 1996). Welfare privatisation indeed corresponds to the liberal orientation of Taiwanese economic technocrats, for at least three reasons. First, more service providers from different sectors mean that the state can reduce its burden of state welfare and the pressures this puts on finance. Second, effectiveness and efficiency should be better assured in the private than the public sector: an important consideration because of limited resources. Finally, more service providers implies more choice and greater empowerment for welfare consumers and thus should encourage greater self-reliance.

Nevertheless, the question of whether or not privatisation offers a unique way out of the welfare crisis is still under examination in Western welfare states (Esping-Andersen, 1996). Some issues arising from privatisation should be noted. The first concerns the role of the state. Privatisation as state policy, meaning that the state is deliberately promoting and maybe subsidizing this process, exposes a structural gap between theory and practice. Privatisation in practice is not so totally private; state intervention is still in evidence. The second issue concerns the defects of privatisation, especially if there is profit motivation in social welfare. Although profits and competition for profits are theoretically able to guarantee effectiveness and efficiency, these could offend against marginal groups of welfare consumers without enough money to pay for services. In a pure market society, the more profits the better and there is no formal mechanism to regulate a reasonable profit level. The private organization tends therefore to reduce its costs, for instance by using unqualified manpower, in order to maximize profits. This could threaten service quality, on the one hand; and, on the other, mean that the needs being satisfied under privatisation were rather the most profitable than the most urgent (see also Chapter 6 below).

Lesson 5: Decentralisation to the community could be another way, but should not become community abandonment

Apart from privatisation, decentralisation - which refers to a top-down devolution of welfare responsibility from central government to local authorities, and even to communities - is another idea attractive to the Taiwanese state. For example, a national conference on community development was held by the Department of Social Affairs under the Ministry of Interior Affairs in 1995, which concluded in favour of the promotion of community-based welfare services (MIA, 1995). Since then five experimental towns around the island have been selected to explore the possibilities of community care (or so-called welfare communitization, in the Taiwanese term).

Yet, although the government advocates its merits with regard to accessibility and acceptability, the matter is not so simple. The government has poured NT$ 15 to 20 million a year into these five experimental towns, each for the construction of community-based service networks. This is a serious amount of money for such small towns, but expenditure has been mainly on meal services, day care, respite care, in-home services, and sending greetings (Yang and Hwang, 1999). This implies there are some limits to community care in Taiwan. First of all, this being an experimental programme, the government treated the five towns as models, thus giving away a lot of money. But this money was neither permanent nor available to all other communities. Hence these services were only temporary and selective. Second, even those towns lucky enough to receive the government money did not use it to construct more care homes in the community. Without such an increase of care beds needy people, especially those who need intensive care or live alone, cannot move out of the slums into better living conditions. Thus we see that all the services actually provided were to help relieve the care burdens of family members only. Family, rather than community or old people's homes in the community, remains the key focus for decision-making about care responsibility.

This stands in contrast to the results of a survey on the needs of the aged population in Taiwan. This demonstrates the following (DSMIA, 1997):

1. There are 15.31 per cent of the elderly with physical or mental disability and of these 76.16 per cent, equivalent to about 200,000 old people, have not reported to the government for help.
2. There are 55.69 per cent of the elderly suffering from poor health and chronic diseases, of which one in ten, about 92,000 old people, need someone else to take care of their daily needs.
3. Of the group of 92,000 old people needing caring services, only 10.27 per cent are living in care homes. About 77.21 per cent are living with their families; and 1.96 per cent are living alone. In addition, however, 10.96 per cent of them, equivalent to about 10,000 old people, are hoping to move into care homes.

We doubt that community care in Taiwan can effectively meet such a demand, especially given the speeding-up of the ageing process. Moreover, the towns selected to promote community care were relatively better equipped with infrastructure and activity. Their successes cannot guarantee its working in other communities, particularly those suffering

radical decline. Three questions stand out:
1.   Whether or not the community is ready to take over welfare responsibility?
2.   Whether or not the community has autonomy to decide for itself?
3.   Whether or not service users are truly satisfied with the change?

The first issue concerns the capacity of the community, including its resources and infrastructure. No community can totally replace the welfare role of the state, and there are in any case different communities with varying degrees of capacity. The second issue concerns the power of the community. Public participation is declining. If the community is dependent on resources and regulation from the state, this could further damage the acceptability of community care. The third issue concerns the satisfaction of consumers. Community care could amount to community abandonment if consumers do not really want this change. If the community will not or cannot play the role of service provider well, then welfare decentralisation could place further burdens on families within communities or specifically on female individuals in families.

Lesson 6: The family is still primary, but its capacity for caring is becoming constrained

In Chinese societies, the family is usually regarded as the final happy home for the elderly and needy; but this now seems to be becoming a myth. First of all, figure 3.1 shows the different age groups as percentages of the total population in Taiwan, from which we can observe a significant ageing process. The proportion of people aged 65 and over has been increasing, from 4.3 per cent of the total population in 1980 to 8.1 per cent in 1997. If we regard 7 per cent as the threshold of an ageing society, then Taiwan has met this criterion since 1993. Meanwhile, the working population was increasing steadily from 63.6 per cent in 1980 to 69.3 per cent in 1997, alongside a sharp decline in the younger generation aged under 15, from 32.1 per cent to 22.6 per cent over the same period. In short, the combination of an increasing aged population and a declining younger population has been the major demographic trend over the past nearly two decades. Although the population remains economically active, given a working population of 69.3 per cent, the combined effect of the demographic trend could undermine this in the future. Before we explore this issue further, we should turn to the dependency ratio in Taiwan, as shown in figure 3.2.

In this figure we find that the dependency ratio of the population (those of dependent age as against those of working age) shows a very interesting trend over the past nearly two decades. First, the general dependency ratio, namely the total population aged under 15 and over 65 against the total population aged between 15 and 64, was declining very fast, from 57.2 per cent in 1980 to 44.3 per cent in 1997. The same was true of the dependency ratio of the younger generation, from 50.4 per cent in 1980 to 32.6 per cent in 1997. Second, however, the dependency ratio of the aged population had moved in a completely contrary direction, increasing from 6.7 per cent to 11.7 per cent over the same period.

Figure 3.1 Demographic trends by age groups, 1980-1997

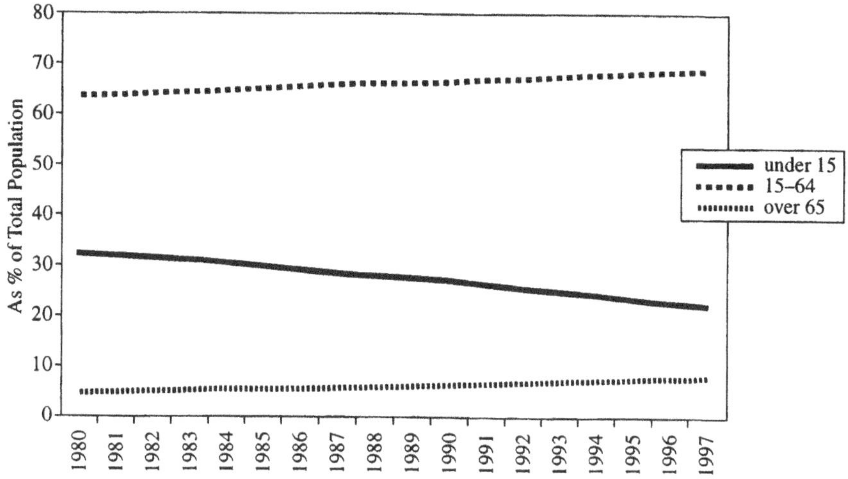

Source: CEPD (1998), *Taiwan Statistical Data Book, 1998.*

There are three conclusions to be drawn from these two sets of figures. First, though life expectancy at birth has increased by about ten years since 1961, reaching 71.95 and 77.83 years respectively for male and female in 1997 (CEPD, 1998), this is not the only reason for the ageing process in Taiwan. In the second place, the decline of the younger generation owing to a sharp fall in the birth rate from 4.66 per cent in 1952 to 1.51 per cent in 1997 (CEPD, 1998), has also had an important effect on the ageing process. Third, the baby boom of the postwar era has matured into an economically active population which has so far underpinned the general dependency ratio without allowing it to worsen (CEPD, 1995, p.7).

Figure 3.2 Dependency ratio, 1980-1997

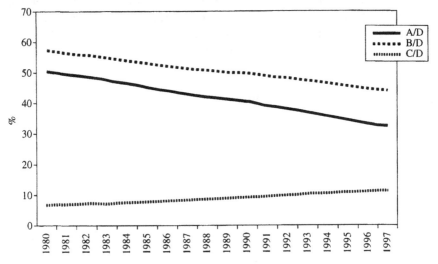

Source: CEPD (1998), *Taiwan Statistical Data Book, 1998.*

A -Total Number of Persons at Dependent Age, 15- & 65+.
B - Number of Persons at Dependent Age 15-.
C - Number of Persons at Dependent Age 65+.

However, as we mentioned at the beginning of this section, the ageing process will be increasingly critical in the future. Due to the combined effect of a declining younger generation which will undermine the future working population, and an increasing aged population set to expand very fast as the postwar baby boom population becomes older, the dependency ratio of elderly to working population in Taiwan should increase considerably. According to the estimate of the CEPD, the percentage of aged people in Taiwan will increase to 10.3 per cent by 2011 and further to 21.7 per cent by 2036. By the same token, the dependency ratio of elderly to working population will be 14.7 per cent and 34.3 per cent respectively (CEPD, 1995, pp.6-7).

Given such an ageing process, whether or not the family can sustain its caring responsibility as usual will become a key issue for policy makers. In answer to this question, we should look at changes in family size and economic structure. Table 3.1 shows general trends, from which we learn that the average number of persons in every household has been decreasing from 4.7 in 1981 to 3.5 in 1997. This implies a trend towards nuclear-type families in which it will be difficult for the elderly and the needy to find someone to take care of them. Furthermore, the increase in the non-agricultural population as a percentage of the total, from 71.9 per cent in 1981 to 82.8 per cent in 1997, also implies a more formalised economic structure, in which risks such as retirement or unemployment are always threatening the economic security and capacity of the elderly as well as their families.

A further question concerns the role of women in the family. As traditional carers, women have been at the heart of family services. So far, this is still the case in Taiwan. A survey conducted by the Taiwanese government on the division of labour within households shows that the family responsibility of the male is as breadwinner whereas that of the female is as housekeeper. In particular, caring for the elderly and children is primarily the responsibility of the female: 2,654 out of 3,008 households surveyed approved of this (DGBAS, 1999, table 7). Even so, the increase in female labour force participation, from 36.6 per cent in 1966 to 45.6 per cent in 1997 (DGBAS, 1998, table 17), has put women under great pressure between their working careers and family roles, and has by the same token constrained the scope for caring within the family. Currently over 41.5 per cent of households in Taiwan are two-career families, meaning that both husband and wife are in formal employment, and this figure even rises to 53.7 per cent of the households with children below 14 years (DGBAS, 1999, tables 14 and 15).

No welfare state pretends it could replace the role of the family in human terms, yet we must recognize the limits of the family in modern society. In particular, changes in demography, family size, and economic structures have constrained the original caring and supportive capacities of the family. A policy to support the family would therefore not be to replace or weaken family functions, as some Taiwanese politicians argue (Ku, 1997a, p.186). On the contrary, it should enable the family to realize

Table 3.1 Household size and non-agricultural population, 1981-1997

Year	Average persons per household	Non-agricultural population as per cent of total population
1981	4.7	71.9
1982	4.6	73.0
1983	4.5	77.0
1984	4.5	77.5
1985	4.4	75.7
1986	4.3	77.9
1987	4.2	79.3
1988	4.1	80.8
1989	4.1	81.7
1990	4.0	78.9
1991	3.9	79.5
1992	3.9	80.3
1993	3.8	80.9
1994	3.8	81.0
1995	3.7	81.6
1996	3.6	82.7
1997	3.5	82.8

Source: DGBAS (1998).

its functions more fully, especially by relieving the pressures on Taiwanese women.

Lesson 7: Voluntary services should be supplementary, rather than the major source of help

As mentioned at the beginning of this chapter, Vice-President Lien Chan has stressed the importance of voluntary services in welfare provisions. However, while it is true that voluntary sector can be an important source of social welfare, it usually suffers problems of sustainability and consistency, especially in financial respects.

By the end of 1997, there were about 12,825 voluntary organizations in Taiwan, of which 3,867 were founded for the purposes of social service and charity (DSMIA, 1998, tables 49 and 50). A significant growth in voluntary organizations took place after political democratization opened up more opportunities for participation in public services. According to some estimates, in 1990 the total expenses of voluntary organizations reached NT$ 13 billion: equivalent to 0.3 per cent of GNP, 10 per cent of the social expenditure of the central government, and 35 per cent of the total governmental expenditure on personal social services in that year. This figure has increased to NT$ 18 billion in 1996 (Wang, 1999).

Yet even though the role of the voluntary sector is becoming important, it is not in a good position to replace the state for at least two reasons. The first concerns its financial characteristics. In Taiwan, a survey has revealed that social donations (39.9 per cent) rank top of the sources of income for voluntary organizations, followed in importance by subsidies from the government (28.7 per cent) (Shih, 1997). However levels of social donation are closely linked to the economic climate, which could reduce the money available for services. Without a more reliable source of income, voluntary organizations find it difficult to develop long-term programmes or to expand service capacity. This in turn will confine the activities of voluntary organizations to those of piecemeal and temporary nature. A much more reliable source of income comes indeed from the government. Along with the development of contracting-out under privatisation, the importance of governmental subsidies is increasing very significantly (Shih, 1997). However, a dilemma emerges. To bid for contracts from the state, voluntary organizations must adjust themselves in line with governmental guidelines. This could lead to (1) loss of independence, (2) a changing shape of the voluntary sector, and (3) a tendency to go wherever the money is (Lewis, 1993). Given such possibilities, the roles and functions of the voluntary sector must be carefully defined, especially with regard to its boundary and relationship with the public sector.

Second, there has been uneven development within voluntary sector so that it is not equally benefiting all the areas and groups. In Taiwan, urban areas have more voluntary organizations. Those organizations with religious conviction are able to collect the most resources (the largest foundation in Taiwan being a Buddhist organization with over 3 million members, equivalent to around 14.3 per cent of the total population). Also, the elderly and children generally attract more attention from the voluntary sector, while women get less. All this makes it difficult to render voluntary services into a universal and comprehensive net for people in need, and thus indicates the necessity for a collective effort at integration.

Lesson 8: More welfare providers does not mean more needs being satisfied

Privatisation, decentralisation, family, and voluntary services are indeed signs that the government is trying to adopt a pluralist approach to social welfare and to share its welfare responsibilities with other sectors. It would be good if more providers from different sectors participate in welfare services. But this is not the happy end of the story. A further issue is emerging, focused on service network and integration.

More service providers can mean an expansion in the resources available to social welfare; yet these could end up too piecemeal and create gaps in welfare provision, so long as there is no collective effort to organize these service providers into an integrated network. We witnessed a similar situation over a hundred years ago in Britain, when the Charity Organization Society tried to organize the charities of London on a more sensible footing, but lacked the authority and hence the necessary co-operation to do so effectively (Fraser, 1984, pp.130-131).

In Taiwan, the gaps are not only between different sectors but also within the public sector. As mentioned under Lesson 1 above, some local authorities controlled by the DPP provide cash allowances to elderly citizens which in effect have discriminated against other elderly citizens living in non-DPP counties. Some richer cities, like Taipei, even run their own child benefit programme and offer free medical services, whereas other cities and counties cannot afford such programme. Without a collective effort the gaps could become even wider in the future, allowing a radical inequality to emerge. But what should be the guideline for mounting such a collective effort?

Lesson 9: Prioritising needs should be the key criterion for resource allocation

We have talked much about the providing side of welfare provision. But are welfare services effective and efficient enough? This last should be examined from the demand side of welfare. In particular, it refers to questions such as: Which need is the most prioritised? How much resource is allocated to such a need? What level of need satisfaction is met? And how?

Unfortunately, mechanisms of need assessment have not yet been properly developed in Taiwan, for two reasons. The first is the incompetence of governmental bureaucracy. The Department of Social Affairs, under the Ministry of Interior Affairs, is the highest authority in charge of national welfare measures, yet it is only staffed to a level of around 60 personnel, compared to the Ministry of Economic Affairs' 3,094 officials, for example. It is impossible to expect a department with such a paucity of staff to make just decisions on need assessment and resource allocation. There is now a growing movement to establish a wholly separate ministry for health and social welfare. If this materialises in the future, the prospects for prioritising needs should be significantly improved.

Second, however, there exists no very clear vision about what the Taiwanese welfare system is to be. Policy is often made in response to immediate political pressures. Amongst the most significant was the election of local authorities by the end of 1993. The DPP's policy proposal of a universal pension system became a common political platform in order to win the election. It was announced that citizens who were 65 years old and over would receive NT$ 5,000 every month from 2 October. The Kuomintang (KMT) fiercely criticized this policy as a collective bribe addressed to elderly voters, yet it pressed ahead to launch some measures of its own for elderly people. On 2 October, the Ministry of Interior Affairs said that a draft policy on a national pension system would be published in November, and on 6 October the allowance for low-income elderly people was increased from NT$ 3,000 to NT$ 5,000 per month. On 7 October, the DPP announced a further pension scheme specific to farmers, leading to President Lee Teng-hui, who was also the leader of the KMT, asking the Executive Yuan (Cabinet) to enact the same scheme as soon as possible. The Cabinet meeting on 21 October announced the allowance for low-income elderly people would be further increased to NT$ 6,000 per month and an extra NT$ 3,000 would be available for middle-low income elderly people. The DPP held a public hearing for its own pension policy on 22 October, while the Ministry of Interior Affairs also published its policy draft on a national pension system. In such a short period - less than one month - pension reform had become the big issue around the island; and the size of the allowance was growing and growing. The more important issues to do with adequacy of benefits and the integration of social security systems were not really listened to by policy makers (Ku, 1997a, pp.247-249).

Such crude decision making risks the misallocation of resources which in turn can damage welfare development in Taiwan. In particular, the 'need' being satisfied in such a process is the politician's need for more votes, rather than ordinary people's need for economic security in old age. In our view this could happen again and again, so long as we have no established priorities with regard to real needs.

Lesson 10: There is no way the state can escape its welfare responsibility

The point is much clearer now. Although the Taiwanese state has made a considerable effort to share welfare responsibility with other sectors, our analysis still finds the role of the state to be a necessary one in welfare provision. The state should not be the only provider of resources, but it is the only entity possessed of sufficiently huge and self-sustaining resources to be able to construct a comprehensive safety net for the public. No other sectors can compete at this level. The mixed economy of welfare might be very helpful in making additional resources available. But this should not become an excuse for the state to reduce its existing commitments. The relationship between the public and other sectors should be complementary and cooperative, geared to enhancing each other, rather than degenerating into a trade-off and zero-sum game.

The state is the only authority in the modern world capable of regulating production and consumption, for all that state capacity varies as a result of different processes of nation-building and national ranking in the world system. Capitalist globalization has put a great constraint upon the state's ability to function well. But this does not mean that the state is powerless in the face of such development. On the contrary, it can readjust institutions and structures, domestically and internationally, in response to transformations of circumstance. Witness the rise of regional bodies such as EU, APEC, and NAFTA (Weiss, 1998). The key problem has been how the state is to balance the requirements of intensified international competition with the rising demands for welfare emanating from its own people. Without the latter, the former would seem to be a mansion built on sand, which must collapse one day. We have learned this much from the very difficult experience of Indonesia; and no one can say this would never happen to ourselves.

In short, there seems no way for the state to escape from its welfare responsibility, for all that this will be no easy task. Whatever the way decided on, the state will have to take an important and positive role in welfare development.

Conclusion

Because of their misunderstanding of Western welfare states, policy makers in Taiwan have been reluctant to admit any possibility of a Taiwanese welfare state. They always accuse welfare states of slowing down economic growth and creating financial deficit. Privatisation and related issues advocated by the New Right have offered Taiwanese policy makers an easy means of escape from the path towards a welfare state; yet these policy makers have forgotten the fact that state welfare in Taiwan, by contrast to European countries and even America and Japan, is relatively underdeveloped. Recent expansions in welfare programmes have often been in response to immediate political pressures. Such temporary measures to pacify people have left the welfare system in a piecemeal condition and created even more inequalities.

At the National Conference on Social Welfare in 1998, the president and the premier both promised a greater effort in state welfare, including the establishment of a new ministry in charge of national welfare development. Unfortunately the vice-president seems to have a different idea, as we remarked at the beginning of this chapter. Whether the promise in the Conference will become solid governmental policy or merely stand as another slogan will be for examination in the near future.

This paper has figured out ten lessons, some of which have particular relevance to Taiwan whereas others have broader relevance. Taiwan is now at the crossroads: to be or not to be a welfare state. This is not merely a matter of intentional choice. Rather, it is the product of developments from the past as well as of the environment the state itself has created. We may not know how to get there, but it is very dangerous if we still have no idea of where to go. Hopefully these ten lessons will help make us wiser, at least as to the reasons why we need a Taiwanese welfare state.

References

Bureau of National Health Insurance (BNHI) (1996), *Introduction to the Bureau of National Health Insurance,* Taipei. (in Chinese).

Chen, C.F. (1996), 'Changes of Poor Households in Taiwan', *Community Development Journal (Quarterly)*, 75, pp. 95-116. (in Chinese).

Chen, Wu-hsiung (1996), 'The Investigation and Prospect of Social Administration Affairs in ROC', *Community Development Journal (Quarterly)*, No. 75: 5-15. (in Chinese).

Council for Economic Planning and Development (CEPD) (1995), *A Planning Report on the Integrated System of the National Pension Insurance*, Taipei. (in Chinese).

Council for Economic Planning and Development (CEPD) (1998), *Taiwan Statistics Data Book, 1998*, Taipei.

Department of Statistics, Ministry of Interior Affairs (DSMIA) (1997), *A Survey of the Elderly in Taiwan, 1996*, Taipei. (in Chinese).

Department of Statistics, Ministry of Interior Affairs (DSMIA) (1998), *Statistical Yearbook of Interior, the Republic of China, 1997*, Taipei.

Directorate-General of Budget, Accounting and Statistics (DGBAS) (1998), *Social Indicators of the Republic of China, 1997*, Taipei.

Directorate-General of Budget, Accounting and Statistics (DGBAS) (1999), *A Survey on Social Development in Taiwan, 1998*, Taipei. (in Chinese).

The Economist, 30 January 1999.

Esping-Andersen, Gosta (1996), 'After the golden age? Welfare state dilemmas in a global economy', in G. Esping-Andersen (ed), *Welfare States in Transition: National Adaptations in Global Economics*, Sage, London, pp.1-31.

Fraser, Derek (1984), *The Evolution of the British Welfare State, 2nd edition*. Macmillan, Basingstoke.

Gordon, D.M., Edwards, R. and Reich, M. (1994), 'Long swings and stages of capitalism', in D.M. Kotz et al. (eds), *Social Structures of Accumulation: The Political Economy of Growth and Crisis*, pp.11-28, Cambridge University Press, Cambridge.

Gough, Ian (1979), *The Political Economy of the Welfare State*, Macmillan, Basingstoke.

Hsueh, Chi (1997), 'Poverty, employment and social welfare', paper presented at the Conference on A Century-Crossing Social Welfare Development in Taiwan, 9 March 1997, Taipei.

Johnson, Norman (1987), *The Welfare State in Transition: The Theory and Practice of Welfare Pluralism*, Wheatsheaf, Brighton.

Jordan, Bill (1996), *A Theory of Poverty and Social Exclusion*, Polity, Cambridge.

Ku, Yeun-wen (1995), 'The development of state welfare in the Asian NICs with special reference to Taiwan', *Social Policy and Administration*, 29, (4), pp. 345-364.

Ku, Yeun-wen (1997a), *Welfare Capitalism in Taiwan: State, Economy and Social Policy*, Macmillan, Basingstoke.

Ku, Yeun-wen (1997b), 'The welfare state under the trend of privatisation: a challenge', *Community Development Journal (Quarterly)*, 80, pp.70-78. (in Chinese).

Ku, Yeun-wen (1998a), 'Who will benefit? The planning of National Pension Insurance in Taiwan', *Public Administration and Policy: A Hong Kong and Asia-Pacific Journal*, 7, (1), pp.33-45.

Ku, Yeun-wen (1998b), 'Can we afford it? The development of National Health Insurance in Taiwan', in R. Goodman, G. White and H. Kwon (eds), *The East Asian Welfare Model: Welfare Orientalism and the State*, Routledge, London, pp.119-138.

Ku, Y.W., Hwang, Y.S. and Chan, C.Y. (1999), *White Paper on Social Welfare: A Preliminary Draft.* Taipei: Ministry of Interior Affairs. (in Chinese).

Lewis, J. (1993), 'Developing the mixed economy of care: Emerging issues for voluntary organizations', *Journal of Social Policy,* 22, (2), pp.173-192.

Marsland, David (1996), *Welfare or Welfare State? Contradictions and Dilemmas in Social Policy*, Macmillan, Basingstoke.

Midgley, James (1997), *Social Welfare in Global Context*, Sage, Thousand Oaks, California.

Ministry of Interior Affairs (MIA) (1995), *Special Issue of the National Conference on Community Development.* Taipei. (in Chinese).

Sachs, D. Jeffrey and Warner, Andrew M. (1996), 'The social welfare state and competitiveness', in World Economic Forum, *The Global Competitiveness Report*, pp. 20-26.

Shih, Chaiw-yi (1997), 'The implementation of privatisation: Current status, problems and strategies', *Community Development Journal (Quarterly),* 80, pp.37-55. (in Chinese).

South China Morning Post, 19 November 1998.

United Daily News, 30 December 1998. (in Chinese).

Wang, Shung-ming (1999), 'The discussion of NPOs and the related issues', *Community Development Journal (Quarterly)*, 85, pp.36-61.

Weiss, Linda (1998), *The Myth of the Powerless State: Governing the Economy in a Global Era*, Polity, Cambridge.

Wilding, Paul (1997), 'Globalization, regionalism and social policy', *Social Policy and Administration,* 31, (4), pp.410-428.

Yang, Yin and Hwang, Yuan-shie (1999), *A Study on Propelling Social Welfare Communitisation – The Case of Lu-Kang, Changhaw.* Taipei: Ministry of Interior Affairs.

4 Modernising social welfare services? Change and continuity in social care and social welfare in Britain
ANN DAVIS

Introduction

At the end of 1998 a government White Paper, *Fit for the Future? Modernising Social Services*, was published outlining future directions and priorities for the social services in England and Wales (Secretary of State for Health, 1998). It promotes a vision for the twenty-first century of how that part of the British welfare system which employs the majority of social workers should be developing. In doing so it argues that this service, alongside others in the public health and welfare sectors, must modernise in order to provide the best possible service to citizens.

In making its case for modernisation the White Paper stresses that in a context where demographic changes and changes in family structures are reshaping British society, the social services are likely to be facing an increased demand for their provision. In order to meet this demand effectively the government contends that it is important to create services which are effective and which break away from the failures of the past. The proposals outlined to achieve this are called a 'third way' for social care and welfare services: a way forward that breaks with the two dominant modes of viewing social services which have characterised the past fifty years. This third way avoids the recent Conservative government's 'devotion to privatisation of care provision [which] put dogma before users' interest and threatened a fragmentation of vital services.' At the same time it rejects previous Labour governments' adherence to 'the near monopoly of local authority provision that used to be a feature of social care and led to a "one size fits all" approach where users were expected to accommodate themselves to the services that existed' (Secretary of State for Health, 1998, p.8). In setting out its

49

alternative to both of these approaches Modernising Social Services claims that government is concerned to move the focus away from who provides the care to 'the quality of services experienced by, and outcomes achieved for, individuals and their carers and families' (Secretary of State, 1998, p.8).

This third way for social welfare and social care represents a small part of the intended reform of Britain's welfare state which the Labour government, elected in May 1997, declared to be one of its major tasks. The third way is being promoted by government ministers as a distinctive approach, which breaks from both the New Right and the previous tradition of the left in Britain: an approach which is going to determine a radically different direction for welfare in the twenty-first century (Giddens, 1998; Powell, 2000).

In considering critically this apparently new mandate for the social care and welfare services, this chapter reviews the development of personal social services in England and Wales over the last fifty years and considers how far the modernising plans of the current government constitute a radically new approach to the delivery of these services. In this review particular consideration is given to the role of social workers since the task of organising social work has been of prime significance in the way in which the British model of the personal social services has developed during this period (Langan, 1993; Harris and McDonald, 2000).

The scope of the personal social services

The personal social services in the United Kingdom are made up of a diverse range of services which have developed since the nineteenth century to care for and control individuals and families who are unable to support themselves. The origins of this welfare sector lie in a range of responses made in nineteenth-century Britain to the divisive, dangerous and distressing impact of industrialisation and urbanisation on the family and the social lives of poor people. These responses by government and non-governmental organisations (NGOs) usually within the framework of the Poor Law gave a remit to social work both to protect and strengthen society and at the same time conditionally to support its most vulnerable and marginalised members (Davis, 1991; Jordan, 1997; Jones, 1998).

The personal social services offer provision across the life cycle for individuals whose behaviour or vulnerability is considered to merit such attention. Personal social services are currently provided in the community as well as in residential institutions and day centres for children, adults of working age, older and disabled people who find themselves unable to manage their lives without additional resources. The majority of families and individuals that receive such services live in poverty and experience social exclusion (Schorr, 1992; Becker, 1997; Barry and Hallett, 1998).

Services have always been provided in this sector by a mix of local government statutory organisations; non-governmental organisations and for profit organisations. The balance between the contributions made by these agencies has changed over time and their work has been sustained by a comparatively small but growing financial investment by central government (Webb and Wistow, 1987; Adams, 1996; Evandrou and Falkingham, 1998).

Figure 4.1   The size of the UK welfare state

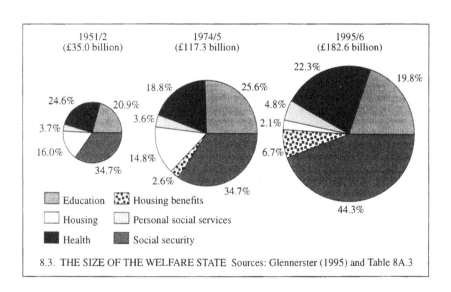

8.3. THE SIZE OF THE WELFARE STATE Sources: Glennerster (1995) and Table 8A.3

Source: Glennerster and Hills, 1998, p.314.

Personal social service expenditure underpins a range of residential, day and community care resources directed at a variety of client groups.

The main areas of expenditure are in services for older people and children.

Figure 4.2   Local authority net current expenditure by client group

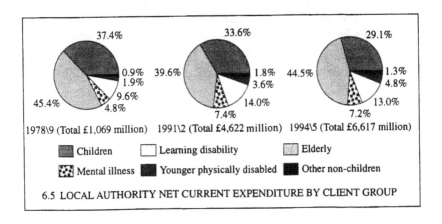

1978\9 (Total £1,069 million)   1991\2 (Total £4,622 million)   1994\5 (Total £6,617 million)

- Children
- Learning disability
- Elderly
- Mental illness
- Younger physically disabled
- Other non-children

6.5 LOCAL AUTHORITY NET CURRENT EXPENDITURE BY CLIENT GROUP

In protecting, supporting and controlling individuals of all ages the personal social services make the kind of provision for a minority of citizens that families are usually expected to make. The operation of this welfare sector therefore raises key questions about the relationship between state and family. The role of the state in substituting for, or supplementing family care of troublesome and vulnerable people has always been a politically and morally contentious area. Social workers play a critical role in determining who should receive assistance from the personal social services, and because of this role they have come to symbolise the changing and often problematic relationship between state welfare services and family life (Parton, 1996; Millar: 1998).

In presenting the latest case for modernisation at national and local levels the White Paper argues that currently social services suffer from six major problems which must be addressed if the services are to improve radically. These are listed as:

- A failure to offer sufficient protection to vulnerable children and adults who are at risk of neglect and abuse;

- A failure to coordinate services sufficiently to ensure that individuals receive individualised responses to their needs;
- An inflexible tendency to offer services that do not fit the individual situations and result in difficulty and exclusion for service users rather than support and integration;
- A failure to be clear about what services can be offered and the standards that individual users of these services should expect to receive;
- A lack of consistency in the provision offered between different local authority departments, and within local authority departments with eligibility criteria for services not being made clear to service users and their families;
- Inefficiency in the way services are run resulting in local authorities not getting full value for the money they spend on services.

These problems are not new; they have been continuously cited at times of review and reform of the personal social services in Britain over the past fifty years. What have changed over this period are some of the solutions proposed by government. Continuity as well as change has, therefore, characterised the development of this welfare sector. In the remainder of this chapter these trends will be considered historically in order to provide a context from which to review the strengths and weaknesses of the most recent modernisation agenda.

The personal social services and the welfare state

The establishment of what became known in the 1950s as the 'welfare state' in Britain was part of an aspiration by government to deliver a comprehensive range of health and welfare services to meet the needs of citizens. In a context in which government pledged itself to maintain full employment to protect its citizens from want, these services were offered to all regardless of their economic standing. It was an approach to welfare provision which attracted support across the political spectrum in Britain for almost thirty years (Marquand, 1988).

The establishment of a comprehensive range of state services in health, social security, housing and education in the late 1940s in Britain raised questions about whether there was a viable future for the range of state and voluntary provision which by then made up the personal social services (Seed, 1973). However, it was considered by Beveridge, amongst others, that the need for such services would probably diminish in the context of a more prosperous and welfare-oriented society; steps were taken to embed a range of social work and social care activities in newly created local government agencies. These services aspired to supplement, directly or indirectly through the voluntary sector, the provision being made by centralised, state-funded welfare bodies for those citizens with particular difficulties. The role that social workers were envisaged as playing in these services reflected the positive way in which their contribution to alleviating the dislocation and distress of wartime had been viewed by the public and politicians.

The new basis given to local authority personal social services at this time broke with the framework of past patterns of provision by the abolition of the Poor Law. This nineteenth-century institution which had previously determined eligibility for many forms of personal social service was considered to be antithetical to a welfare state which proclaimed its intent to establish social citizenship rights for all (Marshall, 1950). The Labour government at this time argued that the abolition of the Poor Law was an essential first step to creating an organisational and legal framework for social care and welfare which would ensure the promotion of fair and just responses to citizens in difficulty. In establishing the case for change politicians and social welfare academics pointed to the evidence of stigma, abuse and neglect which had been suffered by vulnerable children and adults in Poor Law institutional care.

The Curtis Committee which reviewed services for children, young people and families at this time, stated: 'we find a strong impression that the stigma attached to Public Assistance...is so clearly ingrained that only a completely new approach will enable the authorities to keep clear of it' (Curtis, 1946, para. 439). Opening the parliamentary debate on the National Assistance Bill which sought to assist adults with a range of welfare needs, Aneurin Bevan, then Minister of Health, argued that it was important to remove the 'taint' of the Poor Law because 'where the individual is immediately concerned, where warmth and humanity of administration is the primary consideration, then the authority which is responsible should be as near to the recipient as possible' (Hansard, 1947, col. 439).

The abolition of the Poor Law and its replacement by a national government scheme for the payment of social security benefits meant that the administration of financial assistance to families and individuals in need was removed from the personal social services. The result was that in Britain, unlike in many European countries and the United States, local authority social workers played no further part in the assessment of means to determine social security payments. This liberation from assessment for help in cash as well as in kind was embraced positively by most social workers in the 1940s who had experienced working with the Poor Law as a constraint on the development of what they considered to be their professional expertise and status (Jordan, 1974).

The role of social work in this new welfare order was to make personalised responses to the crises and difficulties facing those individuals and families who lacked sufficient personal and social resources. This involved social workers in exercising control in respect of people's behaviour as well as in delivering care and assistance. In recognition of the new challenges which the postwar welfare settlement had placed on social workers, government funded a growing number of professional training and education opportunities for this expanding, and so far largely untrained, welfare workforce. This investment, together with the dismantling of large scale institutional responses to those in need, did much to ensure the gradual expansion rather than the contraction of the personal social services, and by the 1960s social work began to show signs of establishing itself as a profession for the first time, alongside other health and welfare professionals such as doctors, teachers and nurses (Langan, 1993).

The unification of social work

The growth in the 1960s in the size and confidence of social work as a welfare profession, together with evidence that it was playing a key role in responding to problems encountered by individuals and families who were 'falling through the net' of the welfare state, played its part in a government review of the organisational base of the personal social services during this decade. Increasingly it was argued that social work would make a more effective contribution to welfare if it was not so organisationally diffuse and if, from a consolidated base, it could direct its expertise at family and community problems at the same time as under-taking specialist casework with individuals in difficulty. Discussions about effectiveness at this time were dominated by concerns about spreading professional expertise. The focus was on whether the specialisms which had been established in social work practice ought to be replaced by a generic approach to assessing need and delivering services to all. Significantly, this was not an era in which effectiveness was being addressed primarily in terms of financial investment. Expenditure on the personal social services actually doubled between 1960 and 1968 (Adams, 1996) and the expectation was that this trend would continue.

The case being made for a more unified, comprehensive and effective professional social work presence that could respond to changing needs was reinforced by those lobbying for a more coordinated organisational base for social work within local authority services. Evidence was provided of the uncoordinated and uneven responses which had been made in the 1950s and 1960s to vulnerable and troubled individuals in need. This, it was argued, was the result of the overlapping mandates of a number of small, politically weak local authority departments and voluntary sector organisations providing services in this area. To address this lack of coordination, as well as the lack of understanding by the public about what the personal social services could offer, it was suggested that

> One single department concerned with most aspects of 'welfare' as the public generally understands the term is an essential first step in making services more easily accessible. They must not be camouflaged by administrative complexity, or their precise responsibilities closely defined (Seebohm: 1968, para. 46).

The reports of the Seebohm Committee on Local Authority and Allied Personal Social Services in England and Wales, and the Kilbrandon Committee on Children and Young Persons in Scotland, in reviewing the state of the personal social services in Britain, succeeded in making the case for radical organisational change and increased state investment in this welfare sector. In the well-established tradition of the British welfare state these committees recommended the establishment of a unified organisational base for the personal social services within local government to provide

> a community-based and family-oriented service, which will be available to all. This new department will, we believe, reach far beyond the discovery and rescue of social casualties; it will enable the greatest possible number of individuals to act reciprocally, giving and receiving service for the well-being of the whole community (Seebohm, 1968, para. 2).

Dubbed a 'fifth social service' by some, the personal social services took their place alongside health, education, social security and housing as a separate distinct agency striving to identify and respond to individual, family and community needs. In 1971, when the new social services departments in England and Wales were established, a new professional qualification for social workers was also introduced which required a general rather than a specialist training. Three years later, once local government had been reorganised in England and Wales, local authority social services departments, headed by Directors, found themselves with increased budgets, an expanding workforce and the need to develop managerial structures designed to plan, deliver and evaluate their diverse range of services. In the words of Younghusband, social work had 'leapt from the margins to the centre' (Younghusband, 1978).

Social work and the mixed economy of welfare

From the early 1970s Britain, along with other advanced capitalist societies, experienced considerable economic, political and social change. In a context of increasing global economic competition, the British economy experienced a marked contraction of its manufacturing base, more so than most comparable industrialised countries. In 1976, in a situation of deepening unemployment, the International Monetary Fund granted Britain a loan to assist it in managing the economic crisis it was facing. In accepting this assistance the government agreed to make cuts in public expenditure. This marked a transformation in the way in which expenditure on public services was politically constructed. As Deakin suggests, public expenditure was no longer viewed as part of the solution for social problems - it became part of the problem (Deakin, 1994). Efficiency in respect of welfare services was increasingly defined as curtailing expenditure in the face of economic decline.

The election in 1979 of a Conservative government headed by Margaret Thatcher, with a strongly declared opposition to public sector welfare, sustained the budgetary constraints that had hit welfare services in the early 1970s. But it also began to transform the terms of the welfare debate and the direction welfare provision.was to take over the next two decades. In its first statement following the 1979 election the Treasury announced that 'public expenditure is at the heart of Britain's present economic difficulties' (quoted in Becker, 1997). This was followed, in 1981, by the government abandoning the setting of guidelines for service provision which had to be achieved by local authority social services departments (DHSS, 1981). Central direction with regard to the setting of priorities in the personal social services was replaced by the language of 'local choice'; this was to be realised within tightening central government controls on local authority expenditure.

Nevertheless, the evidence shows that despite their rhetoric around welfare expenditure successive Conservative administrations did not succeed in reducing public expenditure on welfare (by 1996, the final year of a series of Conservative administrations, the share of GDP spent on state-funded welfare was greater than in 1974). However, New Right thinking had became increasingly influential in government circles and it did not limit itself to issues of curbing welfare expenditure. Its ideas about the nature of state welfare and recipients of state welfare changed the ways in which welfare, and those seeking state welfare were framed in public, political and professional arenas (Clarke, 1996). Notions of collective responsibility for those who were vulnerable in increasingly insecure and uncertain times were replaced by ideas about promoting individual choice, responsibility and independence from state intervention.

The welfare state as it had been conceived in the 1940s was blamed for creating a dependency amongst those using it, which was economically and morally undermining for the individuals involved, as well as for society in general. Alternatives to state welfare, for example, the family, self-help groups, private and non-government organisations, were promoted as superior to statutory welfare provision, and heralded as the major future providers of welfare services.

The working through of these ideas was played out in negative comments by politicians and the media on the personal social services. The latter came to be seen as exemplifying all that was problematic about welfare dependency. Social work in particular was identified as a profession which fostered outmoded notions of state assistance. The problems experienced by the most marginalised in society were diagnosed by government ministers not so much as a consequence of an increasingly unequal social order but more as evidence of the wilfully different and deviant behaviour of individuals intent on undermining prevailing moral standards (Murray, 1990; Lister, 1996). At the same time social workers came under criticism both for failing to protect children and vulnerable adults in dangerous situations and also for stepping into situations too readily to use their statutory powers to remove children deemed to be at risk.

These changes in the welfare climate emerged in the 1980s and 1990s, a time when income inequality was increasing faster in the UK than in any other industrialised country except for New Zealand (Barclay, 1995, p.14). By the late 1990s one in four of the population of Britain (just below 14 million people) lived on income below half of the national average, with around 10 million living on income support (Walker and Walker, 1997). Evidence from the European Union in the early 1990s showed that the proportion of children living in households with less than half of the average income was 32 per cent - higher than in any other European Union country (Dean and Melrose, 1999, p.4). Furthermore, amongst the poorest fifth of Britain's population, people from minority ethnic groups as well as women, children and older people were disproportionately represented (Amin and Oppenheim, 1992; Glendinning and Millar, 1992; Hills, 1995).

This growing inequality led to increased demands being made on local authority social services departments. Faced with this they moved away in the 1980s and 1990s from addressing issues of unemployment and poverty in poor communities. The family-oriented community-based generic approach to the personal social services was replaced by services organisationally divided between specialist services for children and families and services for adults. In children and family services the predominant policy response was in reaction to all the publicity given to evidence of child abuse and neglect. The guidelines drawn up on child protection procedures and the establishment of 'at risk registers' ensured that budget-constrained social work with families and children became risk and crisis-driven. Admittedly, the Children Act of 1989, with its emphasis on partnerships with families, children's needs and rights and family responsibility, was an attempt to reorder the priorities of local authority children and family social workers from protection to preventive work. However, there is little evidence to date that it has been effective in achieving this.

In the other major area of social work provision - adult services - Conservative governments from 1979 to 1997 sought to encourage the break-up of the 'state monopoly' provision of this sector of the personal social services. The approach was to stimulate the growth of a mixed economy of welfare provision by encouraging the family, together with the independent and private sectors, to virtually replace local authority provision of community care services for adults who needed care and assistance. This encouragement was initially underpinned by financial incentives to the independent and private sectors to enter this market. At a later stage central government constrained the way in which local authorities could invest in their own provision in this area.

From 1984 government signalled that the future for local authority personal social services was to be as regulators and purchasers of care rather than providers. The Griffiths Report on Community Care (DHSS, 1988) argued for local authority social services departments to become brokers to a range of suppliers of care services. The National Health Service and Community Care Act 1990 enacted these recommendations, bringing in the most far-reaching changes in finance, organisation and delivery of social care services since the 1940s.

Many commentators have suggested that this piece of legislation changed social work more fundamentally than the reforms of the Seebohm Committee. Not only did social services departments cease to be the main providers of services, with non-government and for-profit agencies moving in to compete for custom, but social work itself was reshaped by the introduction of care management as well as by business management principles (Clarke and Newman, 1997; Harris and McDonald, 2000).

Personal social services in the twenty first century: Modernisation and the third way

The modernisation agenda for welfare services in Britain promises a 'third way' for welfare, characterised by the government as promoting networks of welfare services developed through public, private and NGO partnerships (Secretary of State for Social Security, 1998; Secretary of State for Health, 1998). The government has announced that central to its concerns are the development of local and regional action to combat social exclusion and to implement change. As part of this it has placed poverty and inequality on the agenda of health and education services, exhorting them to develop partnerships to deliver local responses to these problems in local communities.

Whilst the *Modernising Social Services* White Paper claims that 'Social services are for us all' (Secretary of State for Health, 1998, p.1), the approach it takes to modernisation does not give this sector of welfare an equivalent role to that being given to the health and education services in respect of social exclusion and poverty. Instead the approach is a managerial one. The solutions to the six problems identified as barriers to service improvement (see page 53 above) are the application of six principles underlying a 'high-quality and effective service'. These are:

- care provided in a way which supports independence and dignity;
- services which meet individual's specific needs in a coordinated way;

- care which is delivered in a fair and consistent way in every part of the country;
- care for children which gives them a decent start in life safeguards for adults and children against abuse by the services;
- care provided by a trained and skilled workforce;
- assured standards of care from local services.

While these are principles which are to be welcomed, given the evidence that they have never been fully realised within the personal social services, they hardly constitute a vision for the future which radically changes the direction in which social services have been travelling since the late *1970s. As* Powell, amongst others, has argued, the 'third way',

> despite some central theme...is not a coherent concept that can be applied more or less uniformly to different policy sectors. It appears to be all things to all people: a poorly specified, pick and mix strategy, largely defined by what it is not. Neither does it appear to be new. Arguably some of its key components...have their historical roots in the New Poor Law and the writings of the New Liberals such as Beveridge (Powell, 2000, p.57).

In applying this approach to the arena of the personal social services the government will fail to reverse the retreat of social services in the face of the increasing needs of those neighbourhoods, families and individuals who have borne the brunt of deepening poverty, inequality and social division in British society. Instead, this White Paper limits the potential response of the personal social services to meeting need in its provision of detailed prescriptions for setting and meeting standards and measuring effectiveness. As a result, the marginalisation of social services begun during the 1980s and 1990s is set to continue, programmed to deliver a residual service to a minority of citizens deemed to be eligible because of the high risk they present.

This approach to modernising social services continues and extends the prescriptive, performance-managed approach to social care and welfare developed under Conservative governments. The rapid succession of policy initiatives, performance indicators, service frameworks, targets and other means of measuring best-value outcomes and inspecting and monitoring services it has set in train, add to rather than resolve long-standing tensions: in particular those between central and local government in respect of trying to reconcile calls for consistency with a considered response to local needs.

At the beginning of the twenty-first century social workers in the statutory and NGO sectors in Britain remain positioned where social inequality shapes choice, direction and the possibilities of life for the least powerful in British society. The themes of family life, poverty and crime still powerfully construct its directions and concerns (Becker, 1997). There have been major changes in the organisational and legal context of this profession over the last fifty years but the majority of social work practitioners remain employed directly or indirectly in publicly funded welfare organisations (Balloch et al, 1998). Working within a complex legislative framework, social workers seem destined to remain preoccupied with managerially constructed mandates to assess, target and ration relatively diminishing and residual resources (Glennerster and Hill, 1998).

The evidence of a national survey of the staff of social services departments undertaken in the mid-1990s (Balloch et al, 1998) suggested that one of the outcomes for social workers of working in a situation of intensifying pressure from poor citizens struggling to access scarce resources has been frustration at the increase in bureaucracy and paperwork involved in targeting and rationing decisions. Staff stress is associated with those aspects of work over which staff feel they have least control, insufficient resources and a perceived inability to provide a good enough standard of service.

As Schorr observed in his review of local authority social services departments in the early 1990s, 'the most striking characteristic that clients of the personal social services have in common are poverty and deprivation' (Schorr, 1992, p.8). Since Schorr's review of social work agencies, their strong connection with poverty has grown. In promoting its 'third way' for welfare the 1997 Labour government acknowledges that issues such as poverty and social exclusion are at the heart of social, health and welfare policies. The creation of a Social Exclusion Unit with its emphasis on the need to 'join up' thinking and action across government departments, is an example of what this change of direction can positively produce. But in its detailed policies for the future of the personal social services the government does not indicate how they will make a distinctive contribution to this critical area.

While the Labour government has taken steps to break the Conservatives' silence around poverty and inequality it continues to promote some of the Conservative policies of the 1980s and 1990s. Government remains concerned to be prudent in relation to welfare expenditure and encourages citizens to take increased responsibility for their own lives, and look to sources outside of public welfare to meet their needs and those of their dependants (see for example, Secretary of State for Social Security, 1998).

Conclusions

The personalised forms of investigation and intervention which are the hallmark of social work in the personal social services mean that social work has the potential to be a prime means for determining not only the allocation of scarce welfare resources but also the allocation of blame to the poorest in society. Poor people in contact with social work services continue to feel that their failure to succeed in maintaining themselves without recourse to state assistance is confirmed, through contact with social workers. Merely as users of social work services, they risk becoming labelled as the 'losers' and 'scroungers' portrayed by government and the media as a drain on, if not a danger to, society. Characterised by this difference they know they risk being publicly stigmatised, if not punished, through their association with public welfare services (Beresford et al, 1999).

Social workers over the 1980s and 1990s have found themselves practising where increasing social inequality has constrained choice, direction and the possibilities of life for the least powerful in society. It has been a bleak landscape in which the organisational and legal contexts in which social workers practise have undergone substantial change. New legislation such as the Children Act 1989 and the National Health Service and Community Care Act 1990 have apparently offered more choice for individual service users, and the potential for them to pursue their rights as citizens in receiving state welfare services. At the same time this extension of choice has taken place as public expenditure on the personal social services have not kept pace with the demand generated by an increasingly unequal social order. Choice has had to be exercised in a stigmatising welfare climate in which labels such as 'underclass' and 'welfare dependency' have continued to be all too readily attached to those using social work services.

It is in this climate that social workers find themselves being exhorted, in such documents as *Modernising Social Services*, to demonstrate through their practice that society is concerned to protect those unable to participate fully as citizens in the competitive and unequal conditions of society. At the same time they find themselves being increasingly directed to enforce targeted, residual and controlling, if not punitive, responses to the difficulties of those deemed to have failed to act as responsible and self-sufficient citizens.

A modernised social services armed with the knowledge that service users have about what they need to increase their own independence and participation would need to be based on a set of principles which addresses fundamental issues of purpose, approach and resourcing. A 'third way' which sought radical change could be built from such principles. Such a way would involve a reformulation of the contribution social services can make to the health and well-being of citizens in the twenty-first century. A reformulation based on what users and their neighbourhoods know about what they need rather than what welfare managers and their organisations judge to be in users' best interests. (Lister, 1998).

Becker, in his work on the personal social services, has concluded that to date they have achieved little more than to label and manage poor families. In doing so they have created structures and procedures which contribute to social exclusion and the maintenance of stigmatising approaches towards service users. In not breaking with this tradition the White Paper is in danger of contributing to the further marginalisation, if not exclusion, of those who turn to local authority social services departments. In taking this road, the danger is that social services departments will find themselves, in the twenty-first century, to be as stigmatising and residual as their nineteenth-century Poor Law equivalents.

References

Adams, R. (1996), *The Personal Social Services: Clients, Consumers or Citizens?*, Longman, Harlow.

Amin, K. and Oppenheim, C. (1992), *Poverty in Black and White: Deprivation and Ethnic Minorities*, Child Poverty Action Group, London.

Balloch, S., Maclean, J. and Fisher, M. (eds) (1999), *Social Services Working Under Pressure*, Policy Press, Bristol.

Barclay, Sir Peter (1995), *Inquiry into Income and Wealth*, vol. 1, Joseph Rowntree Foundation, York.

Barry, M. and Hallett, C. (eds) (1998), *Social Exclusion and Social Work: Issues of Theory, Policy and Practice*, Russell House, Dorset.

Becker, S. (1997), *Responding to Poverty*, Longman, London.

Beresford, R., Green, D., Lister, R. and Woodard, K. (1999), *Poverty First Hand: Poor People Speak for Themselves,* Child Poverty Action Group, London.

Clarke, J. (1996), 'After social work?' in N. Parton (ed), *Social Theory, Social Change and Social Work,* Routledge, London.

Clarke, J. and Newman, J. (1997), *The Managerial State,* Sage, London.

Curtis Report, Home Department (1946), *Report of the Care of Children Committee,* Cmd. 6922, HMSO, London.

Davis, A. (1991), 'A structural approach to social work', in J. Lishman (ed), *Handbook of Theory for Practice Teachers in Social Work,* Jessica Kingsley, London.

Deakin, N. (1994), *The Politics of Welfare,* Harvester Wheatsheaf, Hemel Hempstead.

Dean, H. and Melrose, M. (1999), *Poverty, Riches and Social Citizenship,* Macmillan, Basingstoke.

DHSS (1981), *Care in Action: A Handbook of Policies and Priorities for the Health and Personal Social Services in England,* HMSO, London.

DHSS (I 988), *Community Care: Agenda for Action* (The Griffiths Report), HMSO, London.

Evandrou, M. and Falkingham, J. (1998), 'The personal social services' in H. Glennerster and J. Hills (eds), *The State of Welfare: The Economics of Social Spending,* Oxford University Press, Oxford.

Giddens, A. (1998), *The Third Way: the Renewal of Social Democracy,* Polity Press, Cambridge.

Glendinning, C. and Millar, J. (1992), *Women and Poverty in Britain: The 1990s,* Harvester Wheatsheaf, Hemel Hempstead.

Glennerster, H. and Hills, J. (eds) (2nd ed) (1998), *The State of Welfare: The Economics of Social Spending,* Oxford University Press, Oxford.

Hansard, House of Commons Debates (I947), Second reading debate on the National Assistance Bill, vol. 444.

Harris, J. and McDonald, C. (2000), 'Post-Fordist welfare in Australia and Britain', *The British Journal of Social Work,* vol. 30, no. 1.

Hills, J. (1995), *Joseph Rowntree Inquiry into Income and Wealth,* vol. 2, Joseph Rowntree Foundation, York.

Jones, C. (1998), 'Social work and society' in R. Adams, L. Dominelli and M. Payne (eds), *Social Work: Themes, Issues and Critical Debates,* Macmillan, Basingstoke.

Jordan, B. (1974), *Poor Parents: Social Policy and the 'Cycle of Deprivation',* Routledge and Kegan Paul, London.

Jordan, B. (1997), 'Social work and society', in M. Davies (ed), *The Blackwell Companion to Social Work,* Blackwell Publishers, Oxford.

Kilbrandon Report (1964), *Report of the Committee on Children and Young Persons* (Scotland) Cmd. 2306, HMSO, Edinburgh.

Langan, M. (1993), 'The rise and fall of social work' in J. Clarke (ed), *A Crisis in Care? Challenges to Social Work,* Sage, London.

Lister, R. (1996), 'In search of the underclass', in R. Lister (ed), *Charles Murray and the Underclass Debate,* 1EA Health and Welfare Unit, London.

Lister, R. (1998), 'In from the margins: Citizenship, inclusion and exclusion' in M. Barry and C. Hallett (eds), *Social Exclusion and Social Work: Issues of Theory, Policy and Practice,* Russell House, Dorset.

Marquand, D. (1988), *The Unprincipled Society,* Fontana, London.

Marshall, T.H. (1950), *Citizenship and Social Class,* Cambridge University Press, Cambridge.

Millar, J. (1998), 'Social policy and family policy', in P. Alcock, A. Erskine and M. May (eds), *The Student's Companion to Social Policy,* Blackwell, Oxford.

Murray, C. (1990), *The Emerging British Underclass,* Institute of Economic Affairs, London.

Parton, N. (ed) (1996), *Social Theory, Social Change and Social Work,* Routledge, London.

Powell, M. (2000), 'New Labour and the third way in the British welfare state', *Critical Social Policy,* vol. 20, no. 1.

Schorr, A. (1992), *The Personal Social Services: An Outsiders View,* Joseph Rowntree Foundation, York.

Secretary of State for Social Security (1998), *New Ambitions for our Country: A New Contract for Welfare,* Cmd. 3805, Stationery Office, London.

Secretary of State for Health (1998), *Fit for the Future: Modernising Social Services,* Cmd. 4169, Stationery Office, London.

Seebohm (1968), *Report of the Committee on Local Authority and Allied Personal Social Services,* Cmd. 3703, HMSO, London.

Seed, P. (1973), *The Experience of Social Work in Britain,* Routledge, London.

Walker, A. and Walker, C. (eds) (1997), *Britain Divided: The Growth of Social Exclusion in the 1980s and 1990s,* Child Poverty Action Group, London.

Webb, A. and Wistow, G. (1987), *Social Work, Social Care and Social Planning: The Personal Social Services since Seebohm,* Longmans, Harlow.

Younghusband, E. (1978), *Social Work in Britain, 1950-1975,* vol. 1, Allen and Unwin, London.

5 The myth and the reality of privatising social welfare services: A case study of Taipei City

HSIAO-HUNG NANCY CHEN

Preamble

A worldwide tide of privatisation

'Privatisation' seems to have become a ubiquitous phenomenon in welfare-advanced countries ever since the 1980s. As to why it has emerged as an apparent worldwide trend, the following summarize some of the main explanations:

1. Using 'market mechanisms' to deal with public affairs may assist better control of the scale and costs of government.
2. 'Privatisation' can provide consumers with more freedom to choose and thus be more responsive to their needs.
3. 'Privatisation' can broaden the participation of the private sector in public services and thus be conducive to their greater efficiency.
4. Also 'privatisation' may help solve some high-spending welfare countries' predicaments.

Nevertheless, 'privatisation', as experienced in Euro-American welfare contexts, has revealed the following problems:

1. The hypothesis of 'perfect competition' simply does not exist in reality. On the contrary, privatisation can in some cases result in monopoly and oligarchy; thus, under a limited - or no - choice situation, there cannot be a complete fulfilment of consumers' needs as expected.
2. Both governments and consumers tend to know little about private-sector levels of service. Given such limited information, it can be difficult for a government to oversee the cost and effectiveness of the

private sector, let alone evaluate its performance. Thus consumers have also to bear a higher risk when they access welfare services in the private sector.

3. Attempting to ensure the quality of services provided by the private sector can result in increased, instead of decreased, administrative costs for government.

4. Various 'moral hazards' - such as shrinkage of service content by the private sector in order to cut running costs; refusal to provide services for disadvantaged groups; appropriation of whole sections of a governmental budget due to political intervention; difficulties over terminating contracts with the private sector - may be prevalent.

In addition, the accountability of the private sector, the balance between centralization and decentralization, the legitimacy of a government's claims to be acting on consumers' behalf, are further issues worth serious consideration in the context of implementing privatisation.

A brief history of privatising social welfare services in Taiwan

Before the 1980s there existed various types of contract between government and the private welfare agencies. However, it was not until July 1983, when the Department of Social Affairs of the Taiwan Provincial Government signed a contract with Christian Children's Fund, that 'privatisation' of social welfare services could be said to have taken off in Taiwan. Thereafter, the Bureau of Social Affairs of the Taipei Municipal Government also contracted to purchase welfare services from the private sector. Reacting to these developments, in 1983, the Department of Social Affairs of the Ministry of Interior enacted [which is a governmental guideline] *Enhancing Collaboration Between the Government and the Private Sector to Promote Social Welfare Implementation*, which clearly sketched out that each county/city government could adopt subsidy, reward or contracting-out methods to collaborate with the private sector in promoting social welfare services. In 1984, Taipei City promulgated its own *Guidelines for Promoting Public and Private Sector Collaboration in the Delivery of Social Welfare Services*. The Ministry of Interior Affairs and the Taipei Municipal Council subsequently announced further related measures in 1989, 1993 and 1997 respectively.

Though the 'privatisation' of social welfare services is still in its infancy - and given that privatisation is certainly no panacea - a study of its pros and cons would seem timely, given that privatisation has become an increasingly dominant trend in Taiwan. The purpose of this chapter is specifically to examine and assess the privatisation experiences of Taipei City with a special focus on publicly owned, privately run social welfare services.

Review of the literature

'Privatisation' defined

Privatisation, according to Savas (1987, 1992) is: 'The way of transferring the function and activities of government to private organizations'.

Savas identified three different types of privatisation: divestment, delegation and displacement. Divestment implies that through sale, free transfer or liquidation, the government transfers the ownership of public enterprises or assets into the hands of the private sector or market. Delegation, on the other hand, means that the government delegates to the private sector responsibility for taking on full or partial production and/or service delivery functions, by means of a contract, franchise arrangement, grant, voucher or mandate. In such cases, government continues to play a supervisory role since, unlike divestment, this is not a one-off act.

Displacement, by contrast with both the previous two types, is essentially indirect and maybe unintended. It happens when government-provided goods and services fail to satisfy general public demand and/or when performance is faulty, prompting consumers gradually to shift to the private sector for help. It can also happen as a result of government mismanagement necessitating the withdrawal of delivery of a service. It can further take place whenever and wherever deregulation makes it possible for the private sector to question a public-sector monopoly.

The research reported here is focused on the 'publicly owned, privately run' type of privatisation, which in a way combines both contract and franchise. The emphasis will be on the government's transfer of public building utilization rights to the private sector, for the provision of social services to the general public.

Pros and cons of privatisation

As suggested earlier, those who support 'privatisation' often urge the following perspectives.
1. *Efficiency and effectiveness:* this stresses that, through 'privatisation' there will be more competition which will not only promote

efficiency, but also provide consumers with more choice, thus being more responsive to differing demands. Furthermore, owing to there being less regulation and supervision in the private sector, services may be able to maintain a higher level of flexibility.

2. *Liberal ideology:* this perspective, culminating in Reaganism and Thatcherism, argues that too much government intervention can damage economic development. The role of the government should be limited and private-sector participation encouraged. By combining with private-sector resources, public-service activity may have scope for restriction: thus allowing, on the one hand, for the stimulation of other forms of economic activity and, on the other hand, for the better detection of false demand and of unnecessary waste of resources.

3. *Public choice:* motivated by self-interest, voters, interest groups, parties, politicians and bureaucrats are all seeking to maximize their own benefit; therefore it is possible that public expenditures could be boosted to an unlimited extent. Whereas through privatisation and the mechanisms of competition, it is believed that such shortcomings of government may in part be remedied.

Notwithstanding the above arguments, there are voices opposed to privatisation. First of all, some scholars argue that, since public services are by their nature a social necessity and a social responsibility, their being run by government is an essential guarantee of their not being terminated. Once privatized, no one can guarantee the safety of such services and their providers may indeed shun all political and social responsibilities. In addition, since most private service providers are profit-driven, they may not be interested in non-profit-making social welfare services. Thus notions of social justice *per se* could be at stake. Meanwhile private agencies, in any case, may tend not to hire professionally qualified staff in order to cut down on running costs, thus further jeopardizing the quality of the services in question.

To be sure, scholars such as Judge, Smith and Taylor-Gooby (1983) have propounded the idea that 'to support social welfare privatisation does not mean to halt the expansion of the government's role in the welfare state'. Rather, 'privatisation' does not of itself permit a government to escape its responsibilities in the area of social welfare. As already remarked, privatisation is no panacea. After privatisation, the total cost of services may not necessarily be any lower; this quite apart from the fact that the transaction costs of the negotiations themselves often add to the hidden costs of a service. Then again, the emphasis thereafter on reducing costs may result in a lowered quality of service. Finally, due to the non-profit-making nature of social welfare activities, it is not easy to ensure real competition. On the contrary, after privatisation, it can be the ability to pay which dictates who will receive the better services. This 'creaming-off effect' may serve further to broaden the social stratification gap.

Relationships between the government sector and the private sector in the course of privatisation

In theory, it is hoped that, through privatisation, the expansion of governmental social welfare and associated manpower commitments can be cut down. In reality, however, the private sector may still be dependent on government, since it (the private sector) may not grow or expand as might originally have been expected. Generally speaking, there exist the following three models when a government plans to purchase services from the private sector.

1. *Competition model:* this assumes that there are a number of suppliers (or potential contractors), so that the government (buyer) may buy the best service with the lowest price. However, in reality there may exist few competitors, the transaction costs may be high, and the government may not be well enough informed about what it really wants.

2. *Negotiation model:* this involves a consensus-building, incremental decision-making process. There may exist not many competitors. Those interested in wooing a government contract have to come up with adequate proposals through negotiation, then reach some kind of agreement. The government still has to bear some administrative burden. This model, though seemingly more flexible, is likely to end up as some kind of political reward.

3. *Cooperation model:* the strengths of this model include:
   a) the fact of stressing efficiency and project management makes it imperative to maintain a flexible contract relationship in an uncertain environment, which itself can often cut through man-made constraints and complicated procedures;
   b) it may more fully utilize suppliers' professional expertise;
   c) given the lack of competition, it might encounter less opportunism and speculation;
   d) long-term cooperation could save considerable transaction costs.

   However, the shortcomings of this model are as follows:
   a) the lack of objective evaluation criteria, and the fact of being

constrained by the number of suppliers, can make it difficult to
evaluate service efficiency;

b)   due to the lack of competitors, the private-sector agency
     involved tends to focus on how to maintain a good relationship
     with government - at the possible expense of quality of service;

c)   the private sector sometimes holds more information than
     relevant government staff, who thus lack the capacity to form a
     professional judgement on the workings of the service. In such
     circumstances, it is very likely that the private sector may
     dominate the entire scene;

d)   political considerations may be involved in the whole process,
     which can   make it very difficult to avoid misuse of political
     resources.

Professor Liu, shu-chyong's studies (1997, 1998) illustrate that the
relationship between the government and the private organization is that
of both 'dependant' and 'opponent'.

From a 'dependency' point of view, the government often provides
the private sector with subsidy, and professional, technical and political
support, thereby enhancing the legitimacy of the private welfare agencies
in question. In return, these private agencies deliver services on behalf of
the government sector, thus increasing political support for, and the
legitimacy of, the government in question.

However, viewed from a negative - 'oppositional' - point of view,
the discretion of both sides is likely to be constrained. Because of
financial dependency, to receive government funds somehow implies
inviting rigid governmental supervision. It is this prospect which
sometimes prompts private agencies to turn to other sources of finance, to
form coalitions or even to create 'creaming-off' mechanisms in order to
balance their budgets. When such processes go too far, the original aims
of the organization itself may be affected. Meanwhile, from a
governmental point of view, when there are needs beyond the public
capacity to meet, and yet limited private agencies capable of rendering the
requisite types of service, privatisation can literally spell monopoly. Due
to limited administrative resources, governmental supervision is in any
case likely to be restricted. All the same, given the high political profile of
social welfare issues, political interference in the process of privatisation
would seem inevitable.

Development, adjustment, coping, cooperation and shunning: Five ways of response from the private sector

Scholars such as Shi, chiao-yu (1998) have found that private organizations might adopt any or every one of the following responsive models in the course of privatisation:

1. *Developmental:* those who have opted to expand their services will adopt a developmental approach to privatisation.
2. *Adjustment:* some underdeveloped organizations, keen to gain experience, may be prepared to 'adjust' the style or scale of their operations to privatisation.
3. *Coping:* some private welfare organizations may not actively involve themselves in the privatisation business, yet may be willing to spare some resources to cope with new demands.
4. *Cooperation:* most immature private organizations will adopt this strategy in the hope of expanding the scope of their services.
5. *Shunning: in the case of:*
   a) those which had experienced unpleasant working relationships with government in the past; or
   b) well-established organizations which, even without any resource assistance from the public sector, were still in a position to survive well; and
   c) those not eligible to enter into a contract with government, either because of their lack of accommodation capability or for other reasons;
   all of which tend to adopt apathetic attitudes toward privatisation.

The aforementioned analysis clearly indicates that the nature of social welfare privatisation is quite different from the privatisation of other government services such as public utilities. This is because, in addition to 'efficiency', social welfare privatisation involves considerations of 'equity'. The relationship between the government sector and the private welfare agencies sector thus carries overtones of both conflict and cooperation. Where suitably qualified private organizations are not already in existence, to privatize regardless could even amount to a dangerous operation.

Research methodology

The work of scholars such as Lin, wan-yi (1997, 1998), Liu, shiu-chyong

(1997, 1998), Ko, San-gi, Wan, yi-wei (1994), and Shi, chiao-yu (1998) indicates that some private organizations, agencies and foundations have indeed been nourished, and overall service provision increased, through privatisation. However, their research findings also depict the following problems encountered by 'privatisation' in Taiwan:

- *Not enough competitors:* since the private welfare sector in Taiwan is not yet fully developed, whenever there are more cases to be contracted out than agencies exist, it can simply be impossible to find enough private agencies qualified to carry out a contract. Thus the first contract may go to the best agency, the second goes to the second best, leaving the third with no takers.
- *Not enough information:* neither government nor the consumers are possessed of sufficient first-hand information concerning privatisation.
- *Supervision difficulties:* lack of manpower and legal backup make the processes of supervision difficult, which in turn adds to the transaction costs.
- *High 'moral hazard':* political intervention and unclear modes of accounting typify the cases in point.
- The unclear line being drawn between 'centralization' and 'decentralization': this can arouse complaints from the private sector.
- *Bureaucratized, commodified and chain-managed styles of delivery:* this is a growing trend amongst private agencies in receipt of a contract.

In line with the above, scholars have suggested that government should stop contracting out social welfare services until there is a more mature private sector in existence. In other words, scholars incline toward an incremental approach to privatisation; insisting that sufficiency of contracted-out budget, quality of supervision and management, and the qualifications of private sector agencies for the tasks in hand, should be made key criteria for privatising social welfare, in Taiwan generally and in Taipei City in particular.

Against such a background, besides drawing on secondary data - such as related literature, research reports, basic information on each of the organizations receiving contracts, the contents of such contracts, the governmental work plan and budgets - this research involved visits to several private agencies in receipt of government contracts and the conduct of in-depth interviews with responsible personnel. Tables 5.1 and 5.2 show the scale of the sampling carried out and the backgrounds of those interviewed from both the government and the private sectors.

Table 5.1 The μ and sample(s) of the research

Category	Elderly welfare	Youth welfare	Children's welfare	Women welfare	Handi-capped welfare	Home-less services	Total
$\mu^{(1)}$	4	4	7	10	14*	1	40
Sample(s)$^{(2)}$	1	1	1	2	3	0	8
%$^{(2)\div(1)}$	25	25	14.3	20	23	0	20

*The exact number of agencies that is in operation is 13 rather than 14, therefore, the percentage is 23 per cent rather than 21 per cent.

Table 5.2 Backgrounds of interviewees from government and private sectors

	Sector indicator	Government sector	Private sector	Total
Sex	Male	3	3	6
	Female	8	7	15
Subtotal		11	10	21
Educational background	Social work related	8	7	15
	Sociology related	1	0	1
	Other related fields*	2	3	5
Subtotal		11	10	21
	Below 5 years	4	2	6
Work experience	6-10 years	1	1	2
	11-15 years	1	2	3
	16 years and above	5	5	10
Subtotal		11	10	21

* 'Other related fields' refers to areas such as special education, health welfare, architecture and rural-urban planning.

N.B. The total in table 5.2 has already been added to that of 21 - Please see the subtotal for each indicator.

Up until the end of January 1999, there were 39 cases of contracting-out in Taipei. Services relating to the handicapped rank highest, making up a total of fourteen cases, nearly one-third of the contracted-out total. Services relating to women rank second, making a total of ten cases, one-fourth of the total of contracted-out services. Altogether, the research project has completed 8 agency interviews, 9 interviews with public organization staff and 2 interviews with high-ranking officials. In addition, 2 focus group discussions were also conducted to gather opinions from scholars, experts, legislators and staff from both government and private sectors.

As a preliminary exercise in evaluation research, this study tried to assess the experience of privatisation in Taipei City by tackling the following issues:

1. the background and purposes of contracting out;
2. the nature of the privatisation in question: e.g. contracting out or merely providing a subsidy;
3. factors and conditions considered by the Bureau of Social Affairs in relation to privatising social welfare services;
4. the contents of the contract;
5. the precise time when the Bureau of Social Affairs decided to contract-out: eg. at the initial stage of a service? after it had been in operation? as dictated by the nature of the service?
6. when and how the Bureau of Social Affairs actually contracts out social welfare services;
7. whether or not the Bureau of Social Affairs has a way of accurately calculating the administrative cost of these;
8. the kinds of organizations or agencies which have already been contracted by the Bureau of Social Affairs: whether or not these concomitantly receive more than one contract; whether or not they are possessed of proper managers, facilities and professional credentials;
9. the difficulties encountered by those organizations or agencies in receipt of the contract during the course of its operation and how such difficulties might be overcome;
10. the models of interaction adopted by public and private agencies during the course of implementing the contract;
11. types of interaction between private agencies in receipt of the contract and other private agencies of the same nature: competition? cooperation? coexistence? no relationships at all?
12. the circumstances under which the public sector will consider

terminating its collaborative relationship with private agencies in receipt of contract; whether or not there have been any examples of such in the past and, if so, with what consequences;

13. the overall assessment of both public-sector and private contracted agencies, regarding the 'contracting out' system.

Findings

Sample characteristics

We may expect some differences when comparing the background and developmental experience of Taiwan's social welfare services' privatisation with that of other developed countries. Most advanced countries opted for privatisation after the public sector had been engaged in the supply of welfare services for some time, and/or in conditions where there was a plentiful supply of NGOs, and/or again in conditions of apparent welfare state crisis. In Taiwan, by contrast, though the demand for welfare is rising, there remains as yet an insufficiency of public sector supply, coupled with the fact that there exist as yet not too many NGOs either. It is because the welfare market has not attained sufficient economies of scale that privatisation seems to have become the answer.

Prior to 1990, owing to the insufficient capacity of private welfare agencies, most social services were delivered by the public sector. Whereas after 1990, once overall economic development had reached a certain level concomitant with rising popular expectations after the lifting of martial law, the welfare budget was set to increase, even though the number of government-employed professional staff remained, ironically enough, far behind the demand for their services, mainly as a result of government attempts to cap expenditure on personnel. Thus it is that privatisation seems to have become the only choice. Apart from contracting-out to entire private organizations, there are also contracting-out arrangements functioning on 'case-by-case' or 'project' basis.

Figure 5.1 offers a flow chart of the study.

Figure 5.1 The motive of the study

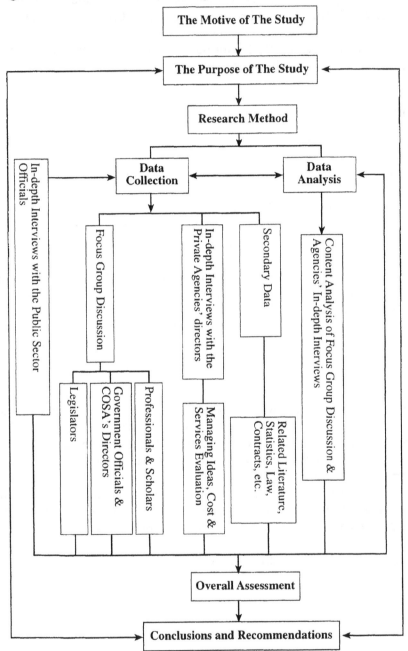

Amongst social welfare services contracted-out on a 'case-by-case' basis, agencies catering for the low-income elderly, children, the handicapped and the mental retarded were quite popular during the 1960s and 1970s. Services contracted-out on a 'project' basis, including those focussed on the child/parental home, on vocational training for the handicapped, early treatment for handicapped children, day care nurses training courses, have been prominent from the late 1970s up to the present day.

However the breakthrough came when 'Contracting out for Statutory Agencies' (COSA) was initiated in March 1985. So far, as a result, there are 39 private agencies in receipt of government contracts in Taipei. Of these, fourteen are handicapped related; ten are concerned with women's welfare; seven are related to child welfare; four each are concerned with the welfare of the elderly and with juveniles, a further one is concerned with services to the homeless. Perhaps as a result of the rapid growth of COSA, the Taipei municipal government started to enact relevant Guidelines from 31 January 1997.

Figure 5.2 Percentage of different welfare programmes managed through COSA in Taipei

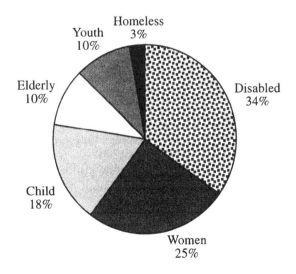

Figure 5.3 Cooperation time between COSA and the Bureau of Social Affairs, Taipei Municipal Government

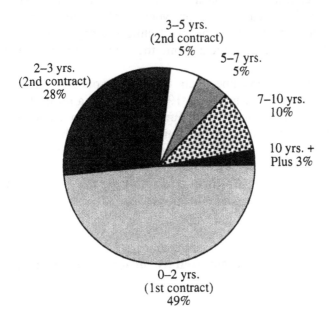

Nineteen out of the 39 private agencies involved were in receipt of a contract for the first time. The average length of existing collaboration cases is less than two years. Another thirteen agencies have signed a second contract, yet only two child welfare centers have worked with the government for more than three years; and only one has entered into a third contract term and has collaborated with the government bureau for more than five years. There are just three private agencies that have obtained a fourth contract, having worked with the government for over seven years. The earliest and the longest COSA is that of Po-Ai Child development center, which has been signatory to a government contract for more than 14 years.

In terms of location, 35 out of 39 COSA are situated in Wan-hwa or Wen-Shan district, accounting for six each; Ta-tung came to the second on the list, obtaining five contracts. Hsin-I and Chung-Cheng follow, covering four cases each; Shug-Shan has three cases, Ta-An has two; Pei-tou, Chung-Shan, Neihu and Nan-Kang have one each. (Wan-hwa and Ta-Tung districts are the oldest and perhaps the least developed/poorest districts of Taipei; Wen-Shan, Neihu, Nan-Kang and Pei-tou districts belong to the newly developed/middle income areas in the outskirts of the city; Ta-An, Shug-Shan, Chung-Cheng, Hsin-I and Chung-Shan districts are considered relatively more developed/richer areas in the city. Nevertheless, though it is true that the least developed areas demand more social services, the location of COSA in Taipei does not necessarily reflect such area characteristics due to the very fact that the city government can only run such programmes on the basis of site availability. In other words, it depends on these districts finding suitable public owned spaces that may be used for COSA.)

Figure 5.4 Percentage of COSA in different administrative districts of Taipei

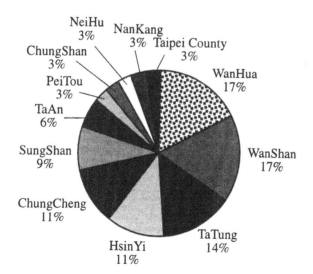

Furthermore, out of 39 contracts, private foundations run 26 of them. So far as the nature of services is concerned, those for the handicapped rank top of the list. Different private associations are in charge of the other thirteen; amongst which women's welfare constitutes the largest single category. It can also be observed from Chart 5 that most private agencies receive only one contract; and that few private organizations have crossed welfare boundaries and obtained more than one contract from the government. (In Taiwan, 'Foundations' refers mostly to those organizations sponsored by Funds which come from a particular enterprise and/or a/group of donors whereas 'Associations' may be formed out of some ideal/common interest/common goal with or without financial support from a specific person or agency. Therefore, associations normally encounter more financial pressures than foundations.)

Figure 5.5 Number of contracts received by contracting-out of statutory agencies in Taipei

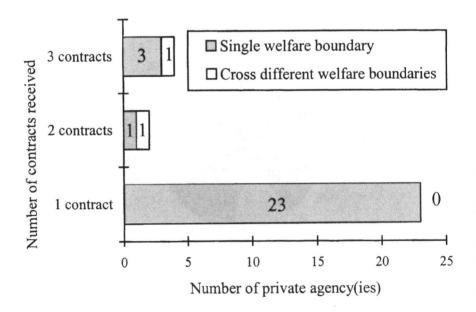

Number of private agency(ies)

In-depth interviews with both the government officials and the private sector's personnel:

As indicated earlier, this study has carried out 21 in-depth interviews with governmental staff and private organizations' personnel. The following are some of the main findings derived from these interviews:

(1) *As to whether the government should continue to contract-out social welfare services to statutory private agencies in the future:*
Government staff's opinions:
Most government staff interviewed maintained a rather conservative stance toward COSA. The reasons given can be summarized as follows:
A. There are simply not enough private agencies in existence for the government to consider contracting-out to:
Most government staffs had experienced pressure: 'once the public announcement concerning the contract-out is posted, there are simply no agencies coming to apply'. Nevertheless, under this policy, some members of staff have to take the initiative for allocating a contract target. So long as the professional ability of the private agencies is made the number one criteria, it is very likely that some private agencies are going to shoulder the burden of more than one contract. This in itself is contrary to the original aim of COSA that the government should guide and/or support as many private agencies as possible.
B. Moreover, with regard to those private organizations interested in COSA, it is said that their professional quality(ies) is/are mostly under doubt.
Most government staff interviewed pointed out that, for those willing to receive government contract(s), their professional qualities are for the most part questionable. To ensure the quality of their services, therefore, the Bureau of Social Affairs, Taipei Municipal Government, has in recent years set aside a budget for two to three professional social workers to attend each relevant private agency. Unfortunately, in the process of evaluation, it has been found that some private agencies did not assign social work to these professionals. Instead, they mostly relied upon volunteers to take care of cases, thus downgrading the level of the quality of services.

(2) Tangible and/or intangible administrative cost are not necessarily reduced

One of the reasons for contracting-out to private organizations has been to expand social welfare services in circumstances when the government is attempting to cut its own budget for personnel. Nevertheless, government staff interviewed reflected that 'if we ran the services by ourselves, each year we could save at least 10,000,000 to 20,000,000'. This relates to the administrative cost only. If one adds the time required for communication and supervision, together with other administrative costs, the total could be even higher.

Private agencies' viewpoints

As to whether COSA should be continued in the future, private agencies' viewpoints tended to be more diverse. Based on the following considerations, some private agency personnel felt that COSA should be continued:

Such opinions, pro COSA, included:

a) The annual subsidy of NT$1,000,000 to NT$2,000,000 (US$1= NT$30.80 as of April 21, 2000) provided by the Bureau of Social Affairs to each private agency involved, does indeed help them a great deal in promoting certain types of social services.

b) Collaborating with the government certainly adds creditability to the private agencies involved.

c) The free use of buildings provided by the Bureau of Social Affairs to contracted private agencies helps greatly in cutting down their running costs, especially when the goal of public and private agencies is in congruence.

d) Modes of supervision, in terms of professional personnel and forms of operation, serve on balance to enhance the quality of services and the growth of those private organizations involved.

However opinions expressed against COSA included:

a) Private agencies' personnel feel that sometimes the government seems not to have 'trust' in the private agencies, resulting in there being a tense relationship between the two. More than one private agencies' person interviewed pointed out that the Bureau of Social Affairs seemed to be afraid that private agencies might utilize public provided buildings for purposes of business other than as designated in the contract. The government is accused of being afraid of private agencies being tempted to use their professional personnel for the conduct of services outside those stated in the contract. There is also suspicion on the part of government over whether private agencies might be levying unnecessary fees for services rendered.

b) Almost all the private agencies felt that they had to devote additional time and manpower, 'inefficiently', to taking care of the paperwork - such as filling in an accounting sheets, writing up minutes or an annual report - as demanded by the Bureau of Social Affairs.

c) Changes in the content of a contract in the midst of its operation - such as in relation to the number of professional personnel that may be subsidized or the kinds of services hitherto agreed upon, due to budget constraints - can create inconveniences for private agencies.

d) Indicators such as 'the amount of services rendered' used by the government sector to evaluate COSA are felt to be inappropriate. So far as private agency personnel are concerned, it may be not an increase of clients but rather a *decrease* in them which should be viewed as proof of better performance. Governmental evaluation should take note of such considerations which, unfortunately, it has so far failed to do.

e) It is stipulated in the contract that, even if there is surplus, this cannot be reallocated back to the mother agencies of the organizations which signed contracts with the Bureau of Social Affairs. This has rendered the operations of some underfunded small agencies unnecessarily problematic. Furthermore, the idea of prohibiting those who have already obtained subsidy(ies) from levying any fee or service charge is also criticized; especially when public agencies are in a position to provide similar services under a different fee regime.

f) The role of the subsidized professional social workers dispatched to private agencies has also caused disagreement between government and the private sector. So far as the private agencies are concerned, it is not at all necessary to have personnel with a social work background imposed on them to act as 'directors of staff'. Psychology, law, even accounting expertise could equally be also considered as suitable for the job. Yet, to ensure professional standards, the public sector insists that social workers are the most suitable personnel for this job in COSA.

g) The annual one-shot, two-to-three hours evaluation of COSA by professors is sometimes viewed by the private agencies as 'too subjective'.

h) The incongruent policies adopted by different divisions of the Bureau of Social Affairs require private agencies in receipt of more than one contract to maintain different expectations vis-a-vis the Bureau. They felt that some consensus in terms of the terms, (subsidies, professional personnel dispatched, budget, etc.) ought first to be established within the Bureau.

Other considerations

Miscellaneous items such as the terms of the contracts, who should pay the utility bill, whether the private agencies can carry their own logo, etc., were also mentioned in the course of the interviews.

Having acknowledged all this, however, some private agencies' personnel are even now worried that, after nine years of contract (the longest contract tenure that the present Guidelines allows), who is going to build on their accumulated experience? What arrangements are there for clients and for professional social workers? In the case of most private agencies, it is believed that the government should continue to play both a supervisory and an assistance role; yet, so far, they feel that the Bureau has played much more of a supervision than an assistance role. Thus it is that, even given the short history of COSA, there are a few private agencies which have already, voluntarily, terminated their contracts with the Bureau; either because they are functionally the stronger partners or because they have other public linkages and hence sources of creditability.

Conclusions and recommendations

Just as COSA in Taiwan is still in its infant stage, both the public sector and the private sector in Taiwan are still at their respective learning (trial and error) stages. Perhaps, we may conclude by offering the following suggestions for both government and private sectors:

Government sector priorities:

1. To decide which area(s) of the social welfare services is most appropriate for COSA:
    Social welfare services related to day-care, nursery, the handicapped

and elderly nursing home services, because of their simplistic nature, market orientation and/or the more specialised personnel required seem the ones more suitable for COSA. Whereas services such as women's welfare (mid-way house excluded) and elderly welfare should be taken care of by the government itself.

2. An incremental approach should be adopted during the course of COSA in order to fulfill the goal of boosting private agencies. To be more accurate, a step-by-step approach such as adopting a 'case' delegation first, followed by a 'project' delegation and lastly adopting COSA, could be a much better way of helping the government and the private sector adjust to each other.

3. In terms of reducing the numbers of government personnel, COSA indeed is quite effective; nevertheless the overall cost of COSA, administrative costs included, requires further investigation.

4. Given the fact that there exist insufficient numbers of qualified private agencies, notwithstanding the fact that providing assistance to COSA has been one of the major goals of the government's contracting-out policy, how are those 'in charge' to get round the fact that large scale private organizations turn out to be the most capable of seizing and even monopolizing limited social welfare resources; and that they especially are liable to be subject to political intervention?

5. Some COSA tasks, though under direct supervision by the Bureau of Social Affairs, are nevertheless related to different branches of city government activity, such as the Bureau of Education, the Bureau of Health, the Bureau of Police, and the Department of Housing and Urban Development. Thus, for an overall high standard of performance to be achieved, it will be essential to strengthen horizontal linkages amongst these departments.

6. The Bureau of Social Affairs is most of the time facing urgent tasks, leaving it very little room for long-term policy consideration. Yet, it is so important for comprehensive planning to be in place in Taipei, for the effective coordination of COSA assignments, there is arguably a need for instituting a higher level committee, directly accountable to the mayor, to integrate all related departments of the city government in this regard.

The Private Sector:

1. Since most directors of private organizations come from a background of involvement in social movements, it is imperative that, besides case, group and community work, they should maximise their own planning and resource mobilization capabilities in order to upgrade their services' provision.
2. Besides planning capabilities, the private organizations ought also to be working to transform the range of their activities in order to cope with environmental changes.
3. Bearing in mind their limited finance, private sector organizations need to pay special attention to the risks of 'creaming-off' 'easy' cases.

References

I. Chinese language references:

Bureau of Social Affairs, Taipei Municipal Government (1993), *Principles on Awarding the Private Social Welfare Agencies in Providing Social Welfare Services,* Taipei Municipal Government.

Bureau of Social Affairs, Taipei Municipal Government, (1998), *Guidelines of Designating City-owned Properties to Private Agencies to Deliver Social Welfare Services.* (Draft)

Bureau of Social Affairs, Taipei Municipal Government (1998), *Guidelines of Designating City-owned Properties to Private Agencies to Deliver Social Welfare Services* (Revised draft).

Bureau of Social Affairs, Taipei Municipal Government (1998), *Conference Materials on Contract-out for Statutory Agencies of Taipei City's Social Welfare.*

Bureau of Social Affairs, Taipei Municipal Government (1998), *Taipei City Social Welfare Association's Proposal on the Revision of the Principles in Designating the City Owned Properties for Private Welfare Agencies in Delivering Welfare Services.*

Bureau of Social Affairs, Taipei Municipal Government (1998), *The Comprehensive Report on Taipei City's Welfare Demand and Supply.*

Bureau of Social Affairs, Taipei Municipal Government (1998), *Handbook on Taipei City's Social Welfare Services: an Introduction.*

Bureau of Social Affairs, Taipei Municipal Government (1999), *Taipei City's Social Welfare Report.*

Chang, Ying-cheng (1999), 'Partnership between business and NPOs', *Journal of Community Development,* vol. 85, pp.62-70.

Chen, Chu (1998), 'The existing situation, problems and strategies of Taipei city's social welfare privatisation', *Journal of Community Development,* vol. 80, pp. 17-25.

Chen, Wu-shun (1998), 'Policy direction and measures of social welfare privatisation of the Republic of China', *Journal of Community Development,* vol. 80, pp.4-9.

Cheng, Tze-yuan (1998), 'Competition and cooperation, dependency and autonomy: relationships between the government and the private sector during the course of social welfare services' privatisation', *Journal of Community Development,* vol. 80, pp.79-87.

Chou, Kuo-rau (1996), 'The practice and evaluation on Taipei City government's privatisation cases', Paper presented at the Administrative Reform and City Administration Participation.

Department of Social Affairs, Taiwan Provincial Government, (1997), *Guidelines of Designating the Private Sector in Delivering Social Welfare Services.*

Department of Social Affairs, Taiwan Provincial Government (1997), *Handbook on Social Welfare Resources in Taiwan Province.*

Hong, The-sen (1997), *Research on Managing the Designated City-owned Properties,* Taipei Municipal Government Research Report.

Kaohsiung City Voluntary Association (1998), *Handbook on Kaohsiung City's Social Welfare Resources.*

Ko, San-gi and Yi-wei Wan (1994), *Social Welfare Services' Delegating Models of the Bureau of Social Affairs, Taipei Municipal Government,* Taipei Municipal Government Research Report.

Ku, Yen-wen (1998), 'The challenge for the state under privatisation: a welfare state view', *Journal of Community Development,* vol. 80, pp.70-78.

Kuo, Ten-tze (1999), Dialogue between welfare and profit-making -another thought on social welfare privatisation', *Journal of Community Development,* vol. 85, pp.142-155.

Lee, Chun-yan (1994), 'Research on social welfare privatisation', Masters Thesis, Graduate Institute of Public Policy, National Chunghsin University.

Lin, Wan-yi (1997), *A Study on the Legislature and Models of Contract-out for Statutory Agencies in Social Welfare Services Provisions.* Ministry of Interior Research Report.

Liu, Shiu-chyong (1998), 'Dependency and opponent-relationship between the government and the private organizations under social welfare services' privatisation', *Journal of Community Development,* vol. 80, pp.113-129.

Liu, Shiu-chyong (1998), 'Research on social welfare 'privatisation' - A case study of Taipei city government', Ph.D. Dissertation, Graduate Institute of Three Principles for the People, National Taiwan University.

Shi, Chiao-yu (1998), 'The status-quo, problems and strategies adopted by the private welfare agencies in reacting to privatisation', *Journal of Community Development,* vol. 80, pp.37-55.

Taipei City Council (1998), *Regulations on Managing the Designation of the City-owned Properties*.

Tan, Shia (1998), The design of government intervention and supervision system after social welfare services' privatisation', *Journal of Community Development*, vol. 80, pp.56-59.

Tang, Chi-ming (1998), 'The existing situation and prospects in promoting social welfare privatisation in Taiwan Province', *Journal of Community Development*, vol. 80, pp.10-16.

The Ministry of Interior (1997), *Guidelines for Promoting Social Welfare Privatisation*.

The Ministry of Interior (1998), *Guidelines of Grants for Promoting Social Welfare Services*.

The Taipei City Voluntary Association (1997), *Handbook on Taipei City's Social Welfare Resources*.

Wang, Si-tu (1999), 'The myth of "contract-out" for statuary agencies: an reassessment from non-profit organization', *Journal of Community Development*, vol. 85, pp.156-165.

Wang, Yu-lin and Wan-yi Lin (1998), 'The impact of purchasing service contracts from private welfare agencies', *Journal of Community Development*, vol. 80, pp. 60-69.

II. English language references:

Ascher, K. (1987), *The Politics of Privatisation: Contracting Out Public Services*, St. Martin's Press, New York.

Braddon, D. and Foster, P. (eds) (1996), *Privatisation: Social Science Themes and Perspectives*, Dartmouth, England.

Clarke, J., Cochran, A. and Mclaughlin, E. (eds) (1994), *Managing Social Policy*, Sage, London.

Dehoog, Ruth Hoogland (1990), 'Competition, negotiation, or cooperation: three models for service contracting', *Administration and Society*, vol.22, no. 3, pp.317-340.

Judge, K. and Smith, J. and Taylor-Gooby, P. (1983), 'Public opinion and the privatisation of welfare: Some theoretical implications', *Journal of Social Policy*, vol.12, no. 4, pp.469-490.

Kramer, R.M., Lorentzen, H., Melief, W.B. and Pasquinelli, S. (1993), *Privatisation in Four European Countries: Comparative Studies in Government - Third Sector Relationships*, M.E. Sharpe, New York.

Martin, G.T. (1990), *Social Policy in the Welfare State*, Prentice Hall, Englewood Cliffs, NJ.

Menefee, D. (1997), 'Strategic administration of non-profit human service organizations: a model for executive success in turbulent times', *Administration in Social Work*, vol. 21, No. 2, pp.1-19.

Morgan, P. (1995), *Privatisation and the Welfare State: Implications for Consumers and the Workforce*, Dartmouth Publishing Company, Brookfield, Vt.

Prokopenko, J. (ed) (1995), *Management for Privatisation: Lessons from Industry and Public Service*, Geneva: International Labour Office.

Taylor-Gooby, P. and Lawson, R. (eds) (1993), *Markets and Managers: New Issues in the Delivery of Welfare*, Open University, Buckingham.

Savas, Emanuel S. (1987), *Privatisation: The Key to Better Government*, Chatham House Publishers, Inc., N.J.

Savas, Emanuel S. (1992), 'Privatisation', *Encyclopedia of Government and Politics*, vol.2, pp.821-836, Routledge, New York.

Tang, Kwong-leung (1997), 'Efficiency of the private sector: a critical review of empirical evidence from public services', *International Review of Administrative Sciences*, vol. 63, no. 4, pp.459-474.

PART II
PENSIONS

6 Is it safe enough? The planning of National Pension Insurance in Taiwan

YEUN-WEN KU
HSIU-HUI CHEN

Introduction

Taiwan is characterized by considerable diversity of social security systems, or, to be more exact, diversity in the systems that are used to provide people with allowances or other benefits when they reach old age or when their income is interrupted owing to disability or to the death of the breadwinner.

This diversity is in part a reflection of the fact that Taiwan is at an uncertain, uneven stage of political and economic development. Since the establishment of National Health Insurance (NHI) in 1995, Taiwan has been moving towards an institutional welfare system, in which a national pension insurance scheme (NPI) is under construction and should be realized by 2000. However, this is not a process devoid of debates, difficulties and conflicts. Rather, it is intensively interwoven with the Taiwanese political economy, especially with democratisation and the primary importance given to economic growth. We can see this very clearly by examining the planning of the pension insurance system.

First of all, this chapter starts by considering the old-age income maintenance programmes in Taiwan, and hence the need for a national pension insurance programme, and proceeds to consider why the matter of pensions has become a political issue. We will further analyse the planning proposals for the NPI and examine it in its social context, to assess its possible impact on the economic security of elderly people in Taiwan.

Old-age income maintenance programmes in Taiwan

The current old-age income maintenance system in Taiwan includes three types of schemes: social insurance, public assistance and work-related retirement payments.

1.   Old-age benefits in social insurance programmes
    (1) Civil Servants' Insurance (CSI)
        (a)   Coverage: employees in public administration agencies; public school teachers and staffs.
        (b)   Rate of contribution: 6.4 per cent of insured salary
            (i)   employer: 4.6 per cent of insured salary;
            (ii) employee: 2.24 per cent of insured salary.
        (c)   Old-age benefit qualifications
            (i)   Compulsory Retirement: age 65 with at least 5 years of contribution;
            (ii) Voluntary Retirement
                (1) at least 5 years of contribution and have reached 60
                (2) over 25 years of contribution.
        (d)   Old-age benefit payment
            (i)   Unit: insured monthly salary at retirement;
            (ii) Units are given as follows:

1-5 insured years	1 unit per year
6-10 insured years	1 unit per year
11-15 insured years	2 units per year
16-19 insured years	3 units per year
20 insured years and over (maximum)	36 units per year

        (e)   Reserve fund for old-age benefit:
The CSI old-age liability reserve had been funded at 14.9 per cent of the premium since July 1960. During the 1963-1968 period, the CSI suffered an increasingly severe deficit, so that the funding rate had to be cut to 10.0 per cent. After 1968, the funding rate was restored to 14.9 per cent. However, since 1971, the number of old-age benefits in payment increased so drastically that the old-age reserve was not sufficient to meet the cost and the insufficiency was made good by the accumulated old-age reserve of previous years, which itself was used up by 1973. After 1974, the old-age reserve fund was still not sufficient to cover the payment of old age benefits each year, but the insufficiency was made good via the CSI's total receipts.

(2) Private School Teachers and Staffs Insurance (PSTSI)
- (a) Coverage: employees in private schools
- (b) Rate of contribution: 4.75 per cent of insured salary
  - (i) general revenue: pays 1.54 per cent of insured salary;
  - (ii) employer: 1.54 per cent of insured salary;
  - (iii) employee: 1.67 per cent of insured salary.
- (c) Old-age benefit and qualifications: same as the CSI.
- (d) Reserve fund for old-age benefit:

By the end of 1997, the old-age reserves for PSTSI showed a grand total of NT$ 6,953 million; consisting of NT$ 1,343 million of premiums revenue; NT$ 2,409 million of interest revenue; NT$ 4,172 million of surplus in the reserves; minus NT$ 1,051 million in respect of old- age benefits paid. For the year 1997, the old-age liability reserve funded NT$ 976 million in total, of which premium receipts provided NT$ 113 million, interest revenue provided NT$ 391 million, and the surplus provided NT$ 472 million, minus NT$ 199 million for old- age benefits paid. The reserve balance for old-age remained NT$ 777 million. By comparison with the corresponding figures for 1996, the old-age liability reserve fund showed NT$ 34 million more, while the cost of old-age benefits in payment had increased by more than NT$ 20 million.

(3) Military Servicemen's Insurance (MSI)
- (a) Coverage: military servicemen
- (b) Rate of contribution: 8 per cent of insured salary
  - (i) employer: 5.2 per cent of insured salary;
  - (ii) employee: 2.8 per cent of insured salary.
- (c) Old-age benefit/qualifications: dependent on military commission.

(4) Labour Insurance (LI)
- (a) Coverage: employees in public and private enterprises and craft workers
- (b) Rate of contribution: 6.5 per cent of insured salary
  - (i) Private enterprise employees
    - (1) general revenue: 0.65 per cent of insured salary;
    - (2) employer: 4.55 per cent of insured salary;
    - (3) employee: 1.3 per cent of insured salary.
  - (ii) Craft workers
    - (1) general revenue: 2.6 per cent of insured salary;
    - (2) Craft worker: 3.9 per cent of insured salary.

    (c) Old-age benefit qualifications
       (i) age 60 for men and 55 for women with at least 1 insured year;
      (ii) age 55 with at least 15 insured years;
     (iii) over 25 insured years.
    (d) Old-age benefit payment
       (i) Unit: average insured wage of last 3 years;
      (ii) Units are given:
           1-15 insured years: 1 unit/year
           16 insured years and over: 2 units/year
           maximum: 45 units.

2. Civil Service Employees' Retirement and Compensation Fund (CSERCF)

   CSERCF is designed for servicemen, civil servants and teaching and administrative staffs in public schools. Retirees are entitled to choose between a lump-sum payment, the payment of a pension or a mix of both. For a lump-sum payment, the number of units is calculated by doubling the basic salary at retirement. For each service year, 1.5 units are given, up to a total of 53 units for 35 years. For pension payment, the replacement rate is 70 per cent for 35 service years. The rate of contribution is 8 per cent of the basic salary, 2.8 per cent from the employee and 5.2 per cent from the agencies employing them.

3. Labour Retirement Payment

   Labour Retirement Payment is regulated by the Labour Standards Law which provides another type of retirement lump-sum payment for public- and private-enterprise employees. Under the Labour Standards Law, retirees are entitled to a 45 units lump-sum unit payment for 30 years or more service in the same workplace. Unit payment is calculated by the average wage of the last 6 months, 2 units a year are given for the first 15 service years, and 1 unit a year for those exceeding 15 service years. The rate of contribution is set at 2.15 per cent of the monthly wage from employers.

4. Social Assistance Schemes for senior citizens:

      Medium-and-low Income Senior Citizens Allowance;
      Senior Peasants Welfare Allowance; and
      Senior Veterans Allowance.

The inadequacies of existing income security provision

Separated systems

There are two distinct kinds of social security system geared to protecting old-age income security in Taiwan. One is social insurance, the other is social assistance. Social insurance takes care of the most important old-age income security provision in Taiwan. Before 1995, there were about fourteen social insurance programmes, in which labour insurance, insurance for civil servants, and insurance for military serviceman, were the three major systems, covering the various risks of maternity, injury and sickness, medical care, disability, old age, death and funeral allowances (Ku, 1995). Since the establishment of National Health Insurance in 1995, maternity benefit and medical benefits have been unified. But the old-age benefits and disability benefits are still calculated along different lines and paid via the different systems. Insurees may transfer between the different social insurance schemes, but insured years are not portable. Old-age benefits are still mostly lump sum payments, not able to offer a steady income to retirees and liable to loss of value as a result of inflation.

Restricted coverage

The most obvious inadequacy of old-age security systems in Taiwan is the incompleteness of their coverage. Existing systems usually exclude the unemployed, homemakers, those employed in enterprises with fewer than five workers, and those with earnings above a specified maximum, such as physicians, lawyers, architects. Numerous countries have been reviewing the coverage of their schemes and expanding coverage is widely regarded as a high priority, because the excluded people are more than likely to have low earnings and little with which to support themselves in old age. However, the extension of compulsory social insurance system coverage to all the unemployed, homemakers and the self-employed will probably invoke another challenge. Even where coverage is in principle compulsory, and the contribution is affordable, many insurants may still evade the payment of contributions.

Financial crisis

Existing social insurance programmes are under financial crisis as a result both of inadequate policy and operational shortcomings. The former is probably the major reason. The real rate of contribution has always been politically underestimated under pressure. Many studies argue that the crisis is strongly related to inadequate policy design, which promises generous benefits and requires only a small amount of contribution.

The public assistance programme for the elderly was introduced in 1993. It is means-tested, providing minimal income support for the low-income elderly. The allowance for low-income elderly people is NT$ 6,000 per month and an extra NT$ 3,000 for middle-low-income elderly people. Another social assistance programme for the elderly is the senior peasants welfare allowance, which is not means-tested. Every senior peasant over 65 years old is eligible for NT$ 3,000 per month. The problem is that the number of beneficiaries has been growing faster than expected; and the coverage of the public assistance programme is bigger than that of the social insurance system. This uneven state of affairs has also given rise to a very unequal outcome. There is incentive to evade paying contributions, given the possibility that the evader will nevertheless be able to collect benefits not contingent on contribution records or on the number of working years.

The growing need for a proper pensions system

Currently, the majority of elderly people in Taiwan are said to live with one or more of their children, but the trend is to supplement traditional informal family support with formal social protection. The main limitation of the family is that it is a relatively small group and, with urbanization and industrialization, the tendency is for families to become smaller and more widely dispersed. Although nearly 50 per cent of old people currently get support from their children, the ratio is going down year by year, with the decreasing number of children and the changes in family style from big to small. Given such a context, every person should prepare for their old age when they are young.

Income and educational levels also play a role. Amongst poor families and those with the lowest educational attainment, people are more likely to expect to rely on sons and daughters in their old age. Some may derive income from the ownership of property, such as house or farm rents, particularly those who have been able to accumulate substantial saving during periods of employment. Others may continue to obtain income from work, particularly in agriculture.

Demographic ageing will take effect quite dramatically in the next few decades. According to long-term population projections conducted by Council for Economic Planning and Development (CEPD), the old-age population rate will reach 10 per cent by the year 2011, rising to 20 per cent by the year 2031: i.e. from 10 per cent to 20 per cent , in only 21 years, faster than anything experienced by most countries in Europe and by the USA. Economic security for the aged thus becomes the priority issue on the social policy agenda. The task of developing adequate systems of income support in old age is therefore an urgent one. But without political agreement it cannot quickly be responded to.

In the 1990s, democratization was confirmed in Taiwan. Political elections are no longer limited to the local level and Taiwanese people can now even vote for their president. Since its foundation in 1986, the Democratic Progressive Party (DPP) has become the major opposition party to the Kuomintang (KMT), the ruling party since 1945. Now, with the coming of every election, the KMT faces great challenges to its policy style. Issues relating to social welfare are often advocated by the DPP in apposition to the 'economics first' stance of the KMT. For example, in the election of legislators in 1992 a debate was provoked between the two sides, as to whether or not Taiwan should make itself a welfare state. Thus social welfare occupied the top of the political agenda for the first time, which served to enlighten people's ideas about the welfare role of the state. In 1993, the DPP published its White Paper on social welfare, proposing (DPP, 1993):

- establishing a universal social insurance system to cover pensions, health, work injury and unemployment benefits;
- family allowances for children and young people;
- increased cash benefits for social assistance;
- expanding welfare services to disadvantaged groups;
- a comprehensive medical care system;
- a housing policy for everyone;
- arrangements for collective bargaining in the workplace;
- establishing a ministry responsible specifically for social welfare in central government;
- incorporating social welfare into national development plans;
- proceeding with resources redistribution across the nation.

In the course of the local authority elections of 1993, the DPP's policy proposal for a universal pension system became a 'common ground' political platform for all those anxious to win the election. The DPP announced that citizens who were 65 years old and above would receive NT$ 5,000 every month on 2 October. The KMT fiercely criticized such a policy as amounting to a collective bribe of elderly voters, but it pressed ahead to launch its own measures for elderly people. On 2 October, the Ministry of Interior Affairs said that a draft policy for a national pension system would be published in November, and on 6 October the allowance for low-income elderly people was increased from NT$ 3,000 to NT$ 5,000 per month. Then, on 7 October, the DPP announced a further pension scheme specific to farmers, leading President Lee Teng-hui (also the leader of the KMT), to ask the Executive Yuan (the Cabinet) to enact the same scheme as soon as possible. The Cabinet meeting on 21 October announced that the allowance for low-income elderly people would be further increased to NT$ 6,000 per month, plus an extra NT$ 3,000 for middle-low-income elderly people. The DPP held a public hearing for its own pension policy on 22 October, at the same time as the Ministry of Interior Affairs published its draft policy on a national pension system.

Over such a short period - less than one month - pension provision had become a big issue around the island, and the size of the allowance was growing and growing (see also Chapter 3 above). This case demonstrates that social welfare is now becoming an issue in Taiwanese politics, and that the KMT has to pay serious attention to the social policy proposals emanating from the opposition, given the likelihood of a growing challenge coming with every election. The first half of the 1990s in Taiwan was packed with social policy debates, along with the adoption of measures geared to the continuing revision and expansion of existing welfare schemes. Social policy competition between political parties has become a main theme nowadays.

In response to this change, the KMT has been trying to achieve a more consistent stance on social policy, as indicated by its publication of the Guiding Principles of Social Welfare Policy in 1994. There are nine principles offered for Taiwanese welfare development, as follows (Ku, 1997, p.248):

- emphasis on the balance between economic and social development;
- the importance of establishing a proper social administration system;
- the family as the centre of social welfare policy;
- the importance of teamwork between the various government departments and emphasis on the role of professional social workers;

- the promotion of harmony and cooperation between employers and employees;
- the institution of a financially independent social insurance system;
- satisfaction of needs in a mixed economy of welfare;
- public housing for lower income families;
- equality of access to medical care.

This is indeed the most comprehensive statement about social policy since the KMT began ruling Taiwan. However, by comparison with the DPP's White Paper, we can appreciate the strength of the KMT's 'economics first' policy orientation. The KMT is arguing strongly for (1) the importance of economic growth in supporting social welfare; (2) sharing welfare responsibilities with family and private sectors; (3) harmonizing industrial relationships; and (4) instituting financially independent social insurance systems such as will not amount to an increasing burden on government. Economic concerns are still the priority of the KMT, for all that it has been forced to expand state welfare under competition from the DPP.

The so-called 'welfare state in crisis' debate has given some Taiwanese economic technocrats a perfect excuse for their neglect of state welfare in past decades and for their continued resistance to state welfare now. Although other studies have found that in reality the welfare state is not being dismantled at all (e.g. Pierson, 1994), this fact has not seized the attention of the economic technocrats, for whom welfare retrenchment is still the main theme. For example, a report published by the CEPD warns of the possible damage done to the economy by state welfare, saying that if the annual average growth rate of state welfare is 10 per cent, the annual average rates of economic growth, inflation and employment will be 6.1 per cent, 3.9 per cent and 1.0 per cent respectively. Where the annual average growth rate of state welfare is 20 per cent, the others will reduce to 5.9 per cent, 4.1 per cent and 0.4 per cent respectively (CEPD, 1996b). These figures will be even worse, it is argued, if the government finds it necessary to raise taxes in order to finance state welfare. Before the full report came out, the CEPD leaked key findings to a national newspaper in Taiwan, which trumpeted in its headline, 'Be careful of your job if welfare grows too fast' (*United Daily News*, 2 October 1995). According to that line of argument, some economic policy makers insist even yet that the introduction of a national pension system should be postponed until the economy is upgraded and strong enough, even though the government had promised in the local election of 1993 to work towards this.

The proposal for a national pension system was therefore still in draft and being held back by the CEPD. But this situation could not last, given that the next local authority elections were looming and the promise of a national pension system was under examination by the public. In order to win the local elections of 29 November 1997, President Lee Teng-hui announced that the KMT would like to establish a universal allowance for those aged 65 years and over at a rate of NT$ 5,000 per month; this being a supplementary measure before the implementation of a national pension system; this, even though he had strongly criticized the same programme as proposed by the DPP in the local elections of 1993. This claim provoked radical political debate, with many commentators thinking this to be a struggle about declining support for the KMT, thanks to its unwillingness to introduce a national pension system. A KMT spokesman blamed the anti-welfare attitudes of the CEPD, which had placed the KMT under direct attack from the opposition. But Premier Hsiao Wan-chang was forced to announce his party's definite intention to introduce a national pension system, to be finalized and realized by 2000 (*China Times*, 5 November 1997).

Even so, the people were no longer content with the KMT's promises, especially its past inefficiency in promoting social development, not only in respect of pensions but also in respect of security and safety in everyday life. The KMT finally lost this local election. In 23 counties, the DPP won 12 seats to the KMT's 8 (3 seats went to independent candidates). For the first time the DPP received more votes (43.32 per cent to 42.12 per cent) than the KMT (*China Times*, 30 November 1997). In effect, the KMT has lost its status as ruling party at the local level. Thus it seems impossible for the KMT to risk postponing the realization of a national pension system any longer; especially since the year of 2000 is also a highly politicized date, being when the first presidential election is due. It was under such political pressure that the CEPD submitted its planning proposal to the Cabinet meeting of 23 January 1998 (CEPD, 1998). We interpret its proposal in detail in the next section.

The CEPD's proposal for NPI

To resolve the issue of old-age income maintenance problems and to meet the needs of population ageing, the CEPD published what was primarily a planning report on the establishment of a national pension system, in which many important ideas and principles were outlined. The Report argues that (CEPD, 1995):

- The system should be for compulsory social insurance, which excludes the possibility of a non-contributory demogrant system.
- The individual should be the insurance unit. People whose age is 25 and over are to be included compulsorily in the NPI, while persons between 15 and 25 might join the NPI voluntarily. But for full-time employees, no matter what their age, membership will be compulsory. The age entitling them to claim a pension is 65.
- The pension should consist of benefits for old age, disability and survivors.
- For the full level of pension, pensioners must have paid contributions for 40 years.
- The basic full pension, in the starting year, will be set at 60 per cent of the average monthly consumption expenditure per person in the preceding two years.
- To claim any pension, a pensioner must have paid contributions for at least 10 years.
- Benefits will be paid monthly or quarterly and be subjected to adjustment in accordance with the growth rate of the real salary/wage and consumer price indices.
- Contributions will be shared by employers and employees: the self-employed and non-working dependants must pay full contributions themselves; low-income households may be allowed to opt out from contributions.
- Basically the government would not subsidize the system, or only subsidize its administration costs, plus no more than 20 per cent of the contributions revenue, if necessary.
- It is to be a state-run system in the short term, but could be privatized in the long term.
- The scheme is to be financially independent, so that government will not be responsible if it goes into deficit.
- The old-age benefits offered by current social insurance programmes will continue with a lump-sum payment.

First, owing to the difficulty of integrating so many current systems, the CEPD proposes a principle called 'Separated Systems with a Unified Benefit', which means that all related old-age benefits will be calculated along the same lines but paid by different systems; leaving the population without any other social insurance to be covered by the NPI. Second, for the population whose ages are over 26 at the start of the NPI, the contribution years entitling them to a full level of pension could, as a concession, be reduced from 40 years to 25 years, because they will not have been able to contribute for 40 years by the retirement age of 65. Third, for those aged 65 and over as the NPI begins, a benefit of NT$ 2,000 monthly will be paid to them as a supplement, because they cannot join the NPI. However, if they were already in receipt of a lump-sum old-age benefit, their entitlement to this supplementary benefit would be postponed until the lump-sum benefit has been spent on the basis of NT$ 2,000 per month (Chan and Chan, 1998; Liu, 1997; *United Daily News*, 24 January 1998).

Is this a fair way of ensuring the economic security of the elderly in Taiwan? The question needs to be examined in its social context, especially with regard to the real situations of the aged population.

The economic situation of the elderly in Taiwan

As a mechanism for securing economic security, the pension issue has become significant for the Taiwanese public. In 1996 a survey, conducted by the Ministry of Interior Affairs on the situation of the elderly in Taiwan, revealed some important opinions on the pension issue. Table 6.1 offers a general profile of public opinion as regards the priority given to various welfare programmes for the elderly, from which we can see that a national pension system stands at the top, only behind medical services. This is even more significant if we consider that the NHI has since been put in place to meet health needs.

Table 6.1 Priorities attached to welfare programmes for the elderly

Items	Scoring	Items	Scoring
Medical Services	40.88	Day Care	7.92
National Pension	34.68	Home Helps	7.49
Medical Services in Home	31.41	Employment	6.73
Medical Services for the Disabled	24.54	Improving Accommodation	6.35
Social Activities	16.82	Counselling	3.87
Education	12.48	Others	0.54

Source: Amended from DSMIA (1997), A Survey of the Elderly in Taiwan, 1996, p.29.

Why are the priorities like this? One reason could be deduced from table 6.2. Although the income of the elderly still depends principally on transfers within the household, these have seen a sharp decline from 65.81 per cent of income in 1986 to 48.28 per cent in 1996. The importance of personal savings has suffered no such sharp decline, but the significance of a pension from employment has overtaken it in importance. In particular, we see the contribution of public transfers growing from 1.24 per cent to 6.37 per cent over the same period. This implies a growing uncertainty over private transfers for securing income, even though the family network is expected effectively to play this role according to Chinese tradition. Nevertheless, the public in general and the elderly in particular have no doubt been aware of the trend in practice, which in part explains why a national pension system has become a top priority, as table 6.1 indicates.

Table 6.2 Income sources of the over-65s in Taiwan in selected years

Year	Transfer from sons and daughters	Personal saving	Occupa -tional Pension	Wages	Widow Pen- sion	Public Trans- fers	Capital Inomes	Aids from Friends	Others
1986	65.81		25.18		4.59	1.24	-	2.03	1.15
1987	64.00		31.86			1.70	-	1.42	1.03
1988	61.82		34.88			1.07	-	1.28	0.96
1989	58.37	15.29	11.87	8.23	2.72	1.23	0.82	0.86	0.61
1991	52.37	15.87	16.07	8.10	2.68	1.57	1.54	1.09	0.70
1993	52.30	17.25	14.76	6.60	4.25	1.61	1.93	0.86	0.45
1996	48.28	13.15	17.55	7.30	4.34	6.37	2.06	0.40	0.54

Source: Amended from DSMIA (1997), A Survey of the Elderly in Taiwan, 1996, p.23.

However, support for the pension scheme does not mean that the NPI as planned for will necessarily be a just system, unless it can meet people's needs and do away with economic insecurity. To examine this, we need most of all to appreciate the economic circumstances of the elderly, especially those who are vulnerable to poverty. In a survey of a sample of 513 middle-low income elderly people from all over Taiwan, Ku and his colleagues have attempted to explore the real configuration of economic insecurity among the elderly, and some important findings can be drawn from the study (Ku et al, 1997, pp.85-89).

The numbers of the elderly in poverty did not diminish in the 1990s, which illustrates the severity of the problem of economic insecurity among the aged population. Significantly, disposable income reaches its highest level at the retirement age of 65 because of the lump-sum old-age benefit. Thereafter it decreases very fast due to the loss of regular income.

Meanwhile, expenditure on medical services by elderly people continues high because of poor health conditions. Only 32.0 per cent of the respondents reported their health to be satisfactory, and 9.9 per cent were handicapped. This rendered medical expenditure second only to expenditure on food.

Poor health also worsened the chances of re-employment and therefore made it impossible for the elderly to secure income from the labour market. Among the respondents only 33 (6.4 per cent) still had a job, mostly in farming.

In such circumstances, the importance of public transfers was becoming significant, whilst the uncertainty of transfers within households was increasing because the younger generation were facing their own economic risks, such as unemployment, which made it even more difficult for them to support their elderly parents.

On the other hand, existing old-age benefits and occupational pensions, if any, were no guarantee of economic security, either. The respondents who had ever had a full-time job before accounted for only 26.3 per cent of the total, with an average record of 32 working years, mostly in unskilled or farming occupations without a proper pension arrangement. For this reason, only 105 (20.5 per cent) out of 513 respondents received old-age benefits when they retired.

The average level of lump-sum old-age benefits received was NT$ 382,000, and over half of the 105 respondents had spent the money within 6 years, simply on daily expenses.

The question remains as to whether or not they could have had supplemental incomes from property or savings accumulated during their working period. But 49.5 per cent of respondents declared they owned neither property nor savings; showing how difficult it could be for them to envisage income from such capital assets. In fact, the lack of full-time and professional jobs over the working lifetime also implied a lifetime of low and irregular incomes, which in turn decreased the possibility of their accumulating enough property or savings for retirement.

The above situation could be even worse if they were forced to quit the labour market earlier than expected, for example because of ill health - the most common factor. Over half (58.5 per cent) of respondents expected the state to play a more significant role in guaranteeing economic security, rather than leaving this to the efforts of individuals and families. However, up to 99 per cent of the respondents said they had no clear ideas about the planned NPI and the impact this might have on their economic security. This implied there had been a lack of open communication and assessment of people's real needs in the planning process.

Is it safe enough?

On the basis of the foregoing discussion, we may attempt to answer whether or not the planned NPI will be a just system for ensuring the economic security of the elderly in Taiwan. Unfortunately, the answer is hardly positive, in our view. As an employment-based social insurance system, the NPI places much emphasis on the interconnection between contribution and benefit, so that the insured population is expected to contribute for 40 years in order to claim a full pension. Four problems emerge from this.

First, those who are now retired or over 26 years old cannot possibly contribute for 40 years and they are therefore excluded from the benefits of the NPI, or can only claim a reduced pension. To fill this gap, the CEPD has introduced two provisions: the first, in relation to the population who are now retired, proposes that a supplemental benefit of NT$ 2,000 per month be paid to them, on condition that they have never been in receipt of a lump-sum old-age benefit. If they have received such a benefit, their entitlement to the supplemental benefit will be postponed until the lump sum benefit had been spent on the basis of NT$ 2,000 per month. Considering the size of the average lump-sum old-age benefit of NT$ 382,000 which the middle- and low-income elderly receive, this means it will be 191 months after their retirement that they become entitled to the supplemental benefit, which means equivalent to when they are 81 years old. In reality, since over half of such recipients exhaust their lump-sum benefits within 6 years, there could be 10 further years in front of them before they qualify for the supplemental benefit, supposing they live long enough. If we further understand that the life expectancy of the Taiwanese is around 75 years (CEPD, 1996a), we can imagine what a small number of the elderly are likely to benefit from this provision.

The other CEPD provision is in regard to the working population currently aged over 26. The concession made to them is to decrease the number of contribution years entitling them to a full pension, down from 40 years to whatever it takes to reach the retirement age of 65. However, this is only a temporary provision. Of the respondents we surveyed, only 26.3 per cent had ever had a full-time job before and with an average of 32 working years, which hardly reach the requirement of 40-year contribution. It will be even more difficult for dependants without a full-time job in the labour market. Thus most of the population are more likely to have a reduced pension only.

Second, the 40-year contribution period seems in any case too harsh to meet. It implies that someone must secure a full-time job immediately after leaving university and that they experience no risks, such as unemployment, throughout their working life. In this case he/she would be a very lucky person. People are not encouraged to undertake further study, for example, because this could take time from the 40-year contribution period. It is ironic that a person who can work for 40 years without risk, can end up not only with a relatively high degree of economic security, because of continuing income, but also be entitled to a full pension. Whereas for those who have high risks and who are in need of public transfers, the pension possibility is reduced. In short, the planned NPI could turn out to be a system on the one hand not so necessary for rich pensioners on full benefit but, on the other hand, not so helpful for poor pensioners on reduced benefit.

Third, even for those lucky enough to be able to claim a full pension, the rate for 1998 is, according to the estimates of the CEPD, to be around NT\$ 9,100 per month. This compares with poverty lines in Taiwan province of NT\$ 7,110, in Taipei of NT\$ 11,443, and in Kaohsiung of NT\$ 8,828. In our view this pension rate is pitched well below an adequate living standard for Taiwan. Without other sources of income, the lucky one with a full pension is still going to be living in poverty, especially in Taipei and Kaohsiung. This is the reason why Ku and his colleagues insist that a dual system, integrating NPI and social assistance, will be essential for guaranteeing the economic security of the elderly (Ku et al, 1997, p.88).

Finally, the old-age benefits administered by current social insurance programmes still take the form of a lump-sum payment. Current insurants will have the right to choose whether to stay in the existing system or join in the NPI within the first two years. For those who choose the current system, their rights and obligations will remain unchanged and, after receiving the old-age lump-sum benefit, they can opt to join in the NPI. But is this really a good alternative during this transition period? Obviously, it is not. As we know, the NPI system is completely different from the existing system. The former is the universal pension system, the latter is the employment lump-sum system. Contribution rates, benefit qualification and benefit payment are all different, so who in each case is to evaluate which is better?

The reluctant attitudes of economic policy makers towards welfare could be a reason, probably the main reason, for such a strange institutional arrangement. In fact, as the major planners of the NPI and dominated by the ideology of economic growth, they have been able to design the system according to their preferences. So we see the superiority of economic rationality in the planned NPI, as reflected in the harsh conditions of contribution and benefit level as well as in the insistence on making it 'financially independent', thereby avoiding state responsibility. Although some scholars have argued that the social function of the NPI - not merely its supposed economic rationality - should be taken more into account (e.g. Ku et al, 1997), this argument has not yet received a positive response.

Conclusion

As a result of demographic, social and political changes the need for income maintenance in old age has become urgent in Taiwan. We have reviewed the need for a national pension system, studied the detailed policy proposals of the CEPD, and examined the latter's function as a mechanism for securing economic rationality in the Taiwanese social context. The dominance of economic rationality in the planned NPI has been exposed. More precisely, the NPI is the product of a mixture of political and economic requirements, which have somehow preceded its welfare implication. This in our view makes the scheme hardly capable of becoming a just system for securing income and maintaining a proper living standard for the elderly in Taiwan. Nevertheless, the NPI seems certain to be implemented in 2000, even though we still doubt its social functionability. If the system remains as planned, those who will benefit from the NPI could be politicians and economic technocrats, rather than the public in general and the poorer elderly in particular.

References

Chan, Ying and Yi-chang Chan (1998), *A Study on the Benefits to Old-age, Disability and Related Groups: Integration to the National Pension Insurance,* Council for Economic Planning and Development, Taipei (in Chinese).

China Times, 5 November 1997 (in Chinese).

China Times, 30 November 1997. (in Chinese).

Council for Economic Planning and Development (CEPD) (1995), *A Planning Report on the Integrated System of the National Pension Insurance,* Taipei (in Chinese).

Council for Economic Planning and Development (CEPD) (1996a), *Taiwan Statistical Data Book, 1996,* Taipei.

Council for Economic Planning and Development (CEPD) (1996b), *Impacts of Social Welfare Expenditure on National Economic Development,* Taipei (in Chinese).

Council for Economic Planning and Development (CEPD) (1998), *The Fourteenth Meeting Record of the Working Team on the NPI,* Taipei (in Chinese).

Democratic Progressive Party (DPP) (1993), *A Just Welfare State: White Paper of the DPP's Social Policy,* Taipei (in Chinese).

Department of Statistics, Ministry of Interior Affairs (DSMIA) (1997), *A Survey of the Elderly in Taiwan, 1996,* Taipei (in Chinese).

Ku, Yeun-wen (1995), 'The Development of State Welfare in the Asian NICs with Special Reference to Taiwan', *Social Policy and Administration,* 29 (4), pp. 345-364.

Ku, Yeun-wen (1997), *Welfare Capitalism in Taiwan: State, Economy and Social Policy,* Macmillan, Basingstoke.

Ku, Yeun-wen, Ying Chan and Yi-chang Chan (1997), *A Study of Economic Security and Pension Insurance for the Elderly in Taiwan,* Ministry of Interior Affairs, Taipei. (in Chinese).

Liu, Anita Yu-lan (1997), 'Establishing a National Pension Scheme with Separated Systems but an Unified benefit', *Social Welfare Bimonthly,* 132, pp. 2-10 (in Chinese).

Pierson, Paul (1994), *Dismantling the Welfare State? Reagan, Thatcher, and the Politics of Retrenchment,* Cambridge University Press, Cambridge.

United Daily News, 2 October 1995 (in Chinese).

United Daily News, 24 January 1998 (in Chinese).

7 Thinking the unthinkable? Pensions policy prospects in Britain

TONY MALTBY

Introduction

This chapter has the principal aim of providing an overview of current trends in social policy on retirement pensions in Britain. More specifically, it reviews critically the present retirement pension provision, assesses the current Labour government plans for pensions,[1] and considers whether such plans are 'thinking the unthinkable' or merely represent a seamless continuation of the past. However, one thing is clear, present policy in this area fails to address the concerns of present pensioners, particularly women (see Waine, 1999; Walker, 1999). The chapter argues that any pensions policy should be bounded by a concern to present a policy that prescribes an adequate income, not only to future pensioners but also to today's pensioners. Yet there has been, in a historical context, of paramount importance to British pension policy, a desire to discover an effective and socially just method to remove 'worn-out workers' from industry. Hence, pension policy is inextricably linked to labour market policy and cannot simply be viewed as the effective yet beneficent transfer of money from the state to senior citizens.

Three trends

In any detailed discussion of British pension policy, there have consistently been three central concerns which have dominated the debate. First, there is the distinct demographic shift towards an older age profile for the population as a whole: what has come to be called the ageing of the population. This in general terms is a result of a combination of declining birth rates and greater life expectancy: 'fewer babies, longer lives'. For example, in 1901 life expectancy at birth was 45 years for men and 49 for women whereas in 1996 the corresponding figures were 75 and

80 years. Hence, there was almost a doubling of life expectancy at birth over the course of the twentieth century with higher numbers of people living twenty years or more in retirement. It has been estimated that the mean age of the UK population will rise from 38 years to a projected 44 years by 2036, and the numbers of people over pensionable age from 10.7 million to 11.8 million in 2010 (Shaw, 1998). Accompanying these demographic shifts, a clear gendered imbalance has been created within the population over sixty: the feminisation of later life.

These changes and in particular the feminisation of later life, raise significant policy dilemmas within the field of pensions policy. Despite an acceptance of these facts, policies in both private and public sectors have consistently been within a framework that pensions should be designed by men with men in mind, and linked to policy on labour force participation: the 'work test' (Shragge, 1984). Women were marginal, at most, to the discussions around the 1908, 1925 and 1946 Acts, and this has constrained future policy making on this issue (Macnichol, 1998). Little acknowledgement is (and was) made of the different work and life histories of women, which often results in their poverty in old age (Arber and Ginn, 1991; Maltby, 1994). The incidence of cohabitation, widowhood and divorce[2] mean that many women cannot rely on the financial support of a husband.[3] Nor can it be assumed that married women will be able to share their husbands' income equally (Ginn, 1998). Consequently, coupled with the feminisation of the older population there exists a feminisation of poverty in old age, a result of the main emphasis on providing for the 'worn-out working man' and his dependent wife that has existed since (at least) the 1908 Act. Moreover, this trend towards population ageing is often viewed with apocalyptic alarm and cast by many as a demon in the shape of the 'demographic time-bomb'. Such a position has been one of the arguments propounded for (particularly) the state to withdraw from funding pensions (and thus assist in reducing public expenditure) (for the UK see, DHSS, 1984; 1985a; 1985b). Many emerging economies, notably and famously Chile, have accepted the rhetoric and already taken this path (see World Bank, 1994). Indeed, just before the last general election in 1997 the Conservative administration had proposed a new scheme, which was modelled on that outlined by the World Bank in this text.[4]

On the contrary, this worldwide trend towards a higher proportion of older people within the population should be viewed as positive development, one of the dramatic outcomes of the social and economic policy enshrined within the 'welfare state' (see Thane, 1989; Walker and

Maltby, 1997). What is required is, in essence, a change of perspective or mind-set on the part of policy makers and pensions advisors towards one that accepts the worldwide ageing of populations as positive, as progress: indeed, an acceptance that the major elements of social and economic policy will in the near future be made *by* older people *for* older people. Moreover, it is clear that the traditional models of, and entry into, retirement, upon which past pensions policies have been developed, are no longer valid (Walker and Maltby, 1997; Phillipson, 1998).

Second, during the twentieth century and accompanying the ageing of the population in the Western industrialised world, the state and government institutions increasingly intervened in the lives of those over 60. This has assisted the creation of the socially constructed notion of retirement and associated with this, the payment of a pension at a defined age (Phillipson, 1982; Townsend, 1986) accompanied by a growing acceptance of older people as 'deserving poor'.

Finally, associated with the development of the concept of retirement and development of a 'retirement pension', there has been a distinct shift towards the withdrawal of (in particular) older men over 65 from the labour market. In the late nineteenth century nearly 75 per cent were still in employment; by the 1950s this had been reduced to one-third and today is as low as 3 per cent (Phillipson, 1998). The trend for those men below the pension age of 65 is equally as marked, with presently just under 50 per cent of them not economically active. Similar although more complex shifts are noted for women over 60 (cf. Walker and Maltby, 1997). Indeed, identical trends are noted for most western industrial nations (Kohli et al, 1991; Atkinson and Rein, 1993; Walker and Maltby, 1997). These labour market effects are discussed more fully later in this chapter.

Development of pensions

To appreciate the nature of pensions policy making today a brief historical outline has to be provided since policy development in this area has adopted an incrementalist approach and present policy reflects the past. The Liberal government, elected in 1906, was the first one to initiate the payment of a means-tested pension from the Exchequer through the passage of the 1908 Old Age Pensions Act (Fraser, 1984). Yet the pension offered was non-contributory, means-tested (those with an annual income above £31 10s[5] were excluded) and paid to those who survived to 70 and who had not 'habitually failed to work'. Thus as Thane (1978, p.103) notes it was a payment to '...the very old, the very poor and the very respectable'. In January 1909, when the first payments were made, 490,000 persons were in receipt of a 1908 pension or as it was popularly known at the time 'the Lloyd George' (Thane, 1978, p.104; Macnicol, 1998, p.162). This scheme continued until 1925, when coverage of the 1908 Act was extended to insured workers and their wives between 65 and 70 by the passage of the Widows, Orphans and Old Age Pensions Act (the 1925 Act) effective from 1928. This again reinforced women's dependency on a male breadwinner and additionally, as the scheme was contributory, upon labour market participation (Macnichol, 1998). Importantly, the 1925 Act established the contributory principle present within the modern state pension scheme. Payments were financed by equal contributions from employer and employee and integrated into the existing framework for health insurance initiated by the 1911 National Insurance Act. Various other Acts of Parliament before World War II offered fine-tuning to the pensions legislation already on the statute book (see Macnichol, 1998; Maltby, 1994).

The National Insurance Act 1946 implemented the main thrust of the proposals outlined in the Beveridge Report (1942) in substance if not in detail (Hess, 1981). This Act established the basis of the post-1945 system of contributory benefits, and hence retirement pensions. A universal contributory retirement pension established by this Act was paid to all contributors conditional on retirement from work at 65 (for men) or 60 (for women) at 26 shillings a week with a lower amount of 16 shillings a week paid to married women. Thus a male breadwinner model was continued into retirement, the wife as secondary and dependent upon her husband; pensions designed by men with men in mind. About the same time, in 1948, the main safety net benefit, then called National Assistance, was enacted and with it the last remnants of the Poor Laws were abolished, although not forgotten by those who administered the scheme. Indeed, many pensioners relied upon National Assistance (the forerunner to 'supplementary benefit' and today's 'income support') for a large percentage of their weekly income (Deacon, 1982).

Titmuss (1955), commenting upon this and the rise and coverage of occupational pensions provision, saw 'two nations in old age': the majority whose pensions were supplemented by National Assistance and the relatively better-off minority, whose supplementation came from an occupational pension. In the light of recent developments, these are prophetic words. The number and coverage of such schemes had increased since 1945 and at present approximately 50 per cent of the workforce is a member of an occupational scheme. The effects of this upon women are considered later in this chapter. In an effort to reduce reliance upon National Assistance payments, the Conservative government introduced the Graduated Pension scheme through the National Insurance Act 1959, implemented from 1961. Under the Graduated Pensions scheme, an additional earnings-related contribution was made on top of the flat-rate of National Insurance 'stamp' (payment) in return for a small earnings-related pension. In this way it was able to supplement the 1946 flat-rate pension. However, the graduated pension was non-indexed and so has lost its relative value as a method of supplementation.

The retirement pensions debate, shuttling between the two major political parties, Labour and Conservative, for 15 years or more, was suspended in 1975 when a compromise was reached, not only between political parties but also with the private sector pensions industry. The Castle plan (*Better Pensions*, Cm 5713) which ultimately resulted in the passage of the Social Security (Pensions) Act 1975 and the creation of the State Earnings Related Pensions Scheme (SERPS), forms the basis of the retirement pension system operating today. This scheme originally provided an inflation-proofed pension (a Basic Pension, which at the time was uprated annually based upon the retail prices index or earnings, whichever was the greater) supplemented by an approved contracted-out occupational pension or earnings-related pension provided by the state (or SERPS). The SERPS pension would be paid out based on the revaluation of the best twenty years' earnings, largely to accommodate the broken career paths of many women. To help the position of those caring for relatives or children the 1975 Act introduced the Home Responsibilities Protection (HRP) from 1978 to enable these people (mainly women) to protect their right to the basic state pension (DSS, 1991a, p.14).

It was Barbara Castle's stated intention that the new pension scheme should provide equal pensions for men and women; that it was 'no longer tolerable to treat women as second-class citizens entitled to third-class benefits' (*Hansard*, 18 March 1975, col. 1492). This specific intention to assist women was indicative of an era in which Parliament would legislate to found the Equal Opportunities Commission through the Sex Discrimination Act 1975. Yet despite the rhetoric of providing assistance for women, the SERPS pensions system was still founded upon 'work-testing': that is upon participation in the paid labour market, paying taxes and contributing through National Insurance (Shragge, 1984).

From 1979 with the election of a 'New Right' government headed by

Margaret Thatcher, many policy documents encouraged the development of pensions provision through a greater emphasis upon the private sector in 'partnership' with the state SERPS scheme. The implementation of this policy of retrenchment commenced in 1981. From this time the basis upon which pensions were indexed was altered from earnings to prices, thus devaluing the basic pension by some 20 per cent up to 1991 (Fry and Stark, 1991, p.67). Today it is worth 17 per cent of average earnings and by 2030, it is estimated it will be worth 8.6 per cent of average earnings.

The Fowler reviews (DHSS, 1985a) were the method by which this retrenchment was legitimised. The reviews estimated that the cost of the SERPS pension would rise from £15.4 billion in 1984/5 to £45 billion in 2033/4 if the pension were adjusted in line with prices and £66.5 billion if adjusted in line with earnings (DHSS, 1985a, p.22). The underlying aim of the policy that developed out of these reviews would, in the words of the then Parliamentary Secretary of State for Social Security, at present the shadow Chancellor of the Exchequer, Michael Portillo (1989, p.192):

> encourage personal independence and return to the old notion of a benefit system which provides a floor on which individuals can build instead of a ceiling which locks them into indefinite dependency.

These are rather prophetic words since they encapsulate the current thinking of the present Labour government's proposals.

The policy that emerged and was finally enacted through the Social Security Act 1986 reduced SERPS entitlement by half (by £12 billion per annum by 2033). This was achieved by altering the principle of earnings relation of 'best twenty years' earnings to that of lifetime earnings. In addition, cutting the value of these earnings from 25 to 20 per cent further reduced the pension. This latter policy has been subject to phasing over a ten-year period (from April 2000) and will devalue the pension earned from 1978 by one-fifth. Additionally, widows who under the 1975 SERPS scheme could inherit the whole of their husband's pension (up to a ceiling) will only be entitled to half.

Additionally, there were important changes to the contracting-out regulations of the 1978 SERPS to accommodate the shift towards private sector provision of the earnings-related additional component. The two main changes were that individual membership of an employer occupational pension scheme was made non-compulsory ar.d the methods through which contracting-out of SERPS was allowed was extended to cover those schemes known in general terms as 'defined contribution schemes'. These are better known as 'appropriate personal pensions' and money purchase schemes: colloquially as personal pensions. The Thatcher government, in the hope of increasing the numbers of people contributing to such personal pensions, paid an additional contribution into these schemes of 2 per cent (variously called a 'bribe' or an 'incentive') for the first five years up to 1993. It subsequently transpired that this 'incentive' was implemented against the advice of the Government Actuary (*The Guardian*, 3 January 1991, p.1). Individuals who remained part of the SERPS scheme (mainly employees of small businesses) could contract out from April 1988. Those whose employers had used the occupational pension scheme to contract-out in 1978 were allowed to utilise their own 'defined benefit scheme' (mainly in the form of an 'appropriate personal pension') for the purposes of contracting out from July 1988.

This privatisation of pensions (Labour Research, 1987; O'Higgins, 1984) gave full voice to the two nations in old age idea first outlined by Titmuss (1955). Because of the reversion to lifetime earnings calculations women have been left in an inferior position as regards their entitlement to the state pension. This is because women's employment careers tend to be disrupted. Typically, it comprises a period in full-time employment up to marriage, a period out of employment whilst having children (euphemistically termed a 'career break') followed by a longer period in part-time employment whilst children are at school, followed by a return to full-time work for brief period up to retirement (Joshi, 1992, p.122; Joshi, 1989; Dex, et al, 1996). Additionally, it has been demonstrated by McGoldrick (1984) that most occupational pension schemes reflect the actuarial and other practices present within the state schemes with respect to gender, the model of pensions designed by men with men in mind. For example, although Section 53(2) of the Social Security (Pensions) Act 1975 made it a statutory requirement to provide equal access for women and men to such occupational schemes, the benefits that are provided are usually differentiated according to gender-specific criteria, partly based upon the greater 'risk' of a longer life expectancy. Furthermore, part-time workers, predominantly women in the UK, are often excluded on the basis that they do not work sufficient hours or that the scheme only provides for full-time employees on an actuarial basis.

The gains made by women towards formal equality of treatment in social security have been due to the application of European Directives and European court rulings to United Kingdom (UK) law, not because of any willingness on the part of the British (UK) governments. For example, following the success of the Barber case in the UK and European courts, the British government was forced to consider equalisation of the pension ages (DSS, 1991b). Only in November 1993 was it decided to equalise the pension age at 65 by phasing this change in over a ten-year period from 2010 (*Hansard*, 30 November 1993, col. 927). Many commentators view this change as being detrimental to the majority of women. Significantly, the decision to equalise at 65 was supported by the Social Security Advisory Committee (SSAC, 1992) and the Confederation of British Industry (CBI, 1991) in their submissions.

Present position of older people

Income after the state pension ages (60 for women and 65 for men) can be derived from three main sources: through occupational or personal pensions; through benefit transfers from the state (the SERPS pension) or from paid work, or a combination of these. Additionally, a small percentage of the older population may have income from investments, for example from stocks and shares, etc. The retirement pensions structure is composed of three pillars, a Basic State Pension; a second pillar comprising either a State Pension (SERPS) or an occupational or private personal pension.[6] The final element, and of increasing importance, is the means-tested safety net benefit called Minimum Income Guarantee (MIG) which is essentially Income Support (social assistance) for pensioners.

In March 1999, the Government announced that this MIG would rise in line with earnings rather than prices so that by April 2000 for a single person it would be £78 and for a married couple £121. They also announced that a one-off payment of £100, raised to £150 in the March 2000 budget would be paid to all pensioner households to assist with higher fuel costs during winter. Added to this all people over 75 will receive a free TV licence (costing £104), a measure that reeks of paternalism. Although welcomed by many pensioners, these changes do mark a shift away from the universalist notion of welfare central to British social policy and a further step, started with the Thatcher administrations, towards a greater reliance upon means testing. For comparison, it should be realised that average adult full-time weekly earnings in 1996 were £351.70. Other research demonstrates that older people need an income of at least £150 per week for a 'modest lifestyle', yet less than a third have incomes at this level (Midwinter, 1997). Indeed, one organisation (Help the Aged) suggested, in response to the March 1999 Budget, that raising the basic pension to £75 would have cost about the same as the £3 billion cost of raising the MIG and the £100 winter payment, but would have helped more people (especially older women) for longer. In 2000, the basic pension rose by just 75 pence per week for a single person. This has been derided by many and been called 'miserly and a depressing contrast to gains in income for those working' (Kohler, cited by Levene, 2000).

The Basic Pension is payable to all those who have made sufficient National Insurance payments over the qualifying period (for men this amounts to a contribution period of 44 years and for women 39 years). Those who fail to qualify for this Basic Pension have to resort to Income Support/MIG. Currently 14 per cent of men and 51 per cent of women fail to qualify for this universal benefit because of an insufficient contribution record (Blackburn, 1999). The Basic Pension is supplemented by a second-tier pension, introduced in 1978 and amended from 1988, which allows for either a SERPS pension from the state or a contracted out (occupational or personal) pension provided by the private sector. Those who contract out of SERPS pay a reduced rate of National Insurance contribution as well as receiving generous tax breaks. Employment income plays a relatively small part in the overall income of older people, although there is considerable variation if one considers this from a European perspective. In recent discussions about the future of pensions systems, the idea of extending the portion of the older population that remains economically active either in full- or part-time employment has received some serious consideration by governments.

Therefore, present policy is a reflection of the recent past. Indeed, Falkingham (1998) has recently noted that despite the presence of state and private provision, later life is now more often associated with financial insecurity than security. Concern for older people's income and, wider, their 'welfare' has historically been predicated upon economic rather than social imperatives, linked to involvement in the labour market and more specifically to paid work. Central to pension policy and particularly since 1948, has been the notion of the 'male breadwinner': pensions designed by men with men in mind. This has had some very significant negative consequences for the income of women in later life (see Arber and Ginn, 1991). For example, nearly all male pensioners receive a full basic pension against approximately 60 per cent of women.

Nevertheless, as Falkingham (1998) also points out, data derived from the Family Expenditure Survey has shown that pensioners' income in real terms has doubled since the early 1960s (Retirement Income Survey 1996). Recent Households Below Average Income statistics (HBAI) (DSS, 1997a) show this trend continuing, with pensioners overall experiencing a higher rise in income (between 55/60 per cent) than those in work (who have seen rises of around 40 per cent). More recent data, derived from the Pensioner Income Series (DSS, 1997b) show that the income of the top 20 per cent of pensioners has increased by 70 per cent since 1979, whereas that of the lowest 20 per cent has risen by only 38 per cent. Although this is a general trend the phenomenon does not appear to be related to any major shift of older people up the income distribution but instead to increasing inequalities among pensioners. This is largely attributable to the increasing numbers of (mainly male) pensioners retiring with good occupational pensions. Field and Prior (1996) show how women have lower access than men to occupational pensions. This is directly related to their position in the labour force (as part-time, low-paid workers) and their continuing role as caregivers within the 'family' (to children and older kin) (see chapter 4, above). Field and Prior have also demonstrated how women are particularly affected by the falling value of the Basic Pension and SERPS and the general shift towards the gender-biased private sector- funded pension schemes. Consistently over recent years both single pensioners and pensioner couples have been over represented in the bottom two-fifths of the income distribution. A quarter of single pensioners and pensioner couples have incomes below half average incomes of the whole population.

Moreover, older people in the UK are less well off than their counterparts in other leading industrial societies. Disposable income of households in the 65 to 74 age group is 76 per cent of the UK household average compared with 93 per cent in the eight other major OECD countries (Bosanquet et al, 1990). Underlying this increasing inequality is the differential rate of increase in the various components of pensioners' incomes. Between 1979 and 1988 social security rose by only 14 per cent in real terms, compared with 99 per cent for occupational pensions and 110 per cent for savings income. A significant part of the explanation for this differential rate of increase is the policy decision by the first Thatcher administration to de-index the basic pension from earnings, along with the positive encouragement and support for a private pensions sector.

Among the poorest older people in the UK are just under 1 million (10 per cent of the older population) living on incomes below the Income Support levels (the main means-tested safety-net social security benefit). Ginn (1998) has shown how in the period 1993-1995, 74 per cent of these Income Support recipients over 65 were women. A significant number of pensioners who are eligible for this benefit do not claim it - nearly one in five of those eligible (DSS, 1995). Research suggests that this is due to a combination of factors including the stigma attached to claiming means-tested benefits and a lack of information. Certainly, it is a long-standing problem that has not been overcome by periodic publicity campaigns designed to increase take-up and appears to be endemic in the means-tested nature of this and other similar benefits.

As for personal pensions (i.e. those introduced as a result of the 1986 Act) the problem here, as the present Blair government has realised, is that only the National Insurance (Basic) pension is assured. The second tier component (i.e. the personal pension) depends on the outcome of investments. As one economist has put it: 'A guarantee is replaced by a lottery' (Atkinson, 1991, p.21). This poses serious questions for the future, concerning the fate of those older people whose investments fail to yield sufficient income to raise the (falling relative) value of the basic National Insurance pension to an adequate level. It could perpetuate the existence for many older people of a life in poverty. Added to this there is the widely reported scandal of the 'mis-selling' of personal pensions by a number of pension providers. Although the Major and Blair governments have taken action over this (largely through the massive and complex Pension Act 1995), it does raise important policy questions over the level of benefits such pensions will accrue when they mature, and the salience and appropriateness of such a policy in the first place.

As indicated earlier, one of the main intentions of the SERPS scheme was to reduce the high reliance of older people on means-tested social assistance benefits and the evidence suggests that it would have had a dramatic impact on poverty in old age. The recent changes in pension policy have seriously undermined the capacity for SERPS[7] to achieve this goal and, as a result, a significant proportion of older people are likely to be living on very low incomes well into the next century. This is particularly the case for older women. Recent research conducted for the Equal Opportunities Commission (EOC) concluded that occupational and personal pensions do not meet the needs of women (see Davidson, 1990). They are more likely than men to have long periods on low incomes, doing part-time work or out of the labour market while raising or caring for family members and, therefore, are disadvantaged by pension schemes linked to levels of earnings, a male career path and length of service.

The myth of the demographic time-bomb

As the above discussion has documented, the issue of population ageing and the notion of a 'demographic time-bomb' have for many years dominated the policy debate in the UK. The general trends in this ageing of the population were mentioned earlier in the chapter and throughout it has been emphasised that this has been the rationale for reducing public expenditure on pensions. However, the effects of the published demographic trends are largely overstated and emphasise many ageist assumptions. First, dependency ratios have been criticised (Falkingham, 1989) for making overly simplistic assumptions about who is 'active' or 'inactive' based on age. Participation in paid work is not the only way in which people make economically valuable contributions. Many older (and younger) people make valuable contributions to the essential services required within their societies and their communities: often unpaid and voluntary. More broadly, arguments based on this demographic burden thesis have been employed largely for party political and ideological purposes. They are an attempt to underline firstly, the alleged benefits of shifting provision from the state towards the private sector and secondly, that the present levels of spending particularly on SERPS pensions are unsustainable.

However, the reality is entirely different, with the UK well placed to absorb the effects of these demographic shifts, as has been the case in the past. Britain's population aged earlier than the rest of Europe and is less exceptional than Italy which will, by 2020 have the highest proportion of older people, the lowest proportion of younger people and the oldest working population in the European Union (Walker and Maltby, 1997). Furthermore, and as Hills (1993, 1997) has shown, over the next fifty years the effect of these much talked-about demographic shifts will result in a minuscule increase in public expenditure of 0.32 per cent of Gross Domestic Product (GDP) per year and a net rise equivalent to 0.8 per cent of GDP over the next 50 years. Thus this emphasis upon the economic burden upon future generations has resulted in the creation of the modern myth of the demographic time-bomb.

Therefore, these recent changes in pension policy in the UK have pre-empted concerns of the kind apparent in some other EU countries about the combined effects of demography and the maturation of pension schemes on public expenditure. The corollary is that UK pensioners are likely to remain relatively worse off than their northern EU counterparts for the foreseeable future. Moreover, the policy of holding the National Insurance Basic Pension at its 1979 (real) level while encouraging the growth of occupational and personal pensions will result in a sharper polarisation in income levels among future pensioners, with low-paid, part-time employees (predominantly women) having the poorest prospects. Titmuss' thesis about 'two nations in old age' has sadly been realised.

A redefinition of the retirement process

Aside from these well-documented trends, there has been a significant transformation in the experience and meaning of old age. As was indicated earlier, for a large proportion of the population retirement and exit from the labour force no longer coincide. Retirement (associated with receipt of a pension) is no longer the recognised entry point to old age it once was, and it is increasingly anachronistic as a method for describing the start of old age. Increasing numbers of older people throughout the European Union are leaving the labour force in different ways, through early retirement, partial retirement, redundancy, unemployment, disability and so on (see Walker and Maltby, 1997). Yet older people are living longer and healthier lives, driving back the threshold of frailty. Added to this is the paradox in which 'official' retirement (with receipt of the state pension) cannot occur before 65 (for men) or 60 (for women), yet a large proportion of mostly male workers have entered retirement. These socio-economic and demographic developments raise important policy questions about the extent to which policy makers and the major economic and political institutions are able to adjust. The established pattern of long work and short retirement is changing to one of increasing length and complexity as a result of a combination of greater longevity and higher rates of long-term unemployment, particularly for men (Phillipson, 1998).

Successive research studies have shown that the employment rate of older workers is lowest among those close to state pension age (Campbell, 1999; Walker, 1985). For example, in 1979 57 per cent of all men aged 64 were working compared with 37 per cent in 1997. After 1979 male employment started to fall at an earlier age, 50 instead of 55, and the lower level of employment among all older workers means that the decline starts from a lower peak, as shown in table 7.1 (Campbell, 1999). Overall female employment has increased dramatically over the last eight years for each age group except for the over 55s, accounting for the expansion of low-paid, 'flexible' part-time work within the service industries.

Table 7.1 Changes in employment, unemployment and economic inactivity rates, 1979-1997 (%)

		Employment	Unemployment	Economic Inactivity
Men aged	*18-24*	*-12.6*	*+6.6*	*+6.0*
	25-49	-7.0	+1.6	+5.4
	50-64	-16.4	+1.0	+15.4
	55-64	-21.2	+0.9	+20.3
All men		-10.2	+1.9	+8.4
Women aged	18-49	+9.8	+0.2	-10.1
	50-59	+4.2	0.0	-4.2
	55-59	-0.5	0.0	+0.5
All women		+8.6	+0.2	-8.8
All	not in last 10 years*	+0.3	+1.2	-1.4
	last 10 years*	-7.5	+0.4	+7.1
All of working age		-1.1	+1.0	+0.1

Note: *refers to the last 10 years of working age (i.e. age 50-59 for women, 55-65 for men).
Source: Campbell, 1999, p.12.

This fall in employment is more a function of higher economic inactivity than the result of an increase in conventionally defined unemployment. Table 7.1 shows how employment and inactivity changes follow one another, with employment falling furthest among men aged 55-64. Table 7.2 shows the contribution of each age group's employment to the total decline in male employment. Older men (and to a lesser extent men aged 18-25) have had a disproportionate share of the decline in male and female employment. Reduced employment among men aged 55-64 accounts for more than one-third of the decline in male employment. Men aged 50-64 account for nearly half of the decline in employment even though they are a relatively small proportion of the total population (Campbell, 1999).

Therefore, the main factors determining the longer-term decline in employment among older workers are demand-related (Taylor and Walker, 1994). For example, older men are likely to work in declining industries, which has increased their risk of redundancy. The available evidence suggests that, in the UK at least, it is not changes in the nature of work or new organisational forms of work but changes in the aggregate supply of employment (or demand for labour) that is still the main influence on the relationship between ageing and work.

Table 7.2 Contribution to changes in employment patterns, 1979-1997 (%)

		Each group's contribution to the change in:		Proportion of population (1997)
		Employment fall	Inactivity increase	
Men aged	18-24	12.9	7.4	10.5
	25-49	41.6	39.0	60.7
	50-54	10.7	11.3	11.7
	55-64	35.5	41.6	17.2
				100.0
		Employment increase	Inactivity fall	
Women aged	18-49	88.9	89.0	78.1
	50-54	11.2	11.0	12.3
	55-59	-0.6	-0.6	9.6
				100.0

Source: Campbell, 1999, p.13.

Present proposals

It is clear that these changes in the nature of retirement, both conceptually and as a process in the late twentieth century, together with the changing demographic and labour market processes mentioned earlier, require policy makers to rethink pensions policy: to rethink the unthinkable. Immediately following the landslide election of the present Labour administration in 1997, the prime minister, Tony Blair, appointed Frank Field as his minister for Welfare Reform. In opposition Field had very effectively chaired the House of Commons Social Security Select Committee. Like his colleague Chris Smith before him (when opposition spokesperson for Social Security) Field was given the task of 'thinking the unthinkable', to radically reform social security policy, including pension policy. Field's resignation in 1998 was partly a reflection of his character and personality, but largely recognition by him that the Treasury had once again, won the battle for ideas and the ear of the prime minister. Prudence had won over 'the unthinkable' alternative. Yet, many of Field's ideas were quintessentially a re-presentation of his numerous pamphlets and articles and were far from radical (see Field and Owen, 1993a; 1993b; 1994).

What transpired from this review was a desire, started in earnest in 1979, for pensions policy to extricate the state from being the sole provider and hence undermine the principles of national insurance (Walker, 1999). An important element of the policy is the centrality of the 'stakeholder pension' idea. Before publication, there were calls from Barbara Castle (now a Labour peer), Peter Townsend, Tony Lynes, Jay Ginn and Alan Walker, and other significant pensions experts for a reinvigoration of SERPS and for a strengthening of the role of National Insurance. There are similarly a number of pensioners' pressure groups (e.g. the National Pensioners Convention and Age Concern England) that convincingly argue for a substantial rise in the rate of the Basic Pension. The evidence is that such an increase would assist the majority of *today's* pensioners and in particular women pensioners (see Parker, 2000). Despite this overwhelming evidence, such requests have been ignored and when the Green Paper (DSS, 1998) was finally published in December 1998, it announced, in essence, a tidying up of the existing system alongside an enhancement of the 'partnership' between the state and private sector. Importantly, it fails to outline any proposals about provision for today's pensioners and only considers future pensioners.

From a political standpoint, what is clear about the Green Paper is that it confirms that the Treasury has firm control of the policy agenda on pensions. The appointment of a 'Treasury man', Alistair Darling, as secretary of state in the Department of Social Security and the departure of Frank Field hinted at such a move, but the Green Paper confirms it. When the paper is implemented, it will continue the shift towards the greater privatisation of pensions, and the continuing rise of what Blackburn (1999, p.5) has termed 'grey capitalism'. It directly reflects the views expressed by the World Bank (1994), which argued (from an economic libertarian view) for a 'multi-pillar approach' with a rejection of pay-as-you-go (because of savings disincentives and costs to public expenditure) and the introduction of mandatory funded private pensions.

It has many similarities with the previous Conservative proposals in this area, which were based upon the World Bank model, referred to earlier.

Overall, the Green Paper (DSS, 1998) suggested that public expenditure by the state on pensions should shift towards the private sector, from 60 per cent at present to 40 per cent by 2050. Improvements in the position of the poorest pensions should be a priority and this will be achieved through provision of the (means-tested) MIG. It further suggested that the Basic Pension (funded on a pay-as-you-go basis) would remain but shrink in real terms (by continuing its annual revaluation with prices). It poured scorn on the call, mainly from pensioner organisations, for an increase in the value of the Basic Pension. The SERPS pension would be replaced from 2002 by a new State Second Pension (SSP) in order, it argues, to boost the pension of the lowest paid, those earning less than £9,000 per annum. The benefits of this SSP would be flat-rate and double, it argues, what can be expected from a SERPS pension today. As now, pension credits will be given for all those caring for dependent relatives or children under five as well as to the long-term disabled with broken employment records.

Those earning above £9,000 per year (which it defines as those on 'middle' incomes), and who are not members of an occupational pension scheme, will be encouraged to take out a funded 'stakeholder pension'. These should be operational from April 2001 and would be low-cost, flexible and provided by the private sector. Clearly this is to allow them to undercut and ultimately reduce, the number of people paying towards a 'personal pension'. As outlined above these were encouraged by the previous government as part of the reforms implemented through the 1986 Act. In order to encourage the shift towards stakeholder pensions, it plans to increase the contracted-out rebate available on National Insurance *rather* than insist upon compulsory inclusion in such a scheme. This is clearly a snub to Field who has always insisted upon compulsion. It further argues that better education, better information and better regulation will all be essential elements of the stakeholder pension structure. It proposes no change for those earning above £18,500 per annum, since correctly the majority in this income bracket are well protected as members of either an occupational or other private schemes.

Although the language of the Green Paper is very encouraging, as Blackburn (1999, p.32) points out providing what it terms 'decent' pensions, although laudable and necessary, can clearly have different meanings. Does 'decent' mean,

(i) alleviation of pensioner poverty; (ii) prevention of pensioner poverty; (iii) giving the retired the resources to play a part in the community; (iv) enabling the retired to retain their pre-retirement standard of living.

Clearly, this question, which has been present in all discussions on pensions since (at least) 1878, is unanswered but hinted at. Based on the principles of social justice, pension policy should at least aim towards the first of this list, although ideally it should start with the second and move towards the third and fourth: the full social inclusion of older people. The present government strategy which emphasises the *alleviation* of poverty through the MIG and eventually the State Second Pension, marks the continuation of successive government thinking since the 1908 Act: nothing has changed. In brief, it marks a shift away from collective provision through National Insurance, towards individual responsibility and means-testing. The Green Paper has been a missed opportunity, particularly to redress the disadvantaged position women face with regard to their pension prospects (Falkingham and Rake, 1999; Rake et al, 1999). Blackburn is correct in suggesting that the absence of any mention of the third and fourth aims (priorities?) on this list emphasises that the government sees such priorities as being no longer the responsibility of the state. Income in retirement must increasingly be the responsibility of the individual and derived from 'the market' not the state. The Green Paper further marks the development of the so-called 'partnership' between state and private sector, the enhancement of 'grey capitalism' 'which offers poor relief for the poor and tax relief to the rich' (Blackburn, 1999, p.34).

Conclusions

This push by most national governments, not just the UK government, towards the private sector for a solution to the pensions debate flies in the face of the evidence. As Walker and Maltby (1997) reported, there is a strong indication of a very powerful intergenerational solidarity and full support across the European Union for the 'social contract'; that is, the payment of contributions or taxes to fund pensions. Furthermore, when questioned about where the responsibility for pensions should lie, with the state, employers or individuals, the majority of respondents in all European Union countries sampled indicated that pensions should be provided by public authorities and funded from contributions or taxes.

What is also evident is that although there is some resentment on the part of Europe's senior citizens about the low level of pensions in some countries, there is widespread agreement among them about the importance of their families and favourable attitudes towards young people.

It is apparent that both Taiwanese and UK current policy (as described in this text) fail to adequately address the high levels of poverty among *today's* pensioners in any systematic and inclusive manner. The priority for such social policy planning is political and economic, about the re-election of a government, rather than the formulation of an integrative social policy solution. What is no less required is the eradication of the harmful effects of poverty and social exclusion, to enable senior citizens to become full participants in their own societies and communities. This requires the removal of existing social and economic barriers with the state becoming the central provider of a citizen's pension funded through taxation, similar to the Danish system. Of vital importance is the provision of an adequate income for all older people, particularly older women, who are often highlighted in the poverty statistics of most countries. In the UK case a first step would be to raise the Basic Pension to at least £90 per week and for governments to utilise the published research evidence when assessing the level of benefits, particularly for older people to eradicate poverty in later life. Combating age discrimination in employment[8] is another priority since this would enhance employment opportunities for all older people and effectively place old age in a new light. Finally, encouraging older people to exercise greater power and influence in the design and implementation of their pension, social services and community care provision would also significantly enhance their level of social integration. The 'Better Government for Older People' strategy, in conjunction with local authorities and academics, which attempts to adopt such processes, is a useful start along this road.

Notes

[1] Now started with the recent passage of the Welfare Reform and Pensions Act, 1999.

[2] The UK has the highest rates of divorce in the European Union, see Walker and Maltby 1997.

[3] Nor should they!! My point is that much of the poverty in old age is a result of the contributory principle and the androcentric (and patriarchal) approach to social

policy in this area of pensions. A pension should be provided as an individual right of citizenship. It is more often provide in the form of deferred earnings.

[4] For a current (re)statement of the World Bank's position see Holzmann, 2000.

[5] Prior to decimalisation, there were 12 pence (d) to each shilling and 20 shillings (s) to the pound (£). This has not been converted into current equivalents since exact conversion does not reflect the true value of the period.

[6] Although many of these personal pensions have yet to mature since they were more widely available with the implementation of the Social Security Act 1986.

[7] If it continues, see below.

[8] For which there is widespread support from electorates within Europe (see Walker and Maltby, 1997).

References

Arber, S. and Ginn, J. (1991), *Gender and Later Life*, Sage, London.

Atkinson, A. B. (1991), *The Development of State Pensions in the United Kingdom*, STICERD Welfare State Programme Paper No. 59, LSE, London.

Atkinson, A.B. and Rein, M. (1993), *Age, Work and Social Security*, Macmillan, London.

Blackburn, R., (1999), 'The New Collectivism: Pension Reform, Grey Capitalism and Complex Socialism', *New Left Review*, 233 Jan/Feb , pp.3-65.

Bosanquet, N., Laing W., and Propper, C., (1990) *Elderly Consumers in Britain: Europe's Poor Relations?* Laing and Buisson, London.

Campbell, N. (1999), *The Decline of Employment Among Older People in Britain*, CASE, London.

Confederation of British Industry, (CBI) (1991), *Pensions post-Barber: equalising occupational pension schemes*, Confederation of British Industry, London.

Davidson, F. (1990), 'Occupational pensions and equal treatment', *Journal of Social Welfare Law*, 5, pp.310-331.

Deacon, A. (1982), 'An end to the means test? Social security and the Attlee Government', *Journal of Social Policy*, 11, no. 3, pp.289-306.

Department of Health and Social Security (DHSS) (1984), *Population, Pension Costs and Pensioner Incomes*, HMSO, London.

Department of Health and Social Security (DHSS) (1985a), *Reform of Social Security Volumes 1, 2, and 3*, Cmnd. 9517, 9518 and 9519, HMSO, London.

Department of Health and Social Security, (DHSS) (1985b), *Reform of Social Security: Programme for Action*, Cmnd. 9691, (White Paper), HMSO, London.

Department of Social Security (DSS)(1991a), *A guide to Retirement pensions*, Leaflet No. NP46, HMSO, London.

Department of Social Security (DSS) (1991b), *Options for Equality in the State Pension Age*, Cm.1723, HMSO, London.

Department of Social Security (DSS) (1995), *The Pensioners Income Series 1993*, DSS Analytical Services Division, London.

Department of Social Security (DSS) (1997a), *Households below Average Income: A statistical Analysis 1979-1994/95*, Government Statistical Office, London, The Stationery Office.

Department of Social Security (DSS) (1997b), *Pensioners' Income Series 1995/6* Analytical Services Division, London.

Department of Social Security (DSS) (1998), *A New Contract for Welfare: Partnership in Pensions*, Cm 4179, The Stationery Office, London. Also available at http://www.dss.gov.uk/hq/pubs/pengp.index.htm.

Dex, S., Joshi, H., McCulloch, A. and Macran, S. (1996), *Women's Employment Transitions Around Childbearing*, CEPR Discussion Paper no. 1408, CEPR, London.

Falkingham, J. (1989), 'Dependency and ageing in Britain: A re-examination of the evidence', *Journal of Social Policy*, 18, no.2, pp.211-233.

Falkingham J. (1998), 'Financial (in)security in Later Life' in M. Bernard and J. Phillips (eds) *The Social Policy of Old Age*, CPA, London, pp.93-111.

Falkingham, J. and Rake, K. (1999), 'Partnership in pensions: Delivering a secure retirement for women?', CASE Paper 24, STICERD/LSE, London.

Field, F. (1998), Ministerial statement to the House of Commons, 26 March, par 14. House of Commons, Hansard.

Field, F. and Owen, M. (1993a), *Private Pensions for All: Squaring the Circle*, Fabian Society Discussion Paper No. 16, July, Fabian Society, London.

Field, F. and Owen, M. (1993b), *Making Sense of Pensions*, Fabian Pamphlet No. 557, March, Fabian Society, London.

Field, F. and Owen, M. (1994), *National Pensions Savings Plan: Universalising Private Pension Provision*, Fabian Society, London.

Field, J. and Prior, G. (1996) *Women and Pensions*, Department of Social Security Research Report Number 49, HMSO, London.

Fraser, D. (1984), *The Evolution of the British Welfare State*, Macmillan, London.

Fry, V. and Stark, G. (1991), 'New rich or old poor: Poverty, take-up and the indexation of the state pension', *Fiscal Studies*, 12, no. 1, pp.67-71.

Ginn, J. (1998), 'Older Women in Europe: East Follows West in the Feminization of Poverty?' *Ageing International*, Vol. XXIV (4), pp.102-122.

Hess, J. (1981), 'The social policy of the Attlee government' in W.J. Mommsen (ed.), *The Emergence of the Welfare State in Britain and Germany*, Croom Helm, Kent, pp.296-311.

Hills , J. (1993), *The Future of Welfare: A Guide to the Debate*, Joseph Rowntree Foundation, York.

Hills, J. (1997), 'How will the scissors close? Options for UK social spending' in A. Walker, A. and C. Walker, *Britain Divided*, CPAG, London, pp.231-248.

Holzmann, R. (2000), 'The World Bank approach to Pension reform', *International Social Security Review*, 53 (1) pp.11-34.

Joshi, H. (1989), 'The Changing Form of Women's Economic Dependency' in H. Joshi (ed) *The Changing Population of Britain*, Blackwell, Oxford, pp.157-176.

Joshi, H. (1992), 'The Cost of Caring' in C. Glendinning and J. Millar, *Women and Poverty in Britain: The 1990s*, Harvester Wheatsheaf, Hemel Hempstead, pp.110-125.

Kohli, M., Rein, M., Guillemard, A.-M. and Gunsteren, H. (1991), *Time for Retirement*, Cambridge University Press, Cambridge.

Labour Research, (1987), 'The privatisation of pensions', July, LRD Publicatons, pp.13-14.

Levene, T. (2000), 'Pensioners who will get a glow', *Guardian*, March 25, Money section p.5.

Macnichol, J. (1998), *The Politics of Retirement in Britain 1878-1948*, Cambridge University Press, Cambridge.

Maltby, T. (1994), *Women and Pensions in Britain and Hungary*, Avebury, Aldershot.

McGoldrick, A. (1984), *Equal treatment in occupational pension schemes*, Equal Opportunities Commission, Manchester.

Midwinter, E. (1997), *Pensioned Off*, CPA, London.

O'Higgins, M. (1984), 'Privatisation and social security', *Political Quarterly*, 55, pp.129-139.

Parker, H. (2000), *Low cost but acceptable incomes for older people: a minimum standard for households 64-74 years in the UK*, Policy Press, Bristol.

Phillipson, C. (1982), *Capitalism and the Construction of Old Age*, Macmillan, London.

Phillipson, C. (1998), 'Changing Work and Retirement. Older workers' discrimination and the Labour Market' in M. Bernard and J. Phillips (eds) *The Social Policy of Old Age*, CPA, London, pp. 76-92.

Portillo, M. (1989), 'The reform of Social Security: A government view', in A. Dilnot and I. Walker, *The economics of social security*, Oxford University Press, Oxford.

Rake, K, Falkingham, J. and Evans, M. (1999), 'Tightropes and Tripwires: New Labour's proposals and Means Testing in Old Age' CASE Paper 23, STICERD/LSE, London.

Shaw, C. (1998), '1996-based national population projections for the United Kingdom and constituent countries', *Population Trends*, 91, Spring, pp.43-49.

Shragge, E. (1984), *Pensions policy in Britain: A socialist analysis*, Routledge and Kegan Paul, London.

SSAC (Social Security Advisory Committee) (1992), *Options for Equality in State Pensions Age: A case for equalizing at 65*, HMSO, London.

Taylor, P. and Walker, A. (1994), 'The Ageing Workforce: Employers' Attitudes Towards Older Workers', *Work, Employment and Society*, vol.8, No.4, pp.569-591.

Thane, P. (1978), 'Non-Contributory versus Insurance Pensions 1878-1908' in P. Thane (ed.), *The Origins of British Social Policy*, Croom Helm, London, pp.84-106.

Thane, P. (1989), 'Old Age: Burden or Benefit' in H. Joshi (ed), *The Changing Population of Britain*, Blackwell, Oxford, pp.56-71.

Titmuss, R. M. (1955), 'Pension systems and population change', *Political Quarterly*, XXVI, no. 2, pp. 152-166.

Townsend, P. (1986), 'Ageism and Social Policy', in C. Phillipson and A. Walker (eds), *Ageing and Social Policy*, Gower, Aldershot, pp.15-44.

Waine, B. (1999), The Future is Private', *Benefits*, 26, Sept./Oct. pp.7-10.

Walker, A. (1985), 'Early Retirement: Release or Refuge from the Labour Market?' *The Quarterly Journal of Social Affairs*, vol.1, No.2, pp.211-229.

Walker, A. and Maltby, T. (1997), *Ageing Europe*, Open University Press, Buckingham.

Walker, A., (1999), 'The Third Way for Pensions (by way of Thatcherism and avoiding today's pensioner's)' *Critical Social Policy*, 67, Vol 19 (4) pp. 511-427.

World Bank (1994), *Averting the Old Age Crisis*, New York, Oxford University Press.

PART III
HEALTH CARE

8 Financing health care for middle-to-low income households in Taiwan

GEORGE CHENG WANG

Introduction

The nature of Taiwan's National Health Insurance (NHI) is a combination of social insurance and social assistance. Currently, premium subsidies to low-income households, in the form of social assistance, cover only 0.5 per cent of the total population. However, in this study, results analyzed from 1984 to 1994's Household Expenditure Surveys suggest that there are approximately 30 per cent of households whose health care expenditures exceed the average of all households, but whose disposable incomes are less than average disposable incomes (table 8.1). This finding reflects the need for equity and efficiency in the reasonable allocation of health care resources, in particular for middle-to-low income households. To reduce the financial burdens of these households, the government should subsidize their premiums.

The NHI in Taiwan is a compulsory programme. The beneficiaries include the insured and his dependants. The insured are classified into 6 categories: employees and employers, union workers, farmers, dependants of military servicemen, low-income families and community-based participants. The government subsidizes premiums for the insured and their dependants except for employers and the self-employed. The contribution share of government for all categories is listed in table 8.2.

The current structure of the insurance fee waiver is based on the principle of social assistance in respect of aid for medical care and that of social insurance regarding proportion of subsidy. There has been less dispute over the subsidy for low income households since it qualifies on the grounds of the ability-to-pay principle From the perspective of policy implementation, it may even be necessary to include middle-to-low income households as a target for subsidies. As for the differential proportionate subsidy for the different occupational groups, a thorough reassessment is essential to rectify its lack of appropriate theoretical

Table 8.1 Household's health care expenditure ratio and corresponding Z score by income decile, 1984-1994

Decile	Average	1	2	3	4	5	6	7	8	9	10
1984											
HCE[a]	5.08	7.36	5.41	5.15	4.79	4.92	4.67	4.75	4.68	4.63	4.49
Z[b]		2.70	0.39	0.08	-0.34	-0.19	-0.49	-0.39	-0.47	-0.53	-0.70
1985											
HCE[a]	5.31	7.85	6.00	5.38	5.09	4.95	4.71	4.98	4.78	4.73	4.63
Z[b]		2.59	0.70	0.07	-0.22	-0.37	-0.61	-0.34	-0.54	-0.59	-0.69
1986											
HCE[a]	5.41	7.95	5.90	5.67	5.18	4.94	4.95	4.79	4.89	4.98	4.86
Z[b]		2.63	0.51	0.27	-0.24	-0.49	-0.48	-0.64	-0.54	-0.45	-0.57
1987											
HCE[a]	5.62	9.41	6.10	5.65	5.05	5.18	5.11	5.10	4.76	4.83	4.82
Z[b]		2.71	0.34	0.02	-0.41	-0.31	-0.36	-0.37	-0.61	-0.56	-0.57
1988											
HCE[a]	5.48	8.39	6.18	5.36	4.96	5.17	5.14	5.03	5.00	4.73	4.69
Z[b]		2.62	0.63	-0.11	-0.47	-0.28	-0.31	-0.41	-0.43	-0.68	-0.71
1989											
HCE[a]	5.25	8.04	6.08	5.14	5.15	4.94	4.80	4.64	4.68	4.65	4.14
Z[b]		2.51	0.75	-0.10	-0.09	-0.28	-0.41	-0.55	-0.51	-0.54	-1.00
1990											
HCE[a]	5.22	8.35	5.65	5.60	4.86	4.98	4.92	4.54	4.44	4.28	4.41
Z[b]		2.60	0.36	0.32	-0.30	-0.20	-0.25	-0.57	-0.65	-0.78	-0.67
1991											
HCE[a]	5.79	8.84	6.50	5.92	5.61	5.41	5.35	5.13	5.08	5.01	4.90
Z[b]		2.58	0.60	0.11	-0.15	-0.32	-0.37	-0.56	-0.60	-0.66	-0.75
1992											
HCE[a]	5.60	9.13	6.30	5.83	5.41	5.09	4.90	5.18	4.81	4.64	4.50
Z[b]		2.59	0.51	0.17	-0.14	-0.37	-0.51	-0.31	-0.58	-0.70	-0.81
1993											
HCE[a]	9.02	15.02	11.48	9.63	8.50	8.04	7.69	7.48	7.44	7.34	7.24
Z[b]		2.40	0.98	0.24	-0.21	-0.39	-0.53	-0.62	-0.63	-0.67	-0.71
1994											
HCE[a]	9.86	16.81	12.96	10.39	9.30	8.66	8.19	8.34	8.39	7.78	7.46
Z[b]		2.37	1.06	0.18	-0.19	-0.41	-0.57	-0.52	-0.50	-0.71	-0.82

Source: 1984-1994's Household Expenditure Surveys.

a: HCE denotes the ratio of health care expenditure to total household expenditure.

b: Z score denotes the difference between decile average ratio and grand average ratio, divided by the standard deviation of the ratios across all deciles.

rationale. It is against this background that this study will attempt the following:

1. To evaluate the current system of insurance fee waiver and social assistance practices with regard to aid for medical care.
2. To examine the role of government in intervening in National Health Insurance policy and the theoretical rationale of the insurance premium subsidy, from the perspective of economics and sociology.
3. To identify and define middle-to-low income households and other relevant social groups as recipients of subsidy; to establish the criteria for subsidy; and to recommend the optimal subsidization rate for target groups as a reference point for the revision of the health insurance policy.

Table 8.2 Percentage of premium contribution under NHI unit

Category		Government Subsidy	Employer	Employee
1st	Private-sector Employees	10	60	30
	Government Employees		60	40
	Private School Employees	30	30	40
	Self-employed/Employers			100
2nd	Union Workers and Sailors	40		60
3rd	Farmers/Fishermen	70		30
4th	Dependents of Servicemen		60	40
5th	Low-income Families	100		
6th	Veterans	100		
	Dependents of Veterans	70		30
	Community-based participants	40		60

The theoretical framework of subsidization, viewed from the perspective of different social values

One of the major objectives of the NHI programme is income redistribution. Hence the subsidy for the insurance fee should target those facing economic difficulties. This study focuses on the equity principle of ability to pay when the subsidy system is accessed. In addition, it attempts to redefine middle-to-low income households by using family medical expenditures in relation to consumption and income deciles. Further investigation is devoted to the relationship between family size and the amount of subsidy. In addition, this study attempts to evaluate the legitimacy of a differential proportion of subsidy being allocated to the different income groups. Finally, it tries to estimate the amount of the government fiscal burden and appropriate methods of financing this.

The NHI plan may be viewed as an in-kind demand subsidy, based on the argument that there are externalities in consumption. If the non-poor wish to subsidize the poor, this will result in a demand for government subsidies. The degree of subsidization will differ, depending upon the values held by the non-poor with respect to redistribution of medical care services. One set of values may indicate minimum provision, meaning that no person in society should receive less than a certain quantity of medical care in case of illness. A second set of values might favour equal financial access to medical care. If these values were the basis for the externalities in consumption, they would suggest an NHI plan that would equalize the financial barriers for all persons. The third set of values that people may share with respect to redistribution of medical care services goes beyond equal financial access to require equal treatment for equal needs. In other words, each person should be able to enjoy equal consumption of medical services regardless of economic or other factors affecting utilization. These different demands for government subsidies reflect varying sets of values that are believed to exist in the population. The first set of values would require the smallest level of subsidization; the third set of values would be the most expensive to achieve.

It is not possible to state which set of values is 'most appropriate'. Whichever set the population selects would be a proper basis for determining the level of government subsidies under NHI. Yet, although it is not possible to determine *a priori* the set of values likely to be chosen by the population, it is possible to determine the most efficient approach for achieving each of the three sets of objectives.

Minimum provision may be achieved by subsidizing those persons whose consumption of medical care is below the minimum, to bring their consumption up to the minimum, as shown in figure 8.1. Assuming that there are three different income groups - high incomes (HY), middle incomes (MY), and low incomes (LY) - their demands for medical care are shown by the three demand curves, HY, MY and LY respectively. The aggregate demand curve of all three income groups is shown by HYMLY. The reason why the three demand curves do not result in the same consumption of medical care at zero price is that there are factors, other than financial ones, that result in differences in demand between the different income groups.

Figure 8.1 The model for the cost of different demand subsidies

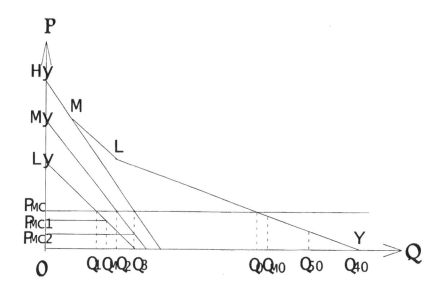

If the current price of medical care is P_{MC}, the utilization of the three income groups would be Q_1, Q_2 and Q_3, and their aggregate utilization would be Q_0, which is the intersection of the aggregate demand curve and the supply of medical care (assuming, for simplicity, perfect elasticity). If society wanted to ensure that no one received less than a minimum amount of medical care, Q_M, a national health insurance system which set the price to zero for everyone (like the NHS system in Britain) would achieve this goal. A system of subsidies that lowered the price of medical care just to those whose consumption is less than the minimum would also achieve this goal. If medical care were free, total consumption would increase from Q_0 to Q_{40}. If, instead, a subsidy were provided by lowering the price for lower-income persons to P_{MC1}, the aggregate consumption would only be increased from Q_0 to Q_{M0}. Since both approaches would achieve the goal of minimum provision, the approach that provided a subsidy only to the lower income group would be less costly than a scheme that reduced the price for everyone.

If society's values with respect to the redistribution of medical care were that all persons should have equal financial access, then this could be achieved by subsidies varied according to income level. Reducing the price of medical care to zero for low-income persons would increase their consumption to Q_3. A subsidy to middle-income groups equal to (P_{MC} - P_{MC2}) would also increase their consumption to Q_3. At consumption level Q_3, the utilization of medical care for the three income groups would be equal. The aggregate increase in medical care use would go from Q_0 to Q_{50}. In short, equal financial access would require a more expensive subsidy system than would a scheme for minimum provision.

Equal treatment for equal needs expresses the third set of values that give rise to a demand for medical care subsidies. As shown in figure 8.1, high-income groups would still consume more medical care at zero price than would those with middle and lower incomes. Thus, a free medical care system (like the NHS) would not be able to achieve that set of values defined as equal treatment for equal needs. The only way this could be achieved would be by 'differential subsidies', varied according to income level. For example, as shown in figure 8.2, lowering the price to zero for both low- and middle-income groups would still not increase their utilization to a point equal to that of the high-income group. Only if the low- and middle-income groups were subsidized further, through a system of negative prices, could their utilization be rendered equal. A negative price could be effected by means of a direct in-kind supply subsidy to low-income groups. For example, establishing clinics and health centres in remote areas and providing incentives for health personnel to practise there would increase accessibility for low-income groups.

Significantly, for each of the sets of values examined - minimum provision, equal financial access, and equal treatment for equal needs - it has been shown that these values can be achieved more efficiently if the subsidy varies by income level rather than occupation categories.

The definition of middle-to-low income households

Currently, official definitions concerning middle-to-low income are not consistent between different local authorities. Actual definitions depend on political considerations, budgetary constraints and policy implementation priorities. One example of such a situation is the broadened standard of living allowance now being offered to the elderly in middle-to-low income households, in response to political pressures (Wang, 1994b; Lan, 1989). Nevertheless, for the purposes of medical subsidy, the definition based on 'The Medical Subsidy Plan for Children, Teenagers,

Figure 8.2 Equal treatment for equal needs through a system of negative prices

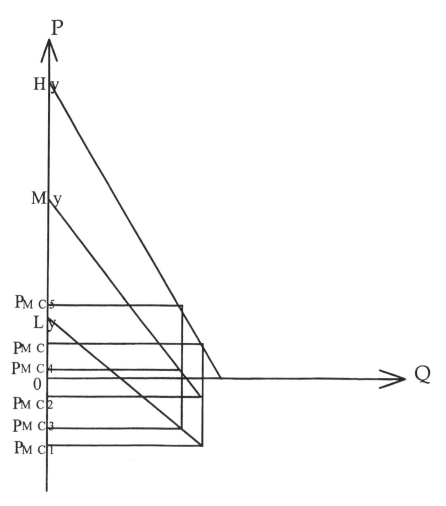

and the Elderly in Middle-to-Low Income Households' is often referred to by the Bureau of National Health Insurance (Yeh et al, 1998). Specifically, the plan defines middle-to-low income households as being those where 'the average income of household member is less than 2.5 times of minimum living expenses'. This last is the official poverty line, which amounts to about 60 per cent of the average consumption level of the previous year.

On careful examination of this definition, first, we find that it does not take into account the facts of resource-sharing and the characteristics of economies of scale in home consumption. Thus the use of average income per capita as the reference point is inadequate, especially for small households (particularly for single-person households). Second, the use of 2.5 times minimum living expenses as the cut-off point has no normative basis and, in any case, is rather impractical to apply. The following estimation based on the survey data for 1994 will be calculated to demonstrate the point.

To determine minimum living expenses, two official poverty lines have been selected and averaged. One from Taiwan Province and Kaohsiung City (NT$5,000) and the other from Taipei City (NT$6,290). If we multiply the 'average' by the number of months (12) and then by a multiplier of 1 to 2.5, the resulting amount estimated ranges from $67,740 to $169,350. It is households with a per capita annual income falling into this bracket which will be classified officially as middle-to-low income households.

According to sample calculations based on 1994 data, there were 7,615 households, encompassing 33,747 persons, who meet the official criterion. After multiplying the sample households by the sampling weight, the number of such households in the total population was estimated at 2,564,745, and the number of persons at 11,376,211; in other words approximately 53.85 per cent of the total population in 1994 (DGBAS, 1994). Evidently, using an upper limit of 2.5 times the official poverty line is unrealistic. If the proportion of the population included in this target group has held constant, then in 1997, the number of persons estimated to be in middle-to-low income households would be 11,692,988. If we assume their premiums to be fully subsidized, the extra amount of government expenditure would be equal to NT$6,340,328,575 per month, which is about one-third of the national health insurance budget.

Z Score comparisons of medical expenditure and income distribution

Who are the poor? A logical place to begin is by asking what is the meaning of poverty. This question has a long history and gives rise to considerable controversy over definition and measurement. The question becomes even more important in this case, when poverty is being discussed in relation to the definition of middle-to-low income households and to the corresponding health care issue.

Once we have identified middle-to-low income households, the next question concerns their health (and health expenditure) relative to the rest of the population. As an economic concept, the poverty to which we refer is some measure of income that indicates 'inadequate' command over material resources. However, there are still some questions to be discussed. Should so-called adequate income be adjusted to allow for the size and composition of the household? Should poverty be defined according to some fixed term (absolute income) or according to position in the income distribution (relative income)? In this chapter, an equivalence scale will be calculated to deal with the economic significance of household size, and a statistical Z score will be used to reflect the relative position of income levels and medical expenditures.

Given the rapid economic growth and social development of Taiwan over the last decade, the nature of poverty in question is not an absolute level of 'primary poverty', but a relative level of 'secondary poverty'. The data analyzed in this study come from Household Expenditure Surveys, 1984-1994, as collected by the Directorate-General of Budget, Accounting and Statistics (DGBAS, 1994). The results of the annual trends in household's health care expenditure are summarized in table 8.1.

As pointed out above, the unit of analysis in this study is based on the household. Classifying survey households into 10 income deciles, we could make comparisons of Health Care Expenditures (HCE) (table 8.1) across 10 income deciles. This procedure has the advantage of making a comparison of medical expenditure and total expenditure in relative rather than absolute terms. Nevertheless, the above procedure can only evaluate the relative position of each decile. It cannot assess the relative position of each decile in the scale of global income distribution within the year and across the year. To be able to assess the position of each decile in more precise relative terms, this study calculates Z scores denoting the relative weights of medical expenditure.

In our national health insurance programme, both the insured and his dependants have to pay the same amount of premium calculated according to the insurance cover of the insured. The household is the enrolment unit in calculating the premium. If we classify the disposable income of all households into 10 deciles, the distribution of medical expenditure per capita shows a U-shaped curve (illustrated in figure 8.3). The lowest part of the curve centres around the fourth to the sixth decile, indicating that these deciles' average medical expenditures (in absolute terms) are lower than the other deciles. Such a pattern has also been found in other countries. For example, Hurst (1985) and Wagstaff et al (1994) found that average health care expenditures for households in both high and low income deciles are higher than those of the middle deciles. It is reasonable to expect higher expenditures for high-income groups, since consumption level increases with income. On the other hand, the underlying reason for low-income deciles having relatively high rates of medical expenditure could be their relatively high demands for health care. Some studies have found that low-income groups have a relatively higher morbidity rate (Le Grand, 1978; Hurst, 1985). However, the types and components of the demands being made by the respective groups might be different.

Figure 8.3   Household health care expenditure by income decile in 1994

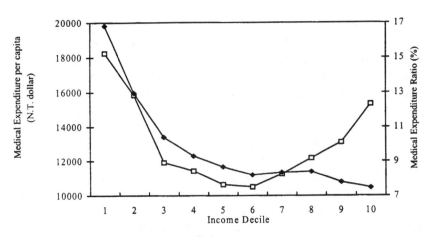

─□─ Medical Expenditure per capita (N.T. dollar)
─◆─ Medical Expenditure Ratio (%)

The above discussion is based on absolute amounts of medical expenditure. To examine health care expenditure in relative terms, we first calculate the ratio of medical expenditure to total expenditure for each household (approximately 16,200 households in total in this study), sum this amount and then divide it by all households in the decile. The resulting amount is then equal to the average ratio (weight) of medical expenditure (HCE). From figure 8.3, we find that the HCE of the first three deciles is higher than the average medical expenditure ratio for the total population. Moreover, this is not a pattern peculiar to the year 1994, being evident in related statistics from other survey years (1984-1993).

In order to find the pattern of relative medical expenditure in terms of total expenditure for lower-income households across the years, Z scores have been calculated (figure 8.4). This measure not only indicates the relative position of medical expenditure ratio for each decile; it also helps identify the relatively disadvantaged (so-called middle-to-low income households) in the health care market. From table 8.3, we find that the Z scores for the first three deciles are positive, except for 1988 and 1989 (which are not statistically significant from zero), whereas the other deciles are negative. If medical expenditure is used as a proxy for both health condition and its demand, then households in the first three deciles not only have relatively low incomes but also relatively poorer health, suffering from the double jeopardy of poverty and illness.

Figure 8.4 Z Score comparison of medical expenditure in 1994

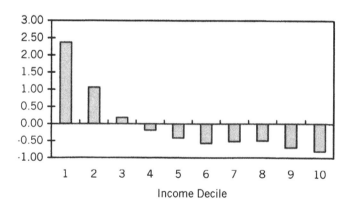

Column 4 (in table 8.3) indicates rising trends in the Z scores for the first three deciles, from 1984 to 1994. A simple regression, $\underline{Y} = \underline{a} + \underline{bT}$, has been conducted, where $\underline{Y}$ and $\underline{T}$ denote the sum of the Z scores and the years respectively. The estimated parameters for $\underline{a}$ and $\underline{b}$ are positive (3.1248 and 0.0309) and significant at the 5 per cent level. The results of the regression test confirm the disadvantage of double jeopardy affecting the first three deciles. Unfortunately, since we haven't found any other foreign studies using the same form of analysis, there is no information for cross-national comparison.

Table 8.3 Relative weights of medical expenditure burden for the lower income decile

Decile	1	2	3	Total	Grand Average Weight
1984	2.70	0.39	0.08	3.17	0
1985	2.59	0.70	0.07	3.36	0
1986	2.63	0.51	0.27	3.41	0
1987	2.71	0.34	0.02	3.07	0
1988	2.62	0.63	-0.11	3.14	0
1989	2.51	0.75	-0.10	3.16	0
1990	2.60	0.36	0.32	3.28	0
1991	2.58	0.60	0.11	3.29	0
1992	2.59	0.51	0.17	3.27	0
1993	2.40	0.98	0.24	3.62	0
1994	2.37	1.06	0.18	3.61	0

Source: 1984-1994's Household Expenditure Surveys.
Note + means above average; - means below average.

The redefinition of middle-to-low income households

Theoretically, households in the first three deciles could be presumed the target group for premium subsidies. Nevertheless, for policy implementation purposes, we should use the household unit instead of the income decile as the baseline for locating middle-to-low income households. In other words, the shift from decile to specific household is necessary in order to allow for the economic scale of family consumption.

Economic scale and equivalences scales in household consumption

The previous plan for medical premium subsidies, designed for the elderly, young people and the disabled in middle-to-low income households, was based on the criterion of per capita income of less than 2.5 times the poverty line. This criterion failed to allow for economic scale in household consumption (Wang and Tsui, 1988). The results from the study of setting a reasonable family poverty line also indicate that, for households with more than five persons, consumption increases at a decreasing rate. In other words, household consumption regressively increases with household size (Wang, 1994). Since the current official system only uses per-capita income as its qualifying criterion, it does have the advantage of making the administrative procedure simple. Even so, this is not fair for households consisting of relatively fewer persons, since it violates the equity principle.

In order to measure the effect of economic scale of consumption on the household size, an equivalence scale will be calculated. In most European countries, poverty scales consist of differential rates, with couples receiving some 160 per cent of the amount for a single person, and children about a third or a half, depending on age. These differentials have a long history, but they have been influenced by research on equivalence scales. Nevertheless, it is shown that the calculation of a differential scale involves some ethical considerations, where judgement plays a significant role.

Central to the discussion of equivalence scales has often been the implicit assumption that a standard of living is common to all members of a given family. Yet intra-family distribution is an important issue, since it is possible for some members of the family (usually women or children) to have a lower level of living than the others. The difficulty is that we know so little about resource distribution within the family.

To calculate our Household Size and Equivalence Consumption scale, we first classified the household survey data into 10 categories according to size (e.g. one, two persons - the last category being ten or more persons). Second, we indexed average consumption expenditure data for a single-person to 1, then calculated the other indices for households with more than one person. For example, to calculate the equivalence index for households with two persons, we divided the total consumption expenditure of two persons by that of single-persons. Finally, for each household size, we took the average of indices for the 11 years (grand average) to smooth out the impacts of differential family composition and intra-family resource distribution. The resulting relationship between household size and the equivalence index is illustrated in table 8.4.

Target population

The target population of middle-to-low income households will be defined according to the first three income deciles. According to the Family

Expenditure Survey data of 1994, the cut-off point for disposable household income between the third and the fourth deciles (i.e. the upper limit for the third decile) is $499,763. Divide this amount by the average house-

Table 8.4 Household size and equivalence consumption scale

House- hold Size	Equivalence Scale for Household Consumption Expenditure											
	1984	1985	1986	1987	1988	1989	1990	1991	1992	1993	1994	Average
1	1.00	1.00	1.00	1.00	1.00	1.00	1.00	1.00	1.00	1.00	1.00	1.00
2	1.64	1.63	1.68	1.71	1.62	1.73	1.66	1.63	1.60	1.66	1.69	1.66
3	2.14	2.14	2.23	2.24	2.20	2.36	2.33	2.25	2.25	2.42	2.49	2.28
4	2.51	2.50	2.58	2.71	2.61	2.77	2.78	2.66	2.71	2.89	3.04	2.71
5	2.54	2.62	2.73	2.87	2.73	2.86	2.83	2.76	2.84	2.99	3.11	2.81
6	2.72	2.73	2.85	2.99	2.83	3.01	2.98	2.92	2.94	3.16	3.23	2.94
7	2.89	2.89	3.07	3.26	2.98	3.19	3.11	3.08	3.16	3.24	3.46	3.12
8	3.20	3.16	3.30	3.45	3.31	3.46	3.46	3.12	3.44	3.52	3.66	3.37
9	3.42	3.35	3.70	3.71	3.72	3.50	3.88	3.56	3.62	4.03	4.21	3.70
10	4.10	3.99	4.36	4.58	4.19	4.47	4.19	4.13	4.50	4.23	4.87	4.33

Source: 1984-1994's Household Expenditure Surveys.

hold size for the third and the fourth decile (average household size is 3.75 and 4.02 persons for the said deciles, respectively) and the resulting amount of per capita income is equal to $128,639. This new definition criterion for middle-to-low income households is much lower than the official ones as indicated in table 8.3. Single-person households with disposable income of less than this amount qualify for premium subsidies. For households with more than one person, it is necessary to multiply the criterion by the associated equivalence scale. The specific procedure is calculated by the following formula and is listed in table 8.5.

$$IC(n) = 128639 \times ES(n)$$

Where $IC(n)$ denotes the criterion for middle-to-low income households with n persons; and $ES(n)$ denotes the scale index of consumption expenditure for each different household size.

By using this new measurement equation, we calculate the target population from the family expenditure survey data for 1994 to be 965 of the households sampled (2,756 persons) who were qualified for premium subsidy. If we multiply the sample households thus classified as disadvantaged by the sampling weight, the estimated total numbers for households and persons are 317,792 and 914,246, respectively. If we then subtract the number of 120,319 persons already classified as low-income persons; the total number of middle-to-low income households as defined in this study is equal to 793,927 persons, which is much lower than the official definition. According to Population Statistics for the Taiwan Area, the total population was 21,125,792 in 1994. In other words, on this

Table 8.5 Equivalence scale and income criterion for middle-to-low income households in 1994

Household Size	Equivalence Scale	Income Criterion	Official Criterion
1	1.00	128,639	169,350
2	1.66	213,241	338,700
3	2.28	292,900	508,050
4	2.71	348,109	677,400
5	2.81	361,121	846,750
6	2.94	378,531	1,016,100
7	3.12	401,534	1,185,450
8	3.37	433,667	1,354,800
9	3.70	476,011	1,524,150
10	4.33	556,788	1,693,500

Source: 1984-1994's Household Expenditure Surveys and Table 2.

reckoning, only 3.76 per cent of the total population should qualify for premium subsidies.

Budget estimation and differential subsidization

If the government decides fully to subsidize middle-to-low income households, the additional fiscal burden will be equal to the premium payments ($546) multiplied by the target population of 793,927; this to be subtracted from current subsidies for the Medical Subsidy Plan for Children, Teenagers and Elderly. The resulting amount of $4.8 billion will be the additional fiscal burden to be borne by government on an annual basis.

When Z scores are calculated as a proxy for the relationship between health and poverty, they show the households in the first three deciles suffering from a double jeopardy of illness and low income. If the target of premium subsidization policy is to reduce Z scores to zero, differential subsidies will be essential for the reason that the Z scores of the first three deciles are different. Two methods of financing the subsidies are simulated, one by taxation, the other by increases in premiums (to be shared in proportion to the disposable income of the other deciles). Judging by the data from 1994, the resulting optimal subsidization rates for the first method will be 100 per cent, 88.9 per cent, and 62.6 per cent for the first three deciles respectively, to be financed from the governmental budget. Meantime, the other optimal subsidization rates are 100 per cent, 82.5 per cent, and 56.1 per cent respectively, to be financed by increases in premiums. Although the subsidized premium of the first decile is already 100 per cent, the Z score does not go down to zero. A 'negative' price is needed for the lowest income group (decile) in terms of equity and efficiency.

Subsidization rates are different according to the method of financing, lower rates being associated with increasing the premiums for higher income groups. Currently, the medical insurance premium is calculated based on the insured amount. The insured amounts of the employees and employers are their declared monthly salary and business income, respectively. Some fixed insured amounts are designated for union workers and farmers. The highest insured amount is set to be only 3.5 times the lowest one, which is lower than the national income distribution scale (that is, approximately 5.8 times in the five income decile distribution) (BNHI, 1999). For policy implication this paper suggests that the scale of insured amounts should be upgraded to assure income redistribution effects.

Conclusion and comments

There are many types of in-kind subsidies in medical care. Some of these are demand subsidies; others are supply subsidies. Some are indirect with regard to the beneficiary groups which they would like to affect; others are direct. The national health insurance programme in Taiwan could be classified as a direct demand subsidy. Although government has long been involved in establishing the rule of resource allocation for medical care, its role in financing and subsidization in health insurance provokes controversy. Given the significant role of government in personal medical service provision, it is important to establish who are the beneficiaries of these subsidies and to estimate the efficiency with which they are distributed. As discussed above, the reason for in-kind subsidies is based on externalities in consumption. As a result, the primary recipients should be those with low and/or middle-to-low income and poor health. If the subsidies are distributed to higher-income groups or provide them with a greater proportionate share of the subsidy, then the medical resources allocation is inefficient.

In general, empirical study shows that the relative medical expenditure ratios for households in the first three deciles are higher than that of other deciles. In addition, normalized Z scores calculated for the measurement of poverty and illness are also higher than the average (positive) for the first three deciles. Thus, this paper suggests that the recipients of premium subsidies, including middle-to-low income households, be confined to these deciles. On gounds of efficiency, differential subsidies might be preferred to minimize costs. On grounds of equity, however, financing by increased premiums is proposed in this paper. The tax subsidy programme (financed by governmental budget) generally benefits those with higher income. As a result, recognizing the redistributive benefits that these subsidy programmes provide to different income groups is the first step in deciding whether the resulting redistributive effects are desirable. It should then be determined whether such subsidies could be provided more efficiently so that they are received by those in greatest financial need. It is, to say the least, questionable that such issues could be fully answered in a study such as this. It is imperative for further research to be done.

References

Abel-Smith, B. (1994), *An Introduction to Health: Policy, Planning and Financing*, Longman Publishing, New York.

Abel-Smith, B. (1992), *Cost Containment and New Priorities in Health Care: A Study of the European Community*, Avebury, Aldershot.

Black, D. (1993), 'Inequalities in Health', in David E. Rogers and Eli Ginzberg (eds), *Medical Care and the Health of the Poor*, Westview Press, Boulder, San Francisco and Oxford, pp.43-60.

Browning, E.K. (1979), 'The Politics of Social Security Reform', in C.D. Campbell (ed), *Financing Social Security*, American Enterprise Institute for Public Policy Research, Washington, D.C.

Cutler, D.M. (1995), 'The Cost and Financing of Health Care', *American Economic Review* (Papers and Proceedings), pp.32-37.

Donaldson, C. and Gerard, K. (1993), *Economics of Health care Financing: The Visible Hand*, St. Martin's Press, New York.

Feldstein, M. (1995), 'The Economics of Health and Health Care: What Have We Learned? What Have I Learned?' *American Economic Review* (Papers and Proceedings), pp.28-31.

Feldstein, P.J. (1993), *Health Care Economics*, Delmar Publishers Inc., New York.

Fuchs, V.R. (1993), 'Poverty and Health: Asking the Right Questions', in David E. Rogers and Eli Ginzberg (eds), *Medical Care and the Health of the Poor*, Westview Press, Boulder, San Francisco and Oxford, pp.9-20.

Hurst, J. (1985), *Financing Health Care in the USA., Canada and Britain*, Kings Fund Institute, London.

Illsley, R. and Le Grand, J. (1987), 'The Measurement of Inequality in Health', in A. Williams (ed), *Health and Economics*, Macmillan Press, London, pp.12-36.

Lan, C.F. (1989), 'A Critical Review of ROC's Health Care Financing and Health Care Delivery: Toward a Regionalized Delivery and Socialized Financing on Health Care', Paper presented on *the International Symposium on Health Care Systems*, Taipei, Dec. 18-20.

Le Grand, J. (1978), 'The Distribution of Public Expenditure: The Case of Health Care', *Economica* 45, pp.125-142.

Le Grand, J. (1986), 'Inequalities in Health and Health Care: A Research Agenda', in Richard G. Wilkinson (ed), *Class and Health: Research and Longitudinal Data*, Tavistock Publications, London and New York, pp.115-124.

Marmor, T.R. (1994), *Understanding Health Care Reform*. Yale University Press, New Haven.

McGuire, A., Fenn, P. and Mayhew, K. (1994), 'The Economics of Health Care', in A. McGuire, P. Fenn, and K. Mayhew (eds), *Providing Health Care: the Economics of Alternative Systems of Finance and Delivery*, Oxford University Press, New York, pp.5-45.

Rowland, D. (1993), 'Health Care of the Poor: The Contribution of Social Insurance', in David E. Rogers and Eli Ginzberg (eds), *Medical Care and the Health of the Poor*, Westview Press, Boulder, San Francisco and Oxford, pp.107-124.

Ryan, A. (1989), 'Value Judgements and Welfare', in Helm (ed) *The Economic Borders of the State*, Oxford University Press, Oxford.

Siegrist, J. (1987), *Social Inequalities in Health: Evaluating the European Region*, World Health Organization Regional Office for Europe, Copenhagen.

Starr, P. (1993), 'The Politics of Health Care Inequalities', in David E. Rogers and Eli Ginzberg (eds), *Medical Care and the Health of the Poor*, Westview Press, Boulder, San Francisco and Oxford, pp.21-32.

Townsend, P. and N. Davidson (1982), *Inequalities in Health: The Black Report*, Harmondsworth: Penguin Books.

Wagstaff, Adam, van Doorslaer, E. and Paci, P. (1994), 'Equity in the Finance and Delivery of Health Care: Some Tentative Cross-Country Comparisons', in A. McGuire, P. Fenn and K. Mayhew *Providing Health Care: The Economics of Alternative Systems of Finance and Delivery*, Oxford University Press, New York, pp.141-171.

Wang, G.C. (1994), 'Issues in Non-Contributory Benefit, Household Equivalence Scales and Poverty Measures', *Socioeconomic Law and Institution Review*, No.13.

Wang, G.C. and W.C. Tsui (1988), *Distribution of Taxes among Households in Taiwan*, Tax Reform Commission, Ministry of Finance, Taipei.

Wolfe, Barbara L. (1994), 'Reform of Health Care for the Nonelderly Poor', in S.H. Danziger, G.D. Sandefur and D.H. Weinberg *Confronting Poverty: Prescriptions for Change*, Harvard University Press, New York, pp.253-288.

9 Current themes and issues in Britain's National Health Service

ROBERT N. MATTHEWS

Introduction

This chapter looks at a series of current issues and themes in the National Health Service (NHS). It does this by exploring the more general area of NHS history, organisational change and development; and then by examining, in more detail, the selected specific topics of rationing and funding, access and 'race', and GP contractors and waiting lists. The chapter does not suggest that these are the only contemporary themes of interest or relevance, merely that they are significant. Examples are chosen, wherever possible, from issues of current concern.

The birth of Britain's NHS

Britain's NHS finally came into being in 1948 as a result of legislation passed in 1946, being the end-product of an evolutionary process. Any notion that the NHS sprang fully-formed into existence, in socialist revolutionary style, as the outcome of the Beveridge Report (Cm 6404, 1942) is misconceived. In fact, the NHS was the culmination of legislation and public health initiatives dating back for more than a century (Ham, 1999: 4). Of particular note are the Poor Law Amendment Act of 1834, which established and legitimated the notion of state intervention in health care, and the Public Health Act 1848 which led to clean water supply and sewerage systems. However, the NHS is unusual, when compared to the health services of most other countries, because it is nationalised, universal and, with minor exceptions, free at the point of use, though, somewhat astonishingly in a service intended to be non-profit-making and for the public good, doctors, opticians, pharmacists and dentists remained outside the NHS as independent contractors rather than employees.

The inception of the NHS involved more than the simple provision of health care and can be perceived as a manifestation of a desire for social integration, in the manner described by Titmuss when he claimed that:

> Social policy...manifests society's will to survive as an organic whole...and is centred [on] those institutions which encourage integration and discourage alienation (Titmuss, 1963, p.39).

Similarly, Bevan saw the NHS as a civilising force, which should not be contaminated by the concept of the individual, remarking that:

> No society can call itself civilised if a sick person is denied medical aid because of a lack of means ...Society becomes more wholesome, more serene and spiritually healthier, if it knows that its citizens have at the back of their consciousness the knowledge that not only themselves, but all their fellows have access, when ill, to the best that medical skill can provide (Bevan, 1961, pp.98-100).

However, an underlying assumption supporting the creation of the NHS was that society contained a finite quantity of ill health which would, in time, be eradicated (Bevan, 1958, pp.xxiii). Needless to say, the associated notion that outlay on the NHS would reduce as the population became healthier proved incorrect (Ham, 1999, p.13) and expenditure has continued to increase, fuelled in part by diverse factors including the development of new treatments which are, inevitably, more costly and have led to the notion of medical inflation, whereby the desire by doctors to use the most recent treatment methods leads to rising costs (table 9.1).

Table 9.1 NHS expenditure 1949-1996

Year	£m
1949	437
1959	826
1969	1791
1979	9046
1989	25491
1996	42155

Source: Office of Health Economics (1997).

The Census of Population for 1951 showed that, while the health of the nation as a whole was improving, there was a perceptible 'health gap' between high and low social classes. This trend was apparent in later censuses, and in a number of surveys, and enquiries confirmed that health care provision was still not equally accessible, nor indeed of the same quality, throughout Britain (see, for example, Griffiths, 1971; Hart, 1971; Cm 7615, 1979, Mays and Bevan, 1987; Black et al, 1992). What had actually been created was a National *Sickness* Service, rather than a health service.

Development and change

The NHS muddled along, not unsuccessfully, during the long summer of political consensus, undergoing persistent change and adjustment to its original design and continuing to provide healthcare for all on the basis of need rather than the ability to pay. This process was largely unchanged by the significant, and very costly reorganisation of 1974 (Ham, 1999, p.19; Baggott, 1998, p.100). However, 1979 saw the election of Margaret Thatcher's first Conservative government (truly a government ideologically aligned with the New Right rather than Conservatism *per se*) which coincided with significant funding difficulties. Mrs Thatcher said that she was reluctant to imagine fundamental changes to the NHS, though she wanted to have a flourishing private sector too (Thatcher, 1993, p.606). Few commentators now believe that this was the case and some suggest that, in fact, a process of 'creeping privatisation' (Ranade, 1997, Chapter 4) was in progress, initially most noticeable in residential and long-stay nursing care for older people.

The Thatcher governments were keen to make the NHS efficient and businesslike (Klein, 1995, Chapter 5) and, to this end they created an 'internal quasi-market' (see, for example, Bartlett and Harrison, 1993) also referred to as the 'purchaser/provider split'. Under these arrangements, implemented from 1 April 1991, organisations that commission healthcare for individuals purchased this care from provider organisations. Holliday (1992, pp.48-49) identified three types of purchasers; District Health Authorities (DHAs), General Practitioner (GP) fundholders and private patients. Likewise, there were three types of providers; NHS Trusts, Directly Managed Units (secondary care hospitals that continued to be managed by the DHA) and the private sector (see figure 9.2).

Though the declared primary aim of these changes was to encourage competition and, thus, increase cost-effectiveness, there is no proof that this was achieved. Rather, available evidence suggests that the reverse was, in fact, the case. Paton et al, for example, notes that there has been a demonstrable growth in NHS administrative costs (1997, pp.24-27) and Glazer, says:

> I cannot assess primary care and GP services but in London it is becoming clear that, either by rationalization or by market forces, hospital services are being curtailed (1995, p.44).

A secondary aim of the changes, set out in the White Paper *Working for Patients* (Cm 555, 1989), was to increase choice within the NHS. However, in practice, choice was exercised on behalf of the individual patient by the GP. During this period, charges were introduced for eye tests and dental check-ups, with the latter leading to the almost total disappearance of NHS dental practices in some areas (British Dental Association, 1998; Silvester, 1999, p.22).

Overall, the internal market must be regarded as a failure (Bartlett and Harrison, 1993, p.92), not least because no competitive market structure was ever created (see, for example, Lee-Potter, 1997 or Appleby, 1998), and the creeping privatisation of the NHS continued with funding continuing to be a crisis issue and the private health sector continuing to expand. William Waldegrave, the then Secretary of State for Health noted, as early as 1991, that '...[it] isn't a market in a real sense...it's not a market in that people don't go bust and all that' (Smith, 1991, p.712).

In addition it is significant that, by 1996, even the then Secretary of State for Health, Steven Dorrell de-emphasised the role of markets and concentrated on management reform (Ham, 1999, p.52; Cm 4325, 1996). Also significant is the imposition of radical reform strategies and the implementation of changes that were '...neither the product of political consensus nor the outcome of bargaining between government and pressure groups' (Ham, 1999, p.49).

It also seems apparent that these changes were not welcomed by the population as a whole (see, for example, *British Medical Journal*, 1990), though one, possibly positive, outcome of the introduction of the internal market was the production of the concept of the patient as a consumer. A 'Patient's Charter' was introduced in 1990, setting out a number of rights and expectations. This document is not without problems, but, for the first time, some patients have felt able to challenge the levels and quality of service provided by the NHS, and there is evidence (Ham, 1999, p.195) that patients' opinions are not now completely discounted.

Figure 9.1   The NHS internal market: simplified structure

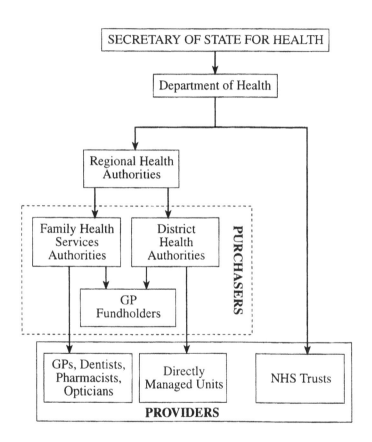

Source: Based on Ham (1999) and Holliday (1992)

New directions in the old

In 1992 the *Health of the Nation* White Paper (Cm 1986) was published, setting a strategy to improve the health of the population and, for the first time, setting specific targets concentrating on cancer, heart disease and stroke, mental illness, accidents and HIV/AIDS and sexual health. The targets were selected from the World Health Organisation's *Target 2000* and were believed to be readily attainable at minimum cost. In the event, the targets were not achieved.

There are, however, signs of continuity between the Conservative governments of the 1980s and 1990s and the New Labour government of 1997. New Labour was making promises about the NHS long before they were elected on 1 May, 1997. Ham (1999, p.53) reports that Chris Smith, the then shadow Secretary of State for Health, proposed a series of guidelines in 1996 which included: the equitable allocation of resources, the need to improve quality of care and to reduce management and administration costs, the need to set service priorities and the need to let primary health care professionals have a say in shaping the agenda. Additionally, there was also a proposal to replace GP fundholders with local commissioning.

Immediately after their election, New Labour set out to assess the situation in the NHS. In July 1997, Sir Donald Acheson was asked to chair an independent inquiry to investigate inequalities in health. The inquiry reported in November 1998, and among its significant findings was that the concept of the health gap between rich and poor remains present. In December 1997, a White Paper was published, *The New NHS: Modern, Dependable* (Cm 3807), which introduced the idea of the 'third way', and 'joined-up working', with an emphasis on partnerships, especially between health care providers and local authorities.

The White Paper set out the principles behind New Labour's plans for the NHS which are to renew the service, making it a genuinely national service, to encourage renewed public confidence and to guarantee excellence. This is to be achieved by requiring the NHS to work in partnership with other agencies and making the delivery of care a matter for local responsibility. New Labour propose that, in order to achieve this there will be a significant reduction in bureaucracy and an increase in efficiency. *The New NHS: Modern Dependable* affirmed that:

> In paving the way for the new NHS, the Government is committed to building on what has worked but discarding what has failed. There will be no return to the old centralised command and control system of the 1970s...But nor will there be a continuation of the divisive internal market system of the 1990s...Instead there will be a 'third way' of running the NHS - a system based on partnership and driven by performance. (Cm 3807, 1997, p.10)

In the Conservatives' internal quasi-market, health authorities had been responsible for commissioning care. *The New NHS* changed this, creating new bodies called Primary Care Groups (PCGs), though some (for example Webster, 1998) contend that they have their origins in the Dawson report of 1920. Despite reassurances given to the professions allied to medicine (for example, physiotherapists, occupational therapists, chiropodists) that they would be represented on PCGs, the final design includes GPs, one representative from Social Services, one community nurse and one lay person. It is significant that doctors have again managed to exercise their power in such a manner that they control their own destinies without being a directly employed part of the structure.

The declared role of health authorities is hence to give strategic leadership and to develop health improvement programmes (HIPs) and support PCGs, which are to be responsible for commissioning and provision of healthcare. Some 481 PCGs (Ham, 1999, p.58) were created in England and Wales. The purpose of PCGs is to combine financial and medical responsibility and, thus, to empower their members to be proactive in creating improvements in healthcare and, at the same time to move towards a clinically managed model of healthcare.

The role of PCGs is intended to be the improvement the health of the community in which they operate by assessing and addressing the health needs of their population, promoting their community's health and working in partnership with other organisations to deliver appropriate and effective care. They are also to develop primary healthcare and community health services. By means of clinical governance (see Buetow and Roland, 1999; Moore, 1999 or *Anaesthesia*, 1999), continuing professional development (CPD), training and education, and investment, they are to increase the quality of services. (A cynic would, perhaps, question the value and effectiveness of clinical governance since it is, essentially, review by peers from the 'brotherhood' of the medical profession, but time will tell.) Additionally, they are charged with commissioning secondary care services, including the majority of hospital services, and the development of NHS service agreements. There are, however, some difficulties associated with the notion of PCGs developing HIPs on the basis of health need in their catchments, when New Labour is keen that identical service availability will exist throughout the country. This is discussed below.

PCGs are intended to develop in order to carry out different functions and responsibilities. In time, they are expected to achieve semi-autonomous trust status and control up to 90 per cent of the NHS budget.

This prospective development is shown diagrammatically in figure 9.2. Beginning in April 2000, many PCGs are expected to become freestanding Primary Care Trusts; however, their structure is not yet clear. The first wave will comprise only 10 trusts, though there is evidence that many more are interested in this change of status (McIntosh, 1999, p.9).

Figure 9.2 PCG levels

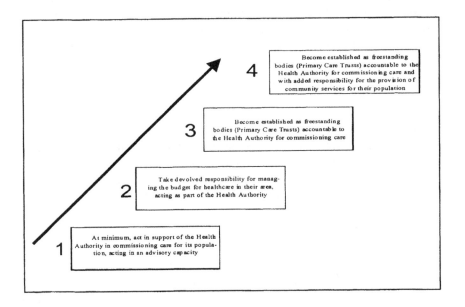

Source: Based on: Cm 3807 (1997).

Additional changes concerned NHS trusts (a product of the purchaser/provider split), who were intended to participate fully in the 'joined-up working' beloved by New Labour. To accomplish this they are expected to work more closely in partnership with local authorities as well as HAs.

In policy terms, the inclusion of local authorities in the planning and delivery structure is an important change; Ham (1999, p.60) argues that this initiative indicates the government's aim to 'break down barriers between agencies and to encourage partnerships not only within the NHS but more widely'.

It is instantly apparent that the radical changes proposed in the 1997 White Paper protract the era of unremitting change initiated by Mrs Thatcher's governments, even though they are to be implemented incrementally over a decade. Thus, there is no evidence that New Labour was willing to accept a post-Thatcher period of consolidation. An epoch of continuous change has resulted in NHS organisations becoming adept at the process and, because the 1997 White Paper offered an outline rather than detailed proposals, there has been much opportunity for the plan to be amended by street-level bureaucrats during its implementation. It is in this way that the composition of PCGs in particular has changed from the government's original intention and now serves arguably to bolster the medical profession's exercise of power (see, for example, Illich, 1990, pp.49-52; Webster, 1998; Wainwright, 1999, pp.6-8).

A change in emphasis?

In February 1998, a Green Paper, *Our Healthier Nation: A Contract for Health* (Cm 3582, 1998), was published. In this document it is, for the first time, acknowledged by a government that there is a link between deprivation and ill health, saying: 'Social and economic issues play a part too - poverty, unemployment and social exclusion' (Cm 3582, 1999, Summary).

The consultation document proposes two key aims: the first is to improve the health status of the entire population by increasing life expectancy and reducing morbidity. The second proposal is to reduce the 'health gap' between rich and poor by improving the health of the 'worst off in society' (Cm 3582, 1999, Summary). Perhaps surprisingly, for a government with 'Labour' in its title, the Green Paper also emphasises the advantages to business from improved health and suggests that health should be achieved through a contract between government, local authorities and individuals. The Paper also suggests targets which, like the Conservatives, *Health of the Nation* (Cm 1986; 1992) concentrate on heart disease and stroke, accidents, cancer and mental health.

Acheson's report (1998, Part 2) confirmed the earlier findings of the *Black Report* (Black et al, 1992 [1980]) and *The Health Divide* (Whitehead, 1992 [1988]) that social deprivation was a major cause of poor health. It is noteworthy that this report has been accepted, almost without comment, by the government, a situation far different from the

alleged suppression of the *Black Report* in 1980.[1] However, there is little
indication of the instigation of policy changes which will be necessary to
implement Acheson's series of proposals for change, his so-called 'thirty-
nine steps'. In particular, Acheson identifies a need to address the social
determinants of health status, for example, poverty and poor education,
confirming that, 50 years on, Beveridge's 'Five Giants' are still active.
Significantly, the Secretary of State for Health, Alan Milburn, has said
that no extra money will be available to address such issues.

Access to treatment: rationing in the NHS

Rationing of service has been a controversial feature of the NHS for many
years; some would argue that it has been intrinsic and inevitable since the
service started. However, there can be little doubt that rationing has
become more overt in recent years, in part because of the establishment of
the internal market (see, for example Klein, 1995, pp.244-245; Ranade,
1997, pp.216-7; Allsop, 1995, chapter 5; Malone and Rycroft-Malone,
1998, pp.325-332). Indeed, there have recently (Boseley, 1999b, p.1) been
allegations that some patients are 'struck-off' family doctor lists for
economic reasons and that older people are sometimes denied hospital
admission until they are very seriously ill (Bright, 1999). In addition, there
is ample evidence (see, for example, *Guardian* staff and Agencies, 1999,
Greengross et al, 1999; Chalmers, 1999, p.6) of huge regional differences
in the availability of treatment.

Arguments to justify rationing specific services are often focused
around the notion of cost-effectiveness. There is some evidence, however,
that other criteria are in use resulting in disparate levels of service
delivery in different parts of the country. This is notably the situation in
the case of assisted conception (commonly referred to as 'infertility
treatment') described by Boseley (1999a, p.1) as 'chaotic'. Hull (1992)
reports that 17 per cent of couples experience difficulty in conception and,
on average, 230 couples in each HA seek treatment each year (National
Infertility Awareness Campaign, 1998, p.1), though effectiveness of
treatment varies dramatically. Friend (1998, p.24) notes that criteria are
applied by different HAs, as shown in table 9.2.

Table 9.2 Health authority fertility treatment criteria

HA criterion	Range
Woman's age	Ranges from under 34 years to not over 43 years.
Man's age	Ranges from not over 45 years to not over 60 years.
Relationship of couple	Some HAs require a stable heterosexual relationship sometimes for a minimum period (up to 5 years).
Residence requirement (within HA)	Varies from zero to 3 years.
Fertility treatment cycles offered	1 –3.
Fertility history (previous relationships).	Enormous variation.

Source: Based on: Friend (1998, p.24).

These types of variation have become known as 'treatment by postcode' (Whitfield, 1999, pp.11-12) because the possibility of obtaining such treatment varies by geographical location. In practice, this often means that social, rather than clinical, measures are in use. In global terms, infertility treatment may seem of little import. However, to the individual it may be an issue of great magnitude, leading potentially to a need for psychological treatment for frustrated couples.

The issue is not dissimilar, though perhaps more serious, in the case of HIV/AIDS. Bellis et al (1999) argue that the funding of HIV/AIDS care in England is inequitable and that, for example, spending per patient in Manchester is one-quarter of that in the NHS North Thames region. In consequence, the death rate from AIDS in the North Thames region is significantly less than elsewhere. Comparative funding levels are shown in figure 9.3.

Figure 9.3   Comparative funding of AIDS/HIV treatment

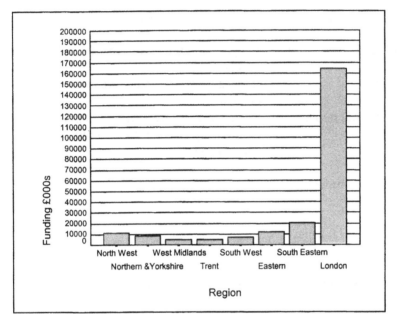

Source: Extrapolated from National Aids Trust (1999).

New Labour suggests, nonetheless, that provision of services and service levels are to be the same throughout the country. This has never been the situation in the past (see above, and for example, Hart, 1971; Hacking, 1996). There have usually been enormous geographical disparities in service provision. If this is not to be the case in the future, the notion of PCGs commissioning care on the basis of the healthcare need (which they are required to assess) of their discrete populations will not be viable since a single level of service cannot meet disparate needs. At the present time, however, there is ample evidence of geographical variations in health (see, for example, Acheson, 1998; Shaw et al, 1999), and it seems that the NHS has a long road to travel if it is to meet this target. There can be little doubt that the period of New Labour govern-ment has seen more high-profile rationing of treatments and drugs than ever before (see, for example, Dyer and Boseley, 1999; Boseley, 1999e, p.12).

Access to treatment: waiting lists

NHS waiting lists have been, for some years, the chosen effectiveness marker of successive governments. Additionally, a significant reduction in the size of waiting lists has been a prominent health aim. It is interesting that it is the numerical size of waiting lists that has been chosen to indicate NHS effectiveness when it would be more logical to examine and evaluate the time an individual spends waiting for treatment. A cynical view would suggest that governments choose the numerical option because it is relatively easy to provide additional finance for certain simple treatments and, thus, reduce dramatically the numbers on waiting lists. This suggests that the numbers of individuals on waiting lists is a poor guide to the efficiency and effectiveness of the NHS, though there are now suggestions that New Labour have decided that '...waiting list [length] - one of its five key pledges at the last election - are not the "be all and end all" of health policy' (Ward, 1999, p.1).

Interestingly, the recent appointment of a new Secretary of State for Health, Alan Milburn, has changed the emphasis a little. McSmith (1999) reported that

> The Government is to launch a revolutionary drive to tackle the twin killers of heart disease and cancer, abandoning reducing waiting lists as its principal health aim.

It can be argued that this initiative is far from 'new' since it mirrors the Conservative government's *Health of the Nation* targets (Cm 1986, 1992) which, in turn, were taken from the targets of the World Health Organisation's *Target 2000* initiative and the numbers of deaths from heart disease have been falling since the 1970s (Boseley, 1999d).

The reduction in waiting list numbers has always been popular with the public and a move away from this process may be politically damaging, especially as it was a manifesto pledge to reduce waiting lists (Labour Party, 1997: 20). The prime minister has already had to respond to criticism that, in fact, he has reduced waiting lists by tampering with the statistics and 'by stopping people getting an appointment to see a doctor in the first place: creating a waiting list to get on the waiting list' (*Health Service Journal*, 1999, p.4).

That the situation around this change in emphasis is perilous, at least in a policy and political sense, is emphasised by Boseley (1999c) and Browne (1999) who note that cancer survival rates in the UK are already among the worst in Europe and that it is not enough to target treatment regimes without dealing with waiting times.

Access to treatment: 'racial' and ethnic determinants

The issue of 'race' in treatment and access to healthcare has become important over recent years. Though the concept of 'race' is contested and has been, to some extent, replaced by the equally contested concept of ethnicity, many commentators (see, for example, Nazroo, 1997; Smaje, 1995) feel that people from minority ethnic populations commonly suffer negative discrimination, particularly in terms of access to healthcare.

There has been little policy concerning access to primary healthcare for the entire population and very little for people from ethnic minorities. There have been attempts at improvement, but these seem often to be empty words since there is little or no evidence of funding allocated to realising them, with the exception of Health Action Zones. Even these are aimed at reducing deprivation for all rather than targeting any specific minority population (Department of Health, 1999c). There are a number of ways in which access to health care can be made more accessible to minority ethnic populations, and some of these are referred to below. It is clear (see, for example, Smith, 1977; Runnymede Trust and the Radical Statistics Race Group 1980) that black people face additional, cumulative disadvantages merely by being visibly different. They are more likely to work in low-paid jobs, experience higher rates of unemployment and to live in poor-quality housing than their white neighbours. This is referred to variously as 'double disadvantage', 'double jeopardy' and 'cumulative disadvantage' and is admirably discussed by Norman (1985, chapter 1).

MORI research (Rudat, 1994, pp.54-60) found that black and minority ethnic groups suffer from 'double disadvantage', but showed that nearly all the population, regardless of the group to which they belonged, were registered with a GP. The lowest figures (94-98 per cent) were among African-Caribbean men. At the same time, this survey shows that members of South Asian and African-Caribbean groups consult significantly more frequently with their GP than does the population as a whole. The data indicated that 28 per cent of the total UK population visit their GP every month, but for African-Caribbean's this figure rises to 33 per cent; for Indians, 36 per cent; for Pakistanis, 44 per cent and for Bangladeshis, 45 per cent. Similarly, the number of GP consultations per year is estimated at: UK population, 3.6, African-Caribbeans, 4.2, Indians,

5.0, Pakistanis, 7.1, Bangladeshis 7.9.

Smaje (1995, p.103) finds similar rates of GP registration and notes that some minority groups, for example South Asian and African-Caribbean, are more likely to consult with their GP than self-refer to hospital, even in an emergency. He points out that,

> ...the GP is if anything an even more crucial point of contact with health services for people from minority ethnic populations than is the case for the majority population and that 'ethnic patterns in health care utilisation are clearly complex'. On the face of it, there is no compelling evidence that people from minority ethnic populations do not *in general* receive adequate levels of care. However,...it cannot be assumed from crude utilisation rates alone that appropriate access exists (original emphasis).

Smaje (1995, pp.104-109) discusses the issue of communication for people whose first language is not English and suggests that the problem manifests itself differently in different communities. For example, Rashid and Jagger's (1992) research found few language difficulties among South Asians in Leicester while considerable problems of fluency in English were detected among South Asians, especially Pakistanis in Bradford, by Ahmad et al (1991, pp.330-341). The results of this survey also showed that South Asians in Bradford would much prefer to consult a South Asian GP and it can be argued that, if one is not available, access is reduced or restricted. Similarly there may be difficulties of access for Muslim women whose religious and cultural 'modesty' makes them disinclined to consult with a male GP (Rashid and Jagger 1992). Ahmad et al, in their Bradford study (1989, pp.153-155) found that 62 per cent of Pakistani women objected to examination by male GPs, though circumstances forced them to accept it. This finding suggests that what Smaje calls 'linguistic concordance', that is, the ability of the patient and the doctor to utilise the same language, is a more important factor than gender and is significant in health access.

Most health promotion policy initiatives in Britain tend to be individualistic and pathological. For example, the Asian Mother and Baby campaign of 1984 (Smaje, 1995, p.115): the laudable intention of this project was to reduce the incidence of rickets (a vitamin D deficiency disease of childhood). In practice it targeted the diet and culture of a specific ethnic group, suggesting that the problem was occurring because the women's traditional dress meant that their level of solar-produced vitamin D was inadequate, an insulting and superficial concept. At the same time, the Health Education Council produced a film of Asian women visiting a GP for a health check. Whilst presumably well-intentioned, it was prejudicial and reinforced negative stereotypes because the women were portrayed experiencing language difficulties.

Overall, the evidence (see for example Nazroo, 1997) suggests that there is little difference in terms of access between ethnic minority populations that are English-speaking and the dominant white population. It seems likely that the ability to communicate is a more important variable (Ameghino, 1999), a position supported by the instigation of NHS Equality Awards (Department of Health, 1999a) and Lord Hunt's assertion that 'equality is central to this Government's agenda and must be integrated into all the NHS does' (Department of Health, 1999b).

Whether the NHS can meet the challenge of providing healthcare for a multicultural society remains to be seen. Positive progress has been made, much remains to be achieved and there is, to date, little assessment of the needs of the fastest-growing population sector in England, that of mixed ethnicity (Smaje, 1995, p.131).

New initiatives for the twenty-first century

When considering access to primary care in general two new schemes have recently begun, but are too new to have been assessed. These are the NHS Direct initiative, which allows individuals to telephone for medical advice without visiting their family doctor and the creation of NHS walk-in centres that 'will help provide quick and convenient access to basic NHS services without the need for an appointment' (Department of Health, 1999b).

It is, perhaps, surprising that family doctors (GPs) have always been contractors to the NHS rather than employees. The reasons for this are historical and based upon the GP Contract of 1913 and the campaigning of the British Medical Association who claimed to be concerned that, if doctors were employees, they would be subordinate to managers and, thus, lose the power to make medical decisions on the basis of clinical need. Though the GP Contract has been revised (in 1948, 1966 and 1990), the GP contractor is being perceived as an increasing problem, even an embarrassment to the NHS. Webster (1999) for example, notes that

> GPs' participation in the NHS as independent contractors has always constituted an awkward anomaly and one of the most damaging inflexibilities within the modern health service.

For the first time, some GPs are becoming NHS employees, for example in Sheffield (Lawson and Heathcote, 1998). This must be seen as a positive move in terms of accountability and openness, especially with the growth of the 'patient as the customer' mentality amongst NHS service users and New Labour's adoption of the concept of a 'contract for health' (Cm 3582, 1998).

Conclusion

Britain is justly proud of its NHS. It provides a high-quality, though not flawless service, and is cost-effective, though, as mentioned above, it is essentially an illness service rather than a health service. It is not without problems, but neither is it without successes. Perhaps the most serious problem it faces is that of almost continuous change with scarcely any opportunity to assess the effects of the change, and the need to adapt to the perceived health needs of an increasingly multicultural, multi-ethnic society. To date, there is little evidence of this adaptability.

Most of the issues discussed in this chapter are far from new, though many have only come to public awareness in relatively recent times. There is no doubt, for instance, that rationing, by a variety of covert or overt means, has been a facet of the NHS since its inception. Similarly, the question of whether doctors should be employees of the NHS has been in contention since the 1930s. However, whilst these issues may excite academic interest and research, it is questionable whether they are of such interest to the service users. Accessibility and appropriateness of service provision are of greater concern to the individual, and the number of people on a waiting list will be of little significance for the older person awaiting surgery for hip replacement; they will be interested in the length of the wait.

Note

[1] The Black Report was commissioned by Callaghan's Labour Government in 1977, but the Research Working Group did not report its findings until April 1980, after the election of the first Thatcher Conservative Government. The publication of such major works is often marked by great publicity and the production of impressively printed documents. In this case, only 260 copies of a duplicated typewritten document were published, no press release or conference was arranged and the copies were sent to some chosen journalists on the eve of August Bank Holiday, presumably as an attempt to ensure the lowest possible publicity. Eventually, the authors of the report arranged publication in 1982 through Pelican Books.

References

Acheson, D. (Chair) (1998), *Independent Inquiry into Inequalities in Health: Report*, Stationery Office, London.

Ahmad, W., Kernohan, E. and Baker, M. (1989), 'Patients' choice of general practitioner: influence of patient's fluency in English and the ethnicity and sex of the doctor', *Journal of the Royal College of General Practitioners*, vol. 39, pp.153-155.

Ahmad, W., Kernohan, E. and Baker, M. (1991), 'Patients' choice of general practitioner: importance of patients' and doctors' sex and ethnicity' *British Journal of General Practice*, vol. 41, pp.330-341.

Allsop, J. (1995), *Health Policy and the NHS: Towards 2000* (2nd ed), Longman, London.

Ameghino, J. (1999), 'Don't suffer in Silence', *Guardian Unlimited Archive*, 5 October. http://www.guardianunlimited.co.uk/Archive/Article/0,4273,39091 77,00.html.

Anaesthesia (1999), 'Editorial: Clinical Governance – what is it all about?', *Anaesthesia*, vol. 54, pp.311-312.

Appleby, J. (1998), 'The internal Market', *Health Service Journal*, 10 September.

Baggott, R. (1998), *Health and Health Care in Britain* (2nd ed) Macmillan, Basingstoke.

Bartlett, J. (1999), 'Do GPs need modernising?', *Fabian Review*, vol. 111: no. 4, Winter, p.15.

Bartlett, W. and Harrison, L. (1993), 'Quasi-markets and the National Health Service reforms' in J. Le Grand and W. Bartlett (eds), *Quasi-Markets and Social Policy*, Macmillan, Basingstoke.

Bellis, M., McVeigh, J., Thomson, R and Syed, Q. (1999), 'AIDS funding: the national Lottery', *Health Service Journal*, vol. 109, no. 5659, 17 June, pp.22-23.

Bevan, A. (1958), 'House of Commons, 30 July 1958' in C. Webster (ed) *Aneurin Bevan on the National Health Service*, Wellcome Unit for the History of Medicine, Oxford.

Bevan, A. (1961), *In Place of Fear*, E P Publishing, London.

Black, D., Morris, J.N., Smith, C., Townsend, P. and Davidson, N. (1992), *The Black Report* (first published 1980), Harmondsworth, Penguin.

Boseley, S. (1999a), 'Infertility treatment on the NHS 'chaotic'', *Guardian Unlimited Archive*, 23 February, http://www.guardianunlimited.co.uk/ Archive/ Article/ 0,4273, 3826113, 00.html.

Boseley, S. (1999b), 'Patients 'struck off by GPs for being uneconomic'', *Guardian Unlimited Archive*, 13 September, http://www.guardianunlimited. co.uk/Archive/Article/0,4273,3901129,00.html.

Boseley, S. (1999c), 'Cancer cure explosion to plunge NHS into crisis', *Guardian*, 21 October, p.1.

Boseley, S, (1999d), '£50m to fight heart disease', *Guardian*, 19 October, p.2.

Boseley, S. (1999e), 'GPs told not to prescribe new flu drug', *Guardian*, 9 October, p.12.

Bright, M. (1999), 'Hospitals challenged on 'death's door' rule for the old', *Guardian Unlimited Archive*, http://www.guardianunlimited.co.uk/Archive/ Article/0,4273,3808991,00.html.

British Dental Association (1998), *BDA Warns of Shortage*, Press Release, BDA, London.

British Medical Journal (1990), 'Poll shows 77% of people against NHS reforms, *BMJ*, vol. 300, 21 April, p.1081.

Browne, A. (1999), 'Health shake-up: Britain fails the war on disease', *Guardian*, 17 October, p.8.

Buetow, S. and Roland, M. (1999), 'Clinical Governance: bridging the gap between managerial and clinical approaches to quality care', *Quality in Health Care*, vol. 8, pp.184-190.

Chalmers, F. (1999), 'NHS operates age discrimination', *Health Matters*, 36, Spring: 6.

Cmd 6404 (1942), *Report of the Inter-Departmental Committee on Social Insurance and Allied Services* (The Beveridge Report), HMSO, London.

Cm. 7615 (1979), *Report of the Royal Commission on the NHS*, London, HMSO.

Cm 555 (1989), *Working For Patients*, HMSO, London.

Cm 1986 (1992), *The Health of the Nation: A Strategy for Health in England*, HMSO, London.

Cm 4325 (1996), *The National Health Service: A Service With Ambitions*, Stationery Office, London.

Cm 3807 (1997), *The New NHS: Modern, Dependable*, Stationery Office, London.

Cm 3582 (1998), *Our Healthier Nation: A Contract for Health*, Stationery Office, London.

Cm 4386 (1999), *Saving Lives: Our Healthier Nation*, Stationery Office, London.

Department of Health (1999a), *Inequality is not just a Black and White issue*, NHS Equality Awards, http://www.doh.gov.uk/equality/eqra.html.

Department of Health (1999b), 'Government committed to equality in the NHS', Department of Health, London, Press Release 1999/0559.

Department of Health (1999c), 'Frank Dobson announces more NHS walk-in centres', Department of Health, London, Press Release 1999/0571.

Department of Health (1999c), 'Trailblazing scheme leads the way in changing the face of healthcare', Department of Health, London, Press Release 1999/0597.

Dyer, C and Boseley, S (1999), 'Viagra rationing 'unlawful'', *Guardian*, 27 May, p.2.

Friend, B. (1998), 'The cost of living', *Health Service Journal*, vol. 108, no. 5674, 23 July, pp.22-26.

Glazer, G. (1995), 'The impact of the NHS reforms on patient care: A view from a London teaching hospital', in R. Murley (ed), *Patients or Customers: Are the*

NHS Reforms Working?, Choice in Welfare Series No. 23, Institute of Economic Affairs, London.

Greengross, S., Hancock, C., Rayner, C. and Sutherland, S. (1999), 'Concern at treatment of old', *Guardian Unlimited Archive*, April 22, http://www.guardianunlimited.co.uk/Archive/Article/0,4273,3856873,00.html.

Griffiths, D. (1971), 'Inequalities and Management in the NHS', *The Hospital*, July, pp.229-233.

Guardian staff and agencies (1999), 'New NHS figures reveal big regional discrepancies', *Guardian Unlimited Archive*, 16 June, http://www.guardianunlimited.co.uk/Archive/Article/0,4273,3875546,00.html.

Hacking, J. (1996), 'Weight watchers', *Health Service Journal,* 2 May, pp.28-30.

Ham, C. (1999), *Health Policy in Britain* (4th ed), Macmillan, Basingstoke.

Hart, J. Tudor (1971), 'The inverse care law', *The Lancet*, 27 February, pp.405-412.

Health Service Journal (1999), 'Prime minister's question time', *Health Service Journal* (News Focus), vol. 109, no. 5672.

Holliday, I. (1992), *The NHS Transformed*, Baseline Books, Chorlton.

Hull, M. (1992), 'Infertility treatment: needs and effectiveness', *Journal of Human Reproduction, 7.*

Illich, I. (1990), *Limits To Medicine: Medical Nemesis: the Expropriation of Health* (first published 1976), Penguin, London.

Klein, R. (1995), *The New Politics of the NHS*, (3rd ed), Longman, Harlow.

Labour Party (1997), *New Labour: Because Britain deserves better* (Labour Party Election Manifesto), Labour Party, London.

Lawson, R. and Heathcote, J. (1998), 'Building to scale', *Health Service Journal*, vol. 108, no. 5602, 18 June, p.28.

Le Grand, J and Bartlett, W (Eds.) (1993), *Quasi-markets and Social Policy*, Macmillan, Basingstoke.

Lee-Potter, J. (1997), *A Damn Bad Business: The NHS Deformed*, Gollancz, London.

Malone, N. and Rycroft-Malone, J. (1998), 'Equity and rationing in the NHS: past to present', *Journal of Nursing Management*, vol. 6, pp.325-332.

Mays, N. and Bevan, G. (1987), *Resource Allocation in the Health Service*, Bedford Square Press, London.

McIntosh, K. (1999), 'Count us in', *Health Service Journal*, vol. 109, No. 5670, 2 September, pp.9-10.

McSmith, A. (1999), 'Waiting lists on hold as NHS fights killer diseases', *Observer*, 17 October, p.8.

Moore, W. (1999), 'Clinical governance: final check-up', *The Guardian*, 17 February, p.8.

Murley, R. (ed) (1995), *Patients or Customers: Are the NHS Reforms Working?*, Choice in Welfare Series No. 23, London, Institute of Economic Affairs.

National AIDS Trust (1999), *1999-2000 HIV/AIDS Budget Allocation*, National AIDS Trust, April.

National Infertility Awareness Campaign, (1998), *Facts and Figures on Infertility and its Treatments*, London, NIAC, www.ein.org/niac.htm.

Nazroo, J.Y. (1997), *The Health of Britain's Ethnic Minorities*, Policy Studies Institute, London.

Norman, A. (1985), *Triple Jeopardy : Growing Old in a Second Homeland*, Centre for Policy on Ageing, London.

Office of Health Economics (1997), *Compendium of Health Statistics,* (10th Ed), Office of Health Economics, London.

Paton, C., Birch, K., Hunt, K. and Jordan, K. (1997), 'Counting the costs', *Health Service Journal*, vol. 107, 21 August, pp.24-27.

Ranade, W. (1997), *A Future for the NHS? Health Care in the Millennium*, (2nd ed), Addison Wesley Longman, Harlow.

Rashid, A. and Jagger, C. (1992), 'Attitudes to and perceived use of health care services among Asian and non-Asian patients in Leicester', *British Journal of General Practice*, vol. 42, pp.197-201.

Rudat, K. (1994), *Black and Minority Ethnic Groups in England*, Health Education Authority, London.

Runnymede Trust and the Radical Statistics Race Group (1980), *Britain's Black Population*, Heinemann, Oxford.

Shaw, M., Dorling, D., Gordon, D. and Smith, G.D. (1999), *The Widening Gap: Health Inequalities and Policy in Britain*, Policy Press, Bristol.

Silvester, S. (1999), 'Filling in time', *Health Service Journal*, vol. 109, 9 September:, pp.22-23.

Smaje, C. (1995), *Health, 'Race' and Ethnicity: Making Sense of the Evidence*, King's Fund Institute, London.

Smith, D.J. (1977), *Racial Disadvantage in Britain*, Penguin, London.

Smith, R. (1991), 'William Waldegrave: thinking beyond the new NHS', *British Medical Journal*, vol. 302, pp.711-714.

Thatcher, M. (1993), *The Downing Street Years*, Harper Collins, New York.

Titmuss, R. (1963), *Essays on the Welfare State* (2nd ed), Allen and Unwin, London.

Wainwright, D. (1999), 'All talk: no action?', *Health Matters*, vol. 36, pp.6-8.

Ward, L. (1999), 'Labour rethinks NHS pledge', *Guardian* 18 October, p.1.

Webster, C. (ed) (1991), *Aneurin Bevan on the National Health Service*, Wellcome Unit for the History of Medicine, Oxford.

Webster, C. (1998), 'The very long history of the PCG', *Health Matters*, vol. 35, p.5.

Webster, C. (1999), 'Time to breach the contract', *Health Matters*, vol. 37, p.5.

Whitehead, M. (1992), *The Health Divide* (first published 1988), Penguin, London.

Whitfield, L. (1999), 'Come in number 35, your time is up', *Health Service Journal*, vol. 109, no. 5670, pp.11-12.

PART IV
FAMILY AND COMMUNITY
CARE AND CONTROL

10 A comprehensive policy for the single-parent family

BETTY Y. WENG

Introduction

Since the late 1970s economic growth has transformed Taiwan from an agricultural into an industrial society, so that Taiwan has gradually become a developed country. Urbanization, democracy, freedom and individualism have accelerated the pace of social change, and traditional Chinese family values have been cruelly challenged. Families themselves have changed, in respect of structure, organizational type and functions. In the processes of industrialization, urbanization, institutional differentiation, and the modernization of scientific technology, traditional family functions are being weakened and family problems have emerged.

The divorce rate in Taiwan is the highest in Asia. The number of broken or single-parent families has increased constantly over the years (Lin and Chin, 1992; Weng, 1998). More and more female-headed families have become low-income families. Broken and single-parent families, especially female-headed households, are usually lacking in financial support. Single parents need to work overtime just to make a living. Sometimes, they even hold two jobs in order to support their children. As a result, the parent-child relationship is weak and the child tends to lack discipline and education, which can lead to deviant behaviour. Problems of juvenile delinquency worsen every year and many juvenile delinquents are from single-parent families (Lee, 1989). Thus the family system in Taiwan faces a tremendous challenge. How is the government going to respond to this? How might family policy help the family to cope with its problems? This article will begin by outlining the current situation, problems and needs of single-parent families. It will follow this by reviewing current welfare policy and programmes for the single-parent family in Taiwan, set against what should be the characteristics of a comprehensive family policy. In conclusion, there will be recommendations for both public and private sectors as to the provision of welfare services for single-parent families.

The single-parent family in Taiwan

Lee (1998) has reported about 4 per cent of the total households of Taiwan to be single-parent households. Some 61.9 per cent of these single-parent households are headed by a female and 38.1 per cent by a male. Divorce gives rise to 44.1 per cent of single-parent households, 38.2 per cent are because of the death of a spouse, 15.7 per cent are due to separation and 2 per cent of lone parents are unmarried. Of female-headed single-parent families, 48.8 per cent are due to death of spouse; whereas, of male-headed single- parent families, fewer than 20 per cent are due to death of spouse, 58.8 per cent of them being due to divorce.

According to *The Social Indices of Statistics of Taiwan* (Executive Yuan, 1993), in 1992, there were 178,818 households which were single-parent families. This represented an 0.33 per cent increase on the previous year. Some 625,540 teenagers, under the age of 18 and unmarried, were living in single-parent families. In other words, the number of under-18 teenagers living in single-parent families was about 8.62 per cent of the total under-18 teenager population of Taiwan (Executive Yuan, 1993).

Chang (1992) reported that 23.5 per cent of low-income families had a lone parent, and 80.4 per cent of these families were female-headed. From the figures, it is apparent that female-headed single-parent families are more likely to become low-income families than are male-headed single-parent families. Chang, et al (1995) stated that the major financial resource of 88.5 per cent of single-parent families was their income. Only 12.9 per cent of single- parent families were in receipt of support from their original families. Some 70 per cent of the families have never received any child support from a previous spouse after divorce or separation. In other words, the parent without guardianship has seldom provided financial support for his/her children. Lee (1998) further reported that female-headed households achieve only about 60 per cent of the income of a two-parent family.

The above statistics indicate that divorce and the death of spouse are the main reasons for single parenthood; that female-headed single-parent households are much poorer than male-headed single-parent households; and that little short of 10 per cent of the children under age of 18 are living in single-parent families.

Single parent family: problems and welfare needs

The needs of a single-parent family are linked to different stages after the specific event. The family, which has just experienced divorce or the death of a spouse, needs assistance the most (Hsu and Chang, 1987). For such a family, the major problems are raising and caring for children, facing up to financial difficulty and psychological adjustment. According to Lin and Chin's survey research on the single-parent family in Taipei City during 1991-1992, about 10 per cent of single parents expressed no need for assistance after the tremendous change (Lin and Chin, 1992). Wang (1991), Wang (1994), Lin and Chin (1992), Chuang (1991), and Shiech and Ma (1989) confirmed that the problems of single-parent families included financial security, childcare, psychological and mental adjustment, work, housing, interpersonal relationships and social isolation. Again, according to Chang, et al (1995), the most urgent living problems of the single-parent family are child-related issues (69.9 per cent); financial problems (62.5 per cent) and work related problems (28.3 per cent): the first two items being way ahead of the third one. Finally Shiech (1995) has reported that the widowed experience particular difficulty in adjustment and that the children from single-parent families can evince some problematic behaviour.

Financial insecurity

For those who had just become single parents, the reality was the decrease of income, or even the loss of the only source of income. The mother, who used to stay at home before the divorce or death of her husband, could need to find a job and earn a living. Approximately three-fifths of single families are headed by females, yet females are usually in a position of economic inferiority. Thus, when females become single parents, financial security tends to become their major concern (Hsu and Chang, 1987; Shiech and Ma, 1989; Tung, 1992; Yeh, 1992). Thus it is that the provision of some form of income security should be one of the most urgent issues for family policy in Taiwan. In 1985, more than half of the female-headed single-parent families were on low incomes, by contrast with only about 12 per cent of male-headed single-parent families (Lin and Wu, 1995). Morgan (1989) likewise reported that 40 per cent of widows and 26 per cent of divorced women depended on public assistance.

Female single parenthood is one of the high-risk factors for long-term poverty, what Millar (1988) called persistent poverty. In Taiwan, no matter whether we take head of household income or total family income, female-headed single-parent households are always the poorest (Hsu and Chang, 1987). Lin and Chin (1992) again reported that, in Taipei City, the income of such households was, on the average, much lower than that of comparable male-headed families. The total family income of single-parent families is in any case much lower than that of dual-parent families. Wang (1991), Hsu and Chang (1987) and Lin and Chin (1992) have thus declared financial security to be the most urgent welfare need for the single-parent family.

The main source of income for the single-parent family is work. Yet, in addition to work income, some single-parent families receive financial support from their original families (Peng and Chang, 1995; Weng, 1998), from their children, and from other relatives (Lin and Chin, 1992).

Nevertheless, the financial problems of the single-parent family, especially for the female-headed family, can easily become severe. In order to make a living, the single parent has to work overtime, has less time to care for the children and does not have extra money to spend on the children's education. Quite a few teenagers drop out of school to find a job in order to support their families. McLanahan (1985) found that the high drop-out rate of the children from single parent families was related to low family income. Children from single-parent families, once they drop out of school and fail to complete their education, will not be able to obtain high-paid jobs either at the time or in the future. The poverty cycle will thus carry over from one generation to the next. If a family can get out of poverty within a year or two, this shouldn't be a problem; whereas if it remains in poverty for a long time, poverty becomes an increasingly complicated issue (McLanahan, 1985). Thus it is that, in order to prevent the financial situation of single-parent families getting worse, some programmes or projects to assist their financial rehabilitation need to be implemented.

Problems of childcare

Single parents have to play multiple roles (Yeh, 1992; Lin and Chin, 1992) and their responsibility for bringing up the children is a very heavy burden. Very often, they feel overloaded by having to play both mother and father, and do not know how to educate their children effectively (Yeh, 1992; Lin and Chin, 1992). Single parents have to care for their children at the same time as they have to worry about their financial situation. According to Lin and Chin, single parents with children under 6 tend to be most concerned about the shortage of time and energy for nurturing their children, worrying about the danger of their child being left at home alone, and about being unable to care for their child when he/she is sick. Additional concerns are over work schedules (which tend not to be flexible enough to allow for transporting children to nursery or school) and the fact that they cannot afford childcare or after-school care. Single parents with children aged 6 to 12 face practically the same problems as those for single parents with children under 6. For single-parent families with teenagers, on the other hand, the issues of most concern tend to be lack of time and energy to educate, lack of knowledge about their children's out-of-home activities, their lack of ability to communicate with their children, and the difficulty of disciplining them. Some of these issues stem from lack of time and energy, which could be due to work and the pressure of multiple roles within the family. However, the other items relate to know-how.

Given that single parents are under such tremendous stress, it is understandable that some of them are going to neglect the supervision and disciplining of their children. Others, however, anxious for a quick result in teaching or disciplining their children, may choose to use an extreme way of discipline which could be over-rigid or over-protective (Liu, 1984; Wang, 1985). In short, single parents have much less time to care for and to understand their children. The parent-child relationship is distorted. Huang (1993) found that children lacking care, protection and supervision are more likely to have accidents, to achieve poor academic results or to manifest deviant behaviour. Demo and Acock (1988) even concluded that the children of these families were less healthy mentally than were the children of dual-parent families. Situations of separation, divorce or desertion are very disadvantageous to teenagers. Lin and Chin (1992) pointed out that single parents worry about raising their children, their children's academic work and discipline. Again, according to Weng (1998), the most stressful parenting issues faced by single mothers are behavioural discipline, academic achievement and daily safety. Naturally, different age groups of children are liable to give rise to different orders of concern.

Emotional and psychological adjustment

Shiech (1995) stated that the widowed not only experienced traumatic change but also difficulties of psychological and social adjustment. Lin and Chin (1992) also reported that single parents always feel depression, loneliness and unhappiness. Hsu and Chang (1987) said that the most common psychological problems of a female single parent concern adjustment after divorce or the sudden death of spouse, a sense of security, experience of discrimination against the divorced, of lack of love and of a sense of belonging.

Since most people still consider the single-parent family to be a 'problem' family, this can make it difficult for such a family to stay or live in the same place. Single parents usually gradually withdraw from their previous social network, or move away from a previous residence or change their employment. The children of such families also have difficulties in making friends and establishing long-term relationships with neighbours and with school teachers. Demo and Acock (1988) cited from Stolberg and Anker's study in 1983 that children from single-parent families due to divorce were likely to adopt abnormal or inappropriate ways of dealing with people, and that their social and interpersonal relationships were usually very poor.

Children of single-parent families are more likely to have psychological and emotional adjustment problems, a low self-concept, find it hard to trust anyone, have a sex-role differentiation problem, poor internal and external control, and be given to deviant behaviour (Aseltine, 1996; Demo and Acock, 1988; Liu, 1988; Lau and Chuang, 1992). Lau and Chuang found that children from single-parent families were more likely to get into inappropriate places for teenagers, more likely to steal, to run away from home, to play truant and/or to join gangs, by comparison with children from dual-parent families. Furthermore, children from single-parent families due to divorce were more likely to get into trouble or manifest deviant behaviour than were children from families caused by the death of one parent. Be this as it may, both single parents and the children from their families experience emotional and psychological problems.

Housing

Those single parents receiving social welfare services do not usually own their residences. Single-parent families usually either rent a home, borrow an apartment from a relative or stay with parents (Weng, 1998). Some single-parent families, due to a decrease in income, cannot afford the more expensive residence they have and must move; and some of them want to move because they desire a new environment and wish to avoid gossip from the neighbours. But in Taiwan, there is a great shortage of public housing, and one has to meet the poverty level in order to be qualified to apply. To rent a house or an apartment is expensive, especially in the urban area. Single-parent families need decent and inexpensive places in which to live, but this is not easy.

Welfare needs of the single-parent family: current policies and programmes for the single-parent family in Taiwan

Many advanced European countries provide for single-parent families through social security and family allowance types of programmes (Chang, 1998; Wu, 1993). According to Lin and Chin's survey research on the single-parent family in Taipei City during 1991-1992, the most urgent welfare needs of these families are, in order, academic assistance for their children, medical assistance, emergency assistance, low-interest loans, child educational support, childcare support, housing subsidy, parent education, and child protection. The first five items are the most needed, and more than half of the respondents expressed such needs (Lin and Chin, 1992). The first item, academic assistance for children, is needed by both male and female single parents; whereas the second through to the fifth items were needed more by female single parents than by their male counterparts. These latter items were all related to the family finance situation, for all that they were different in essence. The welfare needs of single parents require interdepartmental cooperation and integration to provide the services.

However, like most of the countries in the world, Taiwan does not have a state policy specially designed for the single-parent family. Policy and welfare programmes have been set up for children, young people, women, the disabled, the elderly and low-income families, etc. Most of the welfare programmes are not of a universal type; applicants need to apply and meet a means test in order to qualify for benefits.

Currently, Taipei City and Kaohsiung City governments each operate their own programmes for single-parent families. There is no programme for the rest of the Taiwan area. Taipei's 'Assistance to the Single-Parent Family Programme' provides a childcare subsidy, a child and youth family subsidy, emergency shelter, a job training subsidy, professional counselling, emergency assistance, medical assistance and an education subsidy. Kaohsiung City's 'Single Parent Assistance Programme' provides family living support, free or low-cost childcare, vocational services, medical assistance, a housing subsidy and counselling services. The two programmes are very similar. Many of the items are conditional on meeting the means test for low income or for poverty: for example, Taipei's childcare support, child and youth family subsidy and Kaohsiung's family living support, childcare and medical assistance. About one quarter of all the low-income families are single-parent families, and four-fifths of these are headed by a female. In other words, female-headed single-parent families are poorer and are more likely to qualify for assistance.

A comprehensive family policy for Taiwan?

The purpose of a family policy is to solve or prevent various family problems and to promote the well-being of the family and its individual members. Zimmerman (1988) pointed out that a family policy should be drawn up from a 'family' point of view; family well-being being the core criterion. Family policy should focus on the establishment of family systems and functions, enabling the family to protect the well-being of its individual members. However, government intervention is a must, to promote family functions. Since medical, educational, housing, working and tax policies are all related to the promotion of family functions, they should all be included in the broad sense of family policy.

However, while there are various welfare laws and welfare programmes operating in Taiwan, we do not have a comprehensive family policy as yet. Most of the social legislation and welfare programmes have been specially designed to meet specific social problems. We could say that family policy is embedded in various governmental and private welfare programmes, but that it lacks any systematization. Welfare policies for children, young people, women, and the elderly all bear closely on the family; while the education, health, labour and police departments might all be described as executive units of family policy (Chen et al, 1992).

Family policy should be instituted in accordance with a consistent value system. In recent years, the pluralization of social values has created confusion, conflicts, and a change of concepts about the family; this has resulted in the pluralization of social structures and changes in their function. On the one hand, some scholars have criticized family policy for being linked to the traditional family type and thus unable to fulfil the current family's needs. On the other hand, they continue to recommend that, beneath the pluralization of family structures, we should nonetheless be able to identify a common quality of family welfare pertaining to the different types of families (Moen and Forest, 1995; Allen-Meares and Roberts, 1995). In truth, the pluralization of family structures creates different types and different compositions of families, and these different types are also within different social classes (Yi, 1998). Single-parent families are usually of a lower social class, and their functioning is not as good as that of dual-parent families. These situations are detrimental to the child in the long run (Lin, 1994; McLanahan and Sandefur, 1994).

These changes in family structure affect women's role and social status (Pai and Wan, 1995). There are various types of families, including the traditional dual-parent family, the single-parent family and the unmarried single parent. If we treat them all as normal family types, we will institute policies and programmes to promote women's social status: for example, equal opportunity for employment, various substitutive social services and income maintenance programmes (Lin, 1994). Such more liberal ideology-oriented policies and programmes will strengthen the ability of women to work outside the family and provide them with opportunities for self-determination.

Community care is the new trend in welfare services delivery around the world. The function of family care is important again. Government and the family are expected to share responsibility for the care of family members (Ferng, 1997; Hegar and Scannapieco, 1995). In order to carry out community care successfully, the family needs to have supportive programmes to strengthen its functioning as a family. Otherwise, community care merely becomes family care. And since women are the main family caregivers, family care will then become women's care, which deprives women, sacrifices their welfare and limits their role to that of family caretaker (Pai and Wan, 1995).

Help with raising and caring for children is needed by both single-parent and dual-parent families in Taiwan. The single parent who has to work or the working mother who chooses to work - they all require some substitutive welfare services. Therefore, when we institute family policy, we should consider the labour market and labour market policy as well. If problems caused by conflicts between work and family can be solved by substitutive welfare programmes, the family function of caring for its members can then be realized (Ditch et al., 1996). Women's participation in the workforce has been the most notable feature in family change in Taiwan. In 1965, women's work participation rate was 31.2 per cent; it increased to 45.3 per cent by 1995 (1966 and 1996 *Labour Statistics Year*

Book, Taiwan). In 1995, about half of the women who worked were also fully responsible for the care of their families. Therefore, nursery care and childcare are the services needed the most. Women may thus continue to stay in the workforce without disruption because of giving birth to a new baby or having to care for young children (Chien, 1997; Chow and Berheide, 1994).

Meanwhile, in addition to women's participation in the workforce, whether the elderly parents stay with their adult children or not is another important issue. According to the Elderly Survey Report of Taiwan (Executive Yuan, 1992), 62.9 per cent of the elderly who are aged over 65 live with their adult children; 14.5 per cent live alone and 18.7 per cent live with their spouse only. Together, women's participation in the labour force and the importance of elderly parents living with their adult children are critical factors to be taken into consideration when we institute our family policy.

Most family policies are centred on families with children (Kammerman and Kahn, 1978), but some scholars have made the criticism that a family policy which is confined to children and young people is not appropriate for an ageing society (Moen and Forest, 1995). To be sure, the children are our future; our tomorrow is counting on today's children; and women's participation in the labour force decreases their ability to care for children. However, when we institute a comprehensive family policy, we have to consider carefully the child, the woman and the whole family. We want to establish a family policy that will help to preserve family functions, and provide various welfare services to keep the family intact. This is a positive preventive measure to keep it safe from disorganization (Ditch et al, 1996), bearing in mind that we do not leave out labour, health and medical, social insurance and welfare, finance and taxation, and housing policies, etc., in the effort to construct a truly comprehensive family policy.

Recommendations

After the above discussion, I personally recommend that a comprehensive family policy for Taiwan should have the following characteristics:
(1) Empowering families. The main functions of a family policy are to solve or to prevent various family problems and to promote both family and individual well-being. A family policy should be able to empower the various types of families. The word 'empower' means to straighten, to restore, to establish the family functions for different types of families.

Even for single-parent families, there are functions which could be straightened in order to save the family as a whole. For dual-parent families, a family policy should assist in enhancing integration, and in protecting families from falling apart by utilizing their own assets. To repeat, the purpose of family policy is to help families and to assist them to empower themselves.

(2) Family-centred family policy. The family is the most important unit in human society. Zimmerman (1988) pointed out that a family policy should be drawn up from a 'family' point of view. Children, young people, the handicapped, and the old are those who need care the most in the family. A family policy that centres on a certain individual may ignore the needs of the rest of the family. A family policy has both a preventive and a rehabilitative function. A family-centred family policy takes the family as a whole, and considers its needs and its preservation, even though this does not mean ignoring individual needs.

(3) Sharing responsibilities perspective. Women's participation rate in the workforce is constantly increasing. Dual-career families face problems of caring for children and caring for the elderly. The role and status of women in the family is changing. Family members need to adjust to this change. If a woman chooses to work outside the home, the state has a responsibility to provide the options for her to do so. Therefore, a family policy has to be attuned to educating the public that both husband and wife are responsible for caring for family members, not just the wife.

(4) An integrative perspective. There are various types of families, requiring different types of assistance and resources to fulfil their needs. These needs include housing, health and medical, social insurance, child-care, income maintenance, job training, transportation, etc. The departments of Labour, Health, Social Affairs, Transportation, Finance and Taxation, etc., together provide these services. We should have cooperation and coordination from these various departments in order to integrate the services provided in the interests of a comprehensive family policy.

Recommendations for the public and private sectors

Family policy has the function of solving family problems and preventing them. For most single-parent families who are already in some kind of difficulty, what can the government do to get them out of hardship? In responding to single-parent family problems and welfare needs in Taiwan, the following measures or programmes are recommended for the public

and private sectors:
(1) Mandatory collection of child support from non-guardian parents (Lu, 1996; Lee, 1998). Single mothers might need to work at two or three low-pay jobs in order to make enough money to support their children (Weng, 1998). The cost of living is a heavy burden for single parents. Chang (1995) reported that, for divorced or separated parents, 5.6 per cent of the non-guardian parents provide half or most of the living cost for their children, 16.3 per cent of them offer a little, and 77.5 per cent of them never provide any child support. Although we have a law which states that both parents have a responsibility to support their children, we don't have a mandatory collection law to enforce this principle of justice.
(2) Universal child allowance. Although Taipei City and Kaohsiung City governments provide child living support, youth living support and child allowance, these are types of public assistance, not universal benefits. Some 82 countries provide the latter child (family) allowances in the world (Chang, 1998). This universal type of child allowance would not have a labelling effect. The financial budget expenditure is an issue decision makers should consider carefully. However, we could control the amount of child allowance and the length of time of its payment, in order to limit the budget implications to some degree.
(3) Survivors' benefit. Many industrial countries provide survivors' benefits under their social security programmes. Most survivors' benefits are of the social insurance type, specially designed for single-parent families. Taiwan had been planning a survivors' benefit, and had promised to put it into effect by the year 2000, prior to the change of the party of government (Chang, 1998).
(4) Housing security. Housing costs are very expensive in Taiwan. The single parent's most upsetting problem is therefore financial (Chang, 1992; Hsu and Lin, 1984; Hsu and Chang, 1987; Shiech, 1995). To find a low-cost living space is very difficult for single parents. The government should offer low-cost living quarters, low-interest loans, or else provide public housing for their housing needs.
(5) Encouragement and assistance to single parents to work, with necessary supplemental or substitutive services. Receiving public assistance can easily make people feel that they are second-class citizens. It is difficult for them to get out of this sense of inferiority. So we should positively encourage single parents to work and provide them with incentive programmes, for example, free or low-cost childcare services, medical insurance, parental leave, and flexible working hours, etc. These services are required for relaxing the stress created by the conflicts

between work and family.

(6) Offer of proper vocational education, job training, and guidance for single parents. In 1980, 28.9 per cent of women with children under the age of 6 participated in the labour force; whereas by 1995 the rate had increased to 45.8 per cent. From such a change, it is clear that more and more women with young children are entering the job market. Single parents have to work for a living. Work income is a positive way to help them get out of poverty (Lee, 1998). Therefore, vocational education and training are more important than cash benefits. A so-called work-centred strategy is preferred.

(7) Cooperation with the school system to provide assistance for children from single-parent families. Children's academic achievement is one of the most stressful problems encountered by single parents (Weng, 1998). Traditional Chinese put much emphasis on children's school performance. Single parents are no exception. However, due to their own often low educational status, they cannot help their own children. Very often, single parents feel that their future rests on their children. Therefore, to assist them to go upward academically is important. The school and social welfare agencies could work jointly to develop programmes to provide assistance for children from single-parent families.

(8) Assistance with parenting and childcare skills. Due to their tight time schedule, single parents cannot spend as much time as they would like with their children and might have problems in knowing how to teach them skilfully. Unfortunately, there are quite a few juvenile delinquents from single-parent families. We could use different ways to pass on information, for example, by handouts, lectures, or by phone, etc.

Conclusion

The aim of a comprehensive family policy is to solve family problems and prevent them from occurring in the future. Even though we do not so far have a social policy explicitly for the family, we do have child, youth, women, elderly and disabled welfare laws and programmes which are closely related to family. However, these laws and programmes have been mainly designed to solve individual problems. It seems as if we assembled them without systematization.

In Taiwan, most women are still expected to care for family members, particularly for the children, the elderly and the sick. Even a working mother cannot be excused from caring for family members or doing domestic work. Therefore, career women have difficulty in adjusting between work and family. Community care is a humane way to provide welfare services. Needy people will be able to stay in their familiar home and environment to receive the necessary care easily and with dignity. But we hope that community care will not turn into women care.

The anti-poverty strategy of England and the single-parent-centred strategy of Norway in assisting the single-parent family have neither of them proven to be as effective as expected. The U.S.A. has also revised its policy on assistance to the single-parent family. The French strategy of comprehensive assistance the child emphasizes the idea of sharing the cost of childcare with society. The Swedish strategy puts emphasis on both labour market and family policy, in order to take care of both work and family (Lee, 1998). Bearing in mind the facts of the high cost of childcare and the gradually growing rate of women's labour participation, the French and the Swedish strategies may be more appropriate for Taiwan, and the Swedish strategy deserves special attention. Given that nuclear families are in the majority and given the increasing number of single-parent families, I here propose a family-centred comprehensive family policy with the emphasis on children's and women's needs. It may be difficult to set up a so-called family policy from scratch, but it is much easier to re-examine and modify existing welfare laws and programmes to fulfil current family needs, and to assist and solve the single-parent family's problems. We are far from comprehensive, but to start working at it is one big step forward.

References

Allen-Meares, P. and Roberts, E. (1995), 'Public assistance as family policy: Choosing of options for poor families', *Social Work*, 40 (July), pp.559-565.

Aseltine, R.H. (1996), 'Pathways linking parental divorce with adolescent depression', *Journal of Health and Social Behavior*, 37, pp.133-148.

Chang, C.F. (1998), 'Single-parent family welfare policies; A comparison from nation to nation', *Social Welfare*, 136, pp.51-57.

Chang, C.F. (1995), 'Singled out for extra concern: A look at one-parent homes', *Sinorama Magazine*. vol. 20, no. 8, Government Information Office, Taipei.

Chang, C.F. (1992), 'Change of poverty and family structure', *Journal of Women and Sexes*, 3, pp.41-58.

Chang, C.F., Shiue, C.T. and Chou, Y.C. (1995), 'Current situation of the single-parent family and coping strategies', Committee on Research, Development and Evaluation, Executive Yuan, Taipei.

Chen, H.H., Cheng, S.Y. and Tsai, H.H. (1992), *Current Family Welfare Services Policy: Strategy and Direction, Community Development Quarterly*, Chinese Community Development Research Centre, Taipei.

Chien, W.E. (1997), *Married Women Employment Type Analysis: Leave and Reenter*, Master's thesis, Sociology Department, Taiwan University.

Chow, E. and Berheide, C.W. (1994), *Women, the Family and Policy: A Global Perspective*, State University of New York Press, Albany, New York.

Chuang, S.C. (1991), *The Family Problems of Female-headed Single-parent Families*, Master's thesis, Department of Sociology, Taipei, Taiwan, Republic of China.

Demo, D.H. and Acock, A.C. (1988), 'The impact of divorce on children', *Journal of Marriage and the Family*, 50, pp.619-648.

Ditch, J., Barneo, H. and Bradshaw, J. (1996), *European Observatory: A Synthesis of National Family Policies*, Social Policy Research Unit, University of York, England.

Executive Yuan (1997), *Statistical Yearbook of the Republic of China, General of Budget, Accounting and Statistics*. Taipei, Republic of China.

Executive Yuan and Economic Development Committee (1995), *Taiwan Manpower Survey Report*, Taipei, Republic of China.

Executive Yuan (1993), *The Social Indices of Statistics of Taiwan*, Taipei, Republic of China.

Executive Yuan (1992), *The Elderly Living Conditions Survey of Taiwan*, Taipei, Republic of China.

Ferng, Y. (1997), *Nursery Service: An Ecological Analysis Point of View*, (revised), Taipei: Chu-Liu.

Hegar, R and Scannapieco, M. (1995), 'From family duty to family policy: evolution of kinship care', *Child Welfare*, 74 (Jan/Feb), pp.200-216.

Hsu, L.H. and Chang, Y.C. (1987), 'Single-parent family in Taiwan: Problems and prospects', *Journal of Chinese Sociology*, 11, pp.121-153.

Hsu, L.A. and Lin, C.C. (1984), 'Family structure and social change: Comparison of Chinese and American single-parent families', *Journal of Chinese Sociology*, 8, pp.1-22.

Huang, F.L. (1993), *Childcare of Single-parent Families in Taipei City*, Master's thesis, Department of Sociology, National Taiwan University.

Kammernam, S. and Kahn, A. (1978), *Family Policy*, Columbia University Press, New York.

Kammerman, S. and Kahn, A. (1988), *Mothers Alone: Strategies for a Time of Change*, Aubarn House, Boston, MA.

Lau, M.C. and Chuang, Y.C. (1992), 'An empirical study on the single-parent families and the factors related to adolescent delinquency', *Tunghai Journal*, vol. 33, Tunghai University, Taichung.

Lee, A. (1989), 'Family and juvenile deviant behaviors'., in C.C. Yin and R.L. Chu (eds), *Taiwan social phenomena analysis*, Central Research Institute, Taipei, pp.247-274.

Lee, S.J. (1998), 'Single-parent family and poverty', *Social Welfare*, 139, pp.33-46.

Lin, W.J. and Wu, G.F. (1995), 'Child welfare policy of single-parent families', in Chinese Child Foundation (eds), *21st Century Child Welfare Policy*, Taichung, Republic of China.

Lin, W.J. (1994), *Single Parent Family: From the Social Policy Point of View: Single Parent Family - Welfare Needs and Coping Strategy Conference.* Chinese Child Welfare Foundation.

Lin, W.J. and Chin, W.L. (1992), *Taipei Single-parent Family Problems and their Coping Strategy: Research Report*, Committee on Research, Evaluation and Development, Taipei City Government.

Liu, S.N. (1984), *The Support System and Living Adjustment of the Widowed Family*, Master's thesis, Department of Sociology, National Taiwan University.

Liu, Y.Y. (1988), *A Comparison Research on Interpersonal Relationships, Behavioural Problems and Self-concept between Children from Single-parent Families and Two-parent Families*, Master's thesis, Department of Education, National Kaohsiung Normal University, Kaohsiung, Taiwan, Republic of China.

Lu, C.C. (1996), 'Child allowances in Germany', *Social Work Journal*, Soochow University, 5, pp.55-110.

McLanahan, S. (1985), 'The reproduction of poverty', *American Journal of Sociology*, 90, pp.873-901.

McLanahan, S. and Sandefur, G. (1994), *Growing up with a Single Parent, What Hurts, What Helps*, Harvard University Press, Cambridge, MA.

Millar, J. (1988), 'The cost of marital breakdown', in R. Walker and G. Parker (eds), *Money Matters: Income, Wealth and Financial Welfare*, Sage, London.

Moen, P. and Forest, K. (1995), 'Family policies for an aging society: Moving to the 21 century', *Gerontologist*, 35, 6, pp.825-830.

Morgan, A. (1989), 'Economic well-being following marital termination: a comparison of widowed and divorced women', *Journal of Family Issues*, 10 (1), pp.86-101.

Pai, N.W. and Wan, Y.W. (1995), 'The relationship between family policy and community women status: from a feminist comparative point of view', *Community Development*, 71,pp.30-41.

Peng, S.H. and Chang, Y.C. (1995), *The Positive Function of the Single-parent Family*, Research report. National Science Committee, Executive Yuan, Taipei.

Shiech, H.F. (1995), 'Taiwan married women's problems and family welfare policy researches', *Social Work Journal*, Soochow University, 1, pp.1-36.

Shiech, H.F. and Ma, C.J. (1989), *The Welfare Needs of Divorced and Widowed Women in Taipei City*, Bureau of Social Affairs, Taipei City Government, Taipei.

Tung, T.C. (1992), *Financial Plight of the Female-headed Single-parent Family in Taiwan*. Master's thesis, Social Welfare Department, Chung-Cheng University.

Wang, L.S. (1995), 'Woman welfare issue and social policy: from a feminism point of view. *Research and Evaluation Bimonthly*, 19, pp.19-26.

Wang, L.S. (1994), *Women's Welfare Needs Assessment in Taiwan*, Research report. Department of Interior, Taipei.

Wang, H.H. (1991), *Single Parents' Support System and Living Adjustment*, Master's thesis. Child Welfare Report, Chinese University,

Wang, P.L. (1988), *Research on the Relationship between Mother's Living Adjustments after Divorce and the Self-concept of School Children*, Master's thesis. Graduate School of Child Welfare, Chinese Culture University.

Wang, P.L. (1985), *Divorced Mothers' Living Adjustment and the Self-concept of their School-age Children*, Master's thesis, Child Welfare Department, Chinese Culture University, Republic of China.

Weng, B. (1998), *Single Mothers Parenting Stress Group Counselling Research*, Ph.D. Dissertation National Changhua University, Changhua, Taiwan.

Worth, R. (1992), *Single Parent Families*, Franklin Watts, New York.

Wu, C.F. (1993), *Single Parents' Living Adjustment and Related Social Policy Research*, Master's thesis. Sociology Department, National Taiwan University.

Yeh, Y.R. (1992), *Low Income Single-parent Family Problems and Needs in NanKaung District*, NanKaung Social Welfare Services Center, Taipei City.

Yi, C.C. and Chu, R.L. (1992), 'Changes in Chinese family structure and functions: comparisons of Taiwan, Hong Kong, China and Singapore', *Western Social Science Theory Transplant and Application Cooperative Conference,* Hong Kong Chinese University, Hong Kong.

Yi, C.C. (1994), 'Childcare arrangements of employed mothers in Taiwan', in Esther N.L. Chow and Catherine W. Berheide (eds), *Women, the Family, and Policy: A Global Perspective,* State University of NY Press, Albany, NY, pp.235-254.

Yi, C.C. (1998), 'Forming of family policy: using a family protection network as example', *Social Welfare*, 136, pp.16-29.

Zimmerman, S.L. (1998), *Understanding Family Policy: Theoretical Approaches*, Sage, Beverley Hills, CA.

11 Family support services: some recent developments
KATE MORRIS

Introduction

Child welfare services have been engaged in considerable debate about the role and function of state support services since the inception of the Children Act 1989. More recently the Government has introduced the consultation document *Supporting Families*. Both the Children Act and the consultation document identify the role of the state in promoting effective parenting and family life. The relationship between these two initiatives is explored in this chapter and it is argued that the ineffective implementation of the Children Act undermines the more recent policy initiatives presented in the consultation document.

The implications of the Children Act and the research surrounding its implementation are considered. *Supporting Families* is then discussed, and these two highly significant policy developments are compared. In conclusion it is argued that many of the issues facing effective implementation of the Children Act have not been addressed, and that these issues continue to inhibit more recent policy initiatives.

This debate is concerned with support services. By this it is meant those services that aim to assist families experiencing difficulties in bringing up their children effectively. Children at risk of harm or abuse are not included within this definition of support services, although it is recognized that childcare services form a continuum and such divisions as these are somewhat false. Attention will be paid to those services that offer practical guidance and support. While the crucial role played by financial and employment policies is acknowledged, they do not form the focus of this chapter.

The content and impact of the Children Act

In 1989 the then Conservative government introduced the Children Act, presenting it as 'the most comprehensive and far reaching reform of child care law to come before parliament in living memory' (Lord Chancellor,

1988).

The changes embedded within the Act were indeed a fundamental alteration in childcare law and practice and can be argued to have been informed by a number of important developments in social work research and practice. The Act met a practical need to draw together a disparate collection of existing legislation. This lack of coherence in the legal framework had allowed practice to emerge that was unhelpful and disempowering to children and their families (Rowe and Lambert, 1973). The new legal framework saw child welfare services drawn largely together into one coherent piece of legislation.

The Act also responded to growing political and public concern that social workers had become over-zealous in their interventions in family life (Parton, 1991). The 'moral panic' generated by such episodes as the Cleveland investigations led to perceptions that professionals were too quick to remove children from the care of their parents and families (Butler Sloss, 1988). In episodes such as these the local authority was argued to have made too great a use of its powers to remove children. The complex issues in the Cleveland experiences - where sexual abuse of children by their families formed the focus of a widespread investigation - were reduced to simplistic debates about the rights of families and the responsibilities of the state. The social workers involved were seen as either over-zealous and missionary in their actions, or innocent messengers of painful truths about family abuse of children (Bell, 1988; Campbell, 1988).

The Children Act sought a better balance - whilst protecting children, the rights and needs of families should be considered sensitively and appropriately. The Act tried to address notions of responsibilities as well as rights and to place the interventionist work of the state in a broader context of prevention and support.

Running alongside this somewhat simplistic public analysis of the role of social work, as evidenced by the Cleveland episode, came the dissemination of a collection of significant research findings (DoH, 1985; 1991). These various studies found that in a range of settings social work services to children and their families were often inadequate and at times damaging. The state was shown to be a poor substitute parent, with children experiencing real difficulties once they entered the public care system.

However, this wave of research also found that good outcomes could be achieved for children, particularly where professionals worked hard to maintain a child's connections with their original family and where efforts were made to plan effectively with children and families for their well-being: 'by the mid-1980s there was cumulative research evidence... showing that the well-being of children cared for by social agencies is enhanced if they maintain links with parents and other family members (DoH, 1991).

The Children Act began to address these many issues. Underpinning the legislation was the intention to work positively, wherever possible, with children and their families. Specifically the Act makes clear:

- the child's welfare is paramount - all other considerations are secondary;
- wherever possible children are best brought up by their families, with the state playing a role in providing any necessary support services when difficulties are identified;
- professionals should aim to work in partnership with children and families and seek to involve all those concerned with planning to meet a child's needs

The Children Act moved towards an image of the state providing helpful, non-punitive services that addressed family difficulties and supported the care of their children. Specifically the Act introduced a duty on local authorities to identify and support what it referred to as 'children in need':

> It shall be the duty of every local authority to
> a) safeguard and promote the welfare of children within their area who are in need: and
> b) so far as is consistent with that duty, promote the up-bringing of such children by their families,
> by providing a range and level of services appropriate to those child's needs.

This duty made clear the responsibility of local authorities to provide families with support services that enhanced a child's quality of life and where possible maintained them within their families:

> ...family support implies a potentially open-ended approach, and one in which the views and preferences of service users are to be given greater weight... (Tunstill, 1997, p.48).

Implementation of services to children in need

However, it can be argued that Section 17 of the Children Act, whilst generating significant debate and research, has produced little in the way of services (Audit Commission, 1994). The broad, indeed vague, terms by which a child in need is defined has enabled authorities to be consistently limited in their implementation of this section of the Act. By failing to define more closely the term 'in need' authorities have considerable flexibility in establishing the criteria and eligibility for Section 17 services. As a consequence, services are tightly rationed and limited resources managed. For many families access to these services has been a frustrating and demeaning experience, as Lindly identifies in her research:

> I rang on several occasions, the last time in tears asking for help. Then things got really bad and social services turned up next day telling me what to do... (Lindly, 1992, p.10).

Central Government reviews of the implementation of the Children Act have identified that substantial numbers of local authorities have failed to develop services reflecting the positive, accessible tone set by the legislation. The Children Act Report soon after the introduction of the Act notes that:

> ..a broadly consistent and somewhat worrying picture is emerging ...further work is still needed to provide across the country a range of family services aimed at preventing families reaching the point of breakdown... (DoH, 1994, p.16).

More recent research would seem to indicate that for many families the only service available is an assessment of possible risk - if the child is perceived not to be at risk of harm, then few if any alternative services are identified (Gibbons et al, 1995). Research and family experiences seem to indicate that local authorities are investing considerable time in determining eligibility for services against tight criteria, rather than in stimulating the development of support services.

The work by Aldgate and colleagues (1994) reveals a further difficulty in the pattern of support services. Local authorities are choosing to define 'in need' as (a child) displaying acute problems. Looked after children, children committing serious offences, and children in need of protection are all common categories of 'in need' when support services are reviewed. This approach that demands that children and families display relatively high levels of acute need before receiving a service undermines the principles and intentions of the Children Act.

Effective support services are not merely a question of resources.

Professional attitudes also play a part. A high status is assigned to child protection work, with family support services seen as less skilled and of lower status. Even when services are developed such attitudes inhibit their usefulness (Jordan, 1997). The process of defining eligibility inevitably allows professional perceptions of service users to affect the type and nature of the service on offer. Some families are judged to be too difficult to work with in partnership or to develop negotiated services with. Again, such attitudes will inhibit the growth of innovative support services (Morris and Shepherd, 1999).

To summarise, the Children Act 1989 gave family support services a useful structure and role. However, there have been difficulties in the struggle to develop services that reflect the principles and intentions of the Act. While resources have played a significant role, professional attitudes about 'need', status and the right to access helpful services have also played their part. The debates about the supportive and preventative potential of the Children Act remain unresolved. More recently, within childcare social work the 'refocusing' debate has emerged. Drawn from recent Government research (DoH, 1995), this debate argues the need to shift the focus away from child protection and towards preventative services. It is argued that by a narrow concentration on risk and harm too many children, and families' needs are unmet. As a result inappropriate services, or services that are too late, are being delivered.

Overall a theme emerges when exploring the practical preventative and support services provided by the state for families with children within the framework of Part 3 of the Children Act. Whatever the causes - and these are multi-faceted - the policy intentions to address need and maintain children within their networks have rarely been matched in reality. For black and ethnic minority families, for families where disability is an issue, for fathers and for lesbian and gay families service provision is even more complex and inaccessible. The inadequate implementation and resourcing of services for children in need means it is impossible to assess the usefulness of the Act, and it is therefore difficult to establish any messages for amending or changing policies and law. Indeed there is considerable argument that the next step should be full implementation accompanied by careful evaluation.

In 1999 the New Labour government launched its consultation document *Supporting Families*. This document outlines New Labour's strategies for 'the practical support the Government can provide to help parents do the best they can for their children...'. Embedded within this document is the government's view that families are the best place for children to grow up, and that the government has an investment in helping parents care effectively for their children. There is a sense of a hierarchy of arrangements for childcare, with marriage being the preferred option. While other settings are recognized, marriage is given particular weight and value.

The document also makes clear the government's intentions to support families positively in the tasks of parenting, and to offer guidance and assistance where appropriate and necessary.

Various new initiatives are proposed/publicised. These include the 'Sure Start' initiative, which has central government funding. This initiative will target those areas defined as having the greatest 'need'. Indicators of this will include unemployment, economic deprivation, and education and health problems. Government funding will make available additional resources to build on and develop existing and new support services. As in previous family support developments, in order to secure a service relatively high levels of need must be demonstrated. While initiatives such as Sure Start are about areas rather than individuals, they bring with them the real possibility of families feeling stigmatized and labelled. We do not yet have sufficient evidence from existing preventative/support services about what works - it is therefore a considerable risk to invest in new approaches. The limited development of family support services to date inhibits the evaluation of their effectiveness, or comments about transferability of various models across various settings.

Supporting Families makes little reference to existing law and policy, or to the messages from research findings about support services. The document uses concepts of need and prevention. It is presented as a positive approach to enhancing family life for children. There are therefore a series of similarities to the Children Act legislation and guidance. Both documents present the basis of support services as being a positive view of family life and a commitment to offering children this opportunity. Both documents talk about 'need' in broad, somewhat ill-defined terms. The documents accept a responsibility on the part of the state to promote and support effective parenting. Both therefore share a benign view of state services and their intentions.

The absence of any reference in *Supporting Families* to existing powers and duties to support families where children are in need is striking. The difficulties encountered in developing such preventative services are not explored. Indeed the document at times presents itself as heralding new thinking in this complex area. The barriers faced in the design and delivery of family support services under Part 3 of the Children Act are important lessons for future initiatives. Any new developments are built on shaky foundations without a full acknowledgement of past difficulties. In the absence of full implementation of existing preventative and support opportunities it is difficult to envisage new initiatives being successful.

Being a parent is not an easy task. Being a parent in poverty, with poor healthcare and few local resources can at times be overwhelming. The Children Act makes clear the important role the state could play in providing helpful services to children and their families. The real difficulties arise in the translation of intentions into realities.

References

Aldgate J., Tunstill J., Ozolins R. and McBeath, G. (1994), *Family Support and the Children Act - The First Eighteen Months*, Report to the Department of Health, University of Leicester, Leicester.

Audit Commission (1994), *Seen but not Heard: Co-ordinating Child Health and Social Services for Children in Need*, HMSO, London.

Bell, S. (1988), *When Salem came to the Boro: The true Story of the Cleveland Child Abuse Crisis*, Pan, London.

Butler Sloss, L.J. (1988), *Report of the Inquiry into Child Abuse in Cleveland 1987*, HMSO, London.

Campbell, B. (1988), *Unofficial Secrets*, Virago, London.

Children Act 1989: *Accompanying Guidance and Regulations*, HMSO, London.

Department of Health and Social Security (DHSS) (1985), *Social Work Decisions in Child Care*, HMSO, London.

Department of Health (DoH) (1991), *Patterns and Outcomes in Child Placement*, HMSO, London.

Department of Health (DoH) (1994), *The Children Act Report*, HMSO, London

Department of Health (DoH) (1995), *Child Protection: Messages from Research*, HMSO, London.

Gibbons, J., Conroy, S. and Bell, C. (1995), *Operating the Child Protection System*, HMSO, London.

Jordon, B. (1997), 'Partnership with service users in child protection and family support', in N. Parton, *Child Protection and Family Support: Tensions, Contradictions and Possibilities*, Routledge, London.

Lindly, B. (1992), *Families Experiences' of the Children Act: The First Report*, Family Rights Group, London.

Morris, K. and Shepherd, C. (1999), *Quality Services for Families in Child and Family Social Work* (forthcoming).

Parton, N. (1991), *Governing the Family: Child Care, Child Protection and the State*, Macmillan, London.

Rowe, J. and Lambert, L. (1973), *Children Who Wait*, Association of British Adoption Agencies, London.

Tunstill, J. (1997), 'Family support clauses of the 1989 Children Act', in N. Parton, *Child Protection and Family Support: Tensions, Contradictions and Possibilities*, Routledge, London.

12 The social construction of ageing: elderly women in Taiwan

LIH-RONG WANG

Introduction

In Taiwan, over the last ten years, interest in issues concerning ageing women has grown steadily. However, the literature provides a basic descriptive picture of women in later life that covers such dimensions as income, employment and retirement, widowhood, social and family life, and health (Hu, 1990; Lee, 1995a). This study explores the experiences of women as they age, from a social construction perspective.

Relevant literature

A social construction perspective on ageing

From the feminist perspective, studies of older women tend to draw parallels between the economic disadvantage of older women - this disadvantage being rooted in lifelong economic dependency and social subordination - and a general social context of ageism and sexism, that makes up an older woman's precarious social status (Aronson, 1990). However, there has been relatively little attention paid to older women's ageing experiences in terms of social construction in the literature.

The social construction perspective focuses on how older people become unnecessarily dependent because of social barriers, such as the division of labour within the family, inadequate retirement wages, poor transportation systems, the high cost of housing, and inadequate community support (Bicher, 1994; Leonard and Nichols, 1994). These factors contribute to the general dependency on the family of elderly people. Bicher (1994) develops a feminist social construction theory to analyse the caregiving relationship between mother and daughter, stating that social structures contribute to this dependent relationship.

Significant issues in this area include caregiving, the gender division of labour, poverty, economic dependency, income insecurity, the historic role and marginality of older people, and social policies that promote dependency (Bicher, 1994).

Leonard and Nichols (1994) clearly set out the significance of structural factors affecting ageing. According to these papers, what older people feel, think and do remains determined by their experience of economic, social and cultural structures. Their experiences impinge upon them throughout their lives in terms of their political participation, family and religious history, level of material existence, the impact of immigration, and the ambiguities involved in the support or rejection of potential caregivers.

Leonard and Nichols claim that the experience of ageing is socially constructed by the relationships and structures within which it occurs. Their study further claims that the experience of ageing is not constructed solely within the major social divisions of gender, class, ethnicity, and these factors' relationship to the state. It claims, rather, that it is also physiologically constructed. The physical experience of ageing, the experience of health and illhealth, of biological deterioration and decline, are undergone within the context of state services, neighbourhood net-works, and the caregiving capacities of families. So, the health of older people has significant structural determinants, but is nevertheless irreducibly biological.

Bicher (1994) examines women's caregiving role and enunciates the assumption that women have been socialized to be caregivers and that this kind of work is undervalued, underpaid - indeed in most cases unpaid - and that it is perpetuated by patriarchy and the material conditions of women. Similarly, Graham (1983), by employing social construction theory, claims that women's role as caregivers leads to economic dependency and poverty; yet it is caregiving which defines both women's identity and their working role in many cultures. Furthermore, Aronson (1985) suggests that factors such as gender division have the potential to impose dependency on both the carers and the cared-for in the following manner:

1. A woman who looks after an elderly family member may have to remove herself from the paid labour force. By doing so, she is likely to become economically dependent on other family members or the state.

2. The elderly family member (mostly women) may be forced to accept this type of care as she may have limited resources and/or live in a

community with limited resources; she may thus feel powerless and indebted to her daughter.

Walker (1983) also states that the caring role of women often creates dependency. According to this study, social policy can be a reinforcer which pushes women who often undertake caregiving responsibilities into dependency status. Many other social constructionists also emphasize the relationship between social constructive forces and ageing or dependency. For instance, Townsend (1981) maintains that the dependency of the elderly adult is created by pressure for early retirement, the legitimization of low income, and the lack of control elderly people have over their lives both in institutions and in the community. However, Smith (1984) avers that the structured dependency of elderly people existed before industrial capitalism and that, historically, elderly people have always been socially isolated and removed from the workplace.

Leonard and Nichols (1994) take the position that the social construction of dependency can only be analysed by first acknowledging that elderly people are marginal to society. This marginality is compounded by gender, class and race/ethnicity. This paper further states that elderly women's status is even more marginalized. It is claimed that, since women are already devalued in society, elderly women are treated with less respect than elderly men (Burnside, 1993; Collins and Paul, 1994).

Other social constructionists, meanwhile, treat social ideology, such as patriarchy and capitalism, as if it were an invisible hand affecting elderly women's dependency. Peace (1986), for instance, holds that the underlying ideologies of both patriarchy and capitalism with their emphasis on male power and male domination have culminated in the use of the family - and of women's traditional role within it - as a control mechanism for reproducing the status quo and for reinforcing social inequalities. Bicher (1994) shares this view, finding that the dependency relationship between an elderly mother and a middle-aged daughter is created by the interaction between patriarchy and economic structures. Ideologies, including those of both patriarchy and capitalism, serve to produce and reproduce the status quo of elderly women.

Ageing, economic security, and well-being

The social factors as stated above have impinged upon the elderly throughout their lives. As a result the retirement-income security of older people is weak. Very few women work for employers who provide pensions or other retirement plans for their employees (Wang, 1997). In fact, not only may elderly female workers who currently lack pension coverage find retirement pensions harder to obtain, but elderly female workers who are covered may also find it increasingly difficult either to retain their current jobs or to secure new ones which provide a pension.

Women move in and out of the labour force with greater frequency, spend longer periods of time away from paid work (Smith, 1984), and change jobs more often than men (Korczyk, 1993; Smith, 1984). Therefore, female workers tend to be concentrated in low-wage occupations and are less likely to work in industries with pension coverage (Korczyk, 1993). They also receive less by way of private pension benefits when they do qualify, and accumulate less in the way of assets and savings (Wang, 1997; A.Lee, 1995a, 1995b; M.L.Lee, 1996).

Bicher (1994) puts a similar case. He further states that women's pension income reflects their earlier poor work record. The causes of this include the male/female wage gap, the reduced and interrupted participation of females in the labour force, females' lower rate of contribution to wage-related pensions, the much lower incidence of private pension-holding among females, and their skewed occupational segregation (De Viney and Solomon, 1995).

For those women working part-time, the lack of pension coverage is particularly worrisome. Indeed part-time work is often treated as an employment option for ageing women; a means of easing back into the labour force. An attachment to the labour force can thereby be maintained when full-time work is unavailable or undesirable, and/or when the individual is phasing into retirement. In such cases women often suffer from economic deprivation because of the kind of work available. Thus, economic security or financial resources are seen by many as crucial to elderly women's well-being.

Atchley (1989) suggested that economic circumstances are factors potentially influencing the social isolation and the negative attitude of widows. Thompson (1992) also found that reduced income was a significant factor in explaining the lower morale of the retired. Lawton (1975) stated that income after retirement could be a crucial factor in mitigating stress due to the loss of the work role.

Elwell, Maltbie and Crannell (1994), utilizing a sub-sample drawn from the National Opinion Research Center (U.S.A.), consisting of 1,660 male and female respondents, all 50 years of age or older, concluded that income, informal and formal group membership are all contributing factors to economic status. Clearly, economic security affects the psychosocial adaptation of the aged.

In sum, elderly females' economic insecurity is directly or indirectly derived from the social and economic structures they live in. The double deprivation of ageism and sexism has been documented as explaining women's economic disadvantage in life. Therefore, at the policy level, promoting elderly women's life satisfaction or bio-psychosocial adaptation requires a structural change in the workplace labour market, that is, the creation of an equitable pay policy, and, in particular, the creation of a protective pension system for elderly women. As Bicher (1994) points out, in order to reduce women's financial dependency, their pension benefits must be improved, suggesting that women should receive credit for all the years they have spent working at home. In addition, since company pension benefits are related to salaries earned, the implementation of an equitable pay policy is urgently needed.

Based on the above literature review, the present study puts forward the following three propositions in relation to women's income dependency and their degree of well-being:

Proposition 1: The lower the income security, the worse the degree of physical well-being.

Proposition 2: The lower the income security, the worse the degree of psychological well-being.

Proposition 3: The higher the income security, the better the degree of social well-being.

Ageing, the social support system and well-being

The effects of social support on well-being and as a stress moderator have been examined extensively (Collins and Paul, 1994; Hobfoll, 1988). The following variable domains have been suggested as being especially important. (1) personal characteristics, (2) quality of personal relationships, and (3) characteristics of the environment. Hobfoll (1986) presented a general stress model, termed the conservation of resources (COR) theory. COR theory suggests that those with fewer personal resources tend to use external resources as needed , but to rely on personal resources only, if these are adequate, rather than relying on social or other external resources.

With respect to the social support of ageing, structural elements and personal factors have come to be equally recognized. Reeves and Darville (1994) found that personal factors such as frequency/type of social contact and family structure affect satisfaction in women's retirement. In this study, social support or contact groups were categorized into the following four sets: family, close friends, other friends, and organizations.

Osgood's study (1982) concludes that a unique social support concept, called 'social climate', is a significant factor affecting the well-being of the elderly. This study holds that life satisfaction is related to the social climate of the retirement community. It has been observed, for instance, that when widows are grouped together in a community in large numbers, the individuals will enjoy a higher sense of well-being because the social climate is more supportive.

Another social contextual factor which has been utilized in analysing support for ageing is social interaction networks. Social interaction with, for example, friends and children also contributes to life satisfaction. Family and outside family networks all provide informal and formal support systems which contribute to the psychosocial well-being of the aged, they argue. Indeed, widows' life satisfaction can be directly related to the frequency of interactions with friends and participation in group activities.

Social interaction networks have also been documented as being a significant element in structuring the relationship between the emotional well-being of elderly persons and their social context. Reeves and Darville (1994) affirm that subjective perceptions of environmental conditions are better predictors of life satisfaction than are objective measures of environmental parameters; but that objective social structural variables can affect well-being indirectly by their impact on subjective perceptions.

In fact, activity theories and life-cycle theories both provide a connection between the social support, social contact and emotional well-being of the elderly population. The greater the degree of social contact, the higher the degree of social support from the social contact environment. Therefore, a lack of social support and social integration could be both personal and structural in nature (Reeves and Darville, 1994).

Similarly, Collins and Paul (1994) attempt to show that social support systems are relationship patterns which play an important role in the maintenance of an individual's physical and psychological integrity over time and which also facilitate or promote mastery of one's environment. The presence or absence of social support in the environment is a key element in the ability to adapt, or even to survive, as well as to attain comfort and well-being (Coyne and Delongis, 1986).

As regards the relationship between social support and functional health status, the differing definitions and sources of measurement make summarizing statements about this relationship difficult. However, functional impairment has been associated with an increased amount and range of help from informal networks, with decreased social contact outside the home, and with social isolation (Arling, 1987; Stoller, 1984).

Concerning the relationship between social support and emotional or social well-being, some studies have also shown considerable evidence of correlation. Lawton (1975) terms this social adjustment 'morale' in elders, which he describes as a measurement of the elder's inner capacity to maintain a positive mental outlook towards self and towards his or her relationship with others. Persons who have high morale enjoy a satisfying interactive relationship with others and do not exhibit symptoms of distress. A relationship between qualitative, but not quantitative, social interaction data and morale/social adjustment exists. A relationship between perceived support and other measures of well-being such as life satisfaction, is also discovered.

The present study thus presents the following three propositions in this respect:

Proposition 4: The greater the social support, the higher the degree of physical well-being.

Proposition 5: The greater the social support, the higher the degree of psychological well-being.

Proposition 6: The greater the social support, the higher the degree of social well-being.

Ageing, the family caregiving role and well-being

In Taiwan, as in western countries, a basic ideological tenet holds families to be responsible for the care of vulnerable members. Very often family care is equal to women's care. It is women more often than men who are the unpaid, informal caregivers for family members of all ages and generations. This has occurred first of all because of the structured division of labour by gender within the family and in the workplace, and, second, because caregiving is assumed to be women's 'natural' work (Dwyer and Coward, 1992).

Hooyman and Gonyea (1995) argue that within-family division-of-labour models try to explain existing gender differences in caregiving. Witt (1994) considers that non-metropolitan daughters tend to perform more of the kind of caregiving tasks which are considered traditional 'women's work'. Metropolitan daughters, meanwhile, perform significantly more work considered to be nontraditional for women. These research findings suggest that providing care is defined more by socialization of gender roles than by women's natural or biological tendencies to 'nurture'.

From a social construction perspective, the ideology of patriarchy is a system of social structure and practice in which men dominate. Women are central to a feminist analysis of gender relations. As an anti-patriarchal ideology, feminism challenges male power and privilege in the social world, and argues for the elimination of the oppression and subordination of women (Hooyman and Gonyea, 1995).

The duty of family care has been a heavy burden for women. In taking on the role of caregiver, they have experienced increased personal health problems including physical exhaustion and the general deterioration of their own health status (Biegel et al., 1994). Sicknesses typically include headaches, stomach complaints, and weight problems.

Comparisons of the self-reported health conditions of caregivers (mostly women) for frail and elderly people with non-caregiving peers, reveal that the former group reports poorer physical health (Biegel et al., 1994), more chronic illnesses and a greater use of prescription drugs (Haley et al., 1987). Moreover, poor physical health or low physical stamina has often been found to be associated with depression, reduced patience, and an impaired ability to cope with caregiving demands.

The responsibilities of caregiving can disrupt family life and strain family relations. In addition, changes in social relationships can extend beyond the household and the family. Individuals who have taken on caregiving roles often report restrictions in their social and leisure activities, such as opportunities to visit or relax with friends, take vacations, engage in hobbies, attend church or community activities, and participate in volunteer work or community service. The loss of such opportunities leads to greater isolation and loneliness among caregivers (Hooyman and Gonyea, 1995). Indeed, social contacts have been shown to have an important mediating influence on the relationship between stress and well-being (Antonucci, 1985).

Caregivers adjust to caregiving demands by giving up time, leaving less time for personal relaxation; the resulting stress then contributes to the decline of the caregiver's health and effectiveness. Alford-Copper (1993) proposes that caregiver burnout is a result of 'cultural lag'. He claims that social values, regarding caregiving and society's solutions to caregiving problems, are changing more slowly than the material conditions exacerbating caregivers' problems.

In the case of older women who have been designated caregivers by social expectation and cultural forces, their bio-psychosocial adjustment problems may be more apparent than those of elderly non-caregiving women. This study presents the following three propositions in this regard which will be tested empirically.

Proposition 7: The greater the strain of the family care role, the lower the degree of physical well-being.

Proposition 8: The greater the strain of the family care role, the lower the degree of psychological well-being.

Proposition 9: The greater the strain of the family care role, the lower the degree of social well-being.

The research

Subjects

The subjects (n = 439) were aged 65 and over, resident in the northern part of Taiwan, specifically in Taipei City, Taipei County, Keelung City, Ilan County, Tao-Yan County, Hsin-Ju County and Hsin-Chu City.

The sample was drawn from the voting directories of the cities and counties stated above. In order to ensure a representative sample, stratified multistage random sampling was utilized. For a purposive survey frame, 7 levels of urbanization were employed as criteria for determining the sample size in different areas. Our sample consisted of 158 respondents (36.0 per cent) aged between 70 and 74; 120 (27.3 per cent) aged between 65 and 69; 85 (19.4 per cent) aged between 75 and 79; 51 respondents (11.6 per cent) aged between 80 and 84; 17 respondents (3.9 per cent) aged between 85 and 89; and 8 respondents (1.8 per cent) aged over 90. Those aged between 65 and 74 comprises 63.3 per cent of the total sample, the rest of the respondents, 36.7 per cent, were at least 75 years of age. All the respondents above were interviewed face-to-face.

Almost half of the women interviewed were illiterate (55.8 per cent); of the rest, 29.2per cent had had an elementary school education, and the remainder (15per cent) a junior high school (or better) education. Most of the subjects had religious belief (88.4 per cent). Almost half of the sample were widows (49.7 per cent); 46.9 per cent of the subjects were married; 2.5 per cent were divorced or separated, while the remaining 0.9 per cent (4 subjects) were single. Of the subjects' reporting living arrangements, 67 per cent (294 subjects) regularly lived with their children, 12.5 per cent (55 subjects) lived with their spouse, 8.9 per cent (39 subjects) lived variously with offspring. The rest lived with friends or in relatives' houses or else in nursing homes and other places. Some 52.4 per cent (230 subjects) reported that they had had work experience and the remaining 47.6 per cent (209 subjects) reported no work experience. Some 87 per cent did not have any pension cover, while the remaining 13 per cent did.

Instruments

Instrumental Activities of Daily Living (IADL). The IADL, used to measure functional health status, is a Sub-Index in the activities of the Daily Living Domain of the Philadelphia Geriatric Center Multilevel Assessment Instrument (PGC MAI). IADL tasks include using the telephone, getting to places beyond walking distance, shopping for groceries, preparing meals, doing housework and handyman work, doing laundry, managing money, and taking one's own medicine. Such task items are scored from 1 to 3, with a 3 indicating that the task can be done without help, a 2 indicating that some help is needed, and 1 indicating that the individual is completely unable to do the task. Total IADL tasks are accumulated, with the lower numbers indicating the difficulty of performing the tasks and the higher numbers the ability to perform the task independently or with minimal help. In our interview questionnaire, IADL has been modified into 13 items which have been adopted by many researchers in Taiwan and Hong Kong. The modified IADL is utilized as a measurement of the physical status of elderly women.

Life Satisfaction Scale (L. S. scale). The life satisfaction scale has been used to measure social-psychological adjustment associated with the ageing process. It is operationalized in this study by a 5 item Likert-type scale which measures the respondent's satisfaction with area of residence, non-work activity, friendship, health and family relationships. With respect to the psychological or emotional well-being of the respondents, a depression scale is also used to measure respondents' psychological condition above research stated physical ability decreases with age.

Social Support Scale (SS scale). The SS scale is composed of 7 items including emotional support, economic assistance, information support, accommodation support, health care, recreation activity support and outgoing care. According to the personal resources of social support, three dimensions of support are identified, including relatives living together, relatives who do not live together with elderly women, and others who are friends or non-friends. The respondents were requested to answer 'yes' or 'no' to show received support from relatives or friends or others. This social support scale is adopted from the Lubben Social Network Scale (LSNS), which was utilized in Hong Kong's 1994 survey of the psychological health and social support of the elderly.

Economic Security. In order to measure respondents' economic security, the subjects were required to consider the following economic conditions: (1) pension support, (2) major economic source, and (3) the degree of income security.

Family Caregiving Role Strain. The family care role is divided into three categories: (1) spouse-caring demand, (2) grandchildren-caring demand, (3) other family members' demand. In measuring the subjective burden which refers to feelings aroused in family members as they fulfil their caregiving functions, the measurement is conceptualized/and defined as 'emotional reactions to caregiving such as worry, tension, sadness, resentment and difficulty sleeping'.

Procedure

Data for this study were collected through structured home interviews. Since elderly women tend to be suspicious of 'outsiders' or 'strangers', written letters were delivered before the formal interview took place. Once the interviewers reached the homes of the prospective participants, very few refused to be interviewed. However, if the prospective participant did refuse, then stand-by samples were used to guarantee the number of subjects required.

All investigations and the supervision of the survey process were carefully conducted in order to ensure the usefulness of the data. The survey interviews were conducted in winter, including in Chinese Lunar New Year, so some of the interviewees were very warmly treated. After the interview, the survey questionnaires were followed up by telephone calls to the homes in order to double-check the results.

The results

Economic stress and well-being in ageing

With respect to economic security, the descriptive statistics are shown in

Table 12.1. Most elderly women (61.3 per cent) had a regular income from their son and daughter-in-law with whom they lived, and more than one-third (36.7 per cent) received an income from their son and daughter-in-law with whom they did not live. Meanwhile, about one-fifth of the sample (21.4 per cent) received a regular income from themselves and spouses. Very few of the respondents (3.2 per cent) had a regular income from personal retirement savings.

Asked about economic adequacy, nearly 40 per cent of respondents felt they had adequate economic means, while nearly 20 per cent felt under economic pressure. In addition, the general attitude toward economic dependency was a 'traditional' one which indicates that sons and daughters are the ones relied on (74.9 per cent), while the spouse is the second choice. However, this result may be partially derived from the fact that widows made up almost half of the respondents. Very few (3.2 per cent) had turned to the government for economic support. The data confirmed that Taiwanese women are very traditional in securing their economic needs.

Pearson correlations were calculated to determine the relationships between economic adequacy and physical condition, economic adequacy and psychological well-being, and economic adequacy and social or psychosocial well-being (See table 12.2). Economic adequacy and psychological well-being scores correlate at the $r = 0.3208^{***}$ level (see table 12.2). Economic adequacy and social well-being were also negative at $r = $ minus 0.2550.

Pairwise correlations were calculated for economic security and the demographic variables of age, education, marriage, living arrangements, satisfaction with living arrangements, work experience, and retirement pension. Education was shown to be a significant factor with a positive relationship existing between education and economic security scores, with the F/ratio = 0.608, p<.05. Marriage and economic security scores were correlated, with the F/ratio = 4.703, p<.01, as were living arrangements with economic security scores, with the F/ratio = 4.745, p<.001. Retirement pension and economic security scores were also correlated, with the F/ratio = 5.637, p<.05. No significant correlations were shown for work experience and work satisfaction, however.

Table 12.1 Economic situation of respondents

	Frequency	%
1. Economic Resources		
Personal Pension	14	3.2
Working Salary	27	5.9
Spouse Income	21	4.8
Personal / Spouse Savings	94	21.4
Son/Daughter In-law Living Together	269	61.3
Son/Daughter In-law Not Living Together	161	36.7
Daughter/Son In-law Living Together	43	9.8
Daughter/Son In-law Not Living Together	80	18.2
Widowhood Compensation	36	8.2
Rent and Interest	25	5.7
Investment	4	0.9
Social Assistance	28	6.2
Relatives and Friends	11	2.5
Other	15	3.4
2. Economic Adequacy		
Very Much Adequate	22	5.0
Adequate	152	34.6
Moderate	184	41.9
Inadequate	76	17.3
Seriously Inadequate	5	1.1
3. Economic Dependency		
Self/Spouse	56	12.8
Son and Daughter	329	74.9
Relatives	8	1.8
Friends/Neighbourhood	7	1.6
Government	14	3.2
Other	7	1.6

Table 12.2 Correlation matrix of socially structured elements and ageing well-being

Variables	Well-being		
	Physical	Psychological	Social
1. Economic adequacy	0.0080	-0.3028	-0.2550
2. Social support	0.0709	0.0485	0.1333
3. Subjective care burden	-0.0974	0.0039	0.0453

Social support and well-being in ageing

The data indicate that as long as elderly women live with relatives such as children, spouse, and so on, most of them receive social support (table 12.3). Of the sample, 84.9 per cent and 82.8 per cent received emotional support and economic support respectively; 60.5 per cent and 60.8 per cent received informal support and health care support, respectively, while other supports such as accommodation, leisure activity support and out-going support were less common for elderly women.

However, when the elderly women do not live with relatives such as children, spouse, and others, a lower percentage of them receive support (see table 12.3). For instance, only 50.1 per cent of respondents receive emotional support, compared to 84.9 per cent in the group of respondents living with relatives; also only 38.5 per cent of these respondents receive economic support from relatives, compared to 82.8 per cent in the other group.

Table 12.2 shows the relationship between social support and the physical, psychological and social well-being of older women; social support and the three scores correlate at $r = 0.0709$, 0.0485, and 0.1333, respectively. However, the correlations are non-significant. Meanwhile, social support from relatives and others may improve elderly women's bio-psychosocial adjustment. This too, however, is not statistically significant.

Table 12.3 Social support from relatives

Indicators	Frequency	%
1. Emotional Support		
a. living together	355	84.9
b. non-living together	220	50.1
c. others	116	26.4
2. Economic Support		
a. living together	346	82.8
b. non-living together	169	38.5
c. others	12	2.7
3. Informal Support		
a. living together	253	60.5
b. non-living together	109	24.8
c. others	38	8.7
4. Accommodation Support		
a. living together	221	52.9
b. non-living together	16	3.6
c. others	5	1.1
5. Health Care		
a. living together	259	60.8
b. non-living together	69	15.7
c. others	10	2.3
6. Recreation Activity		
a. living together	176	42.1
b. non-living together	58	13.2
c. others	58	13.2
7. Outgoing Assistance		
a. living together	187	44.7
b. non-living together	38	8.7
c. others	21	4.8

Pair-wise correlations were also calculated for social support and demographic variables including age, education, marriage, living arrangements, satisfaction of living arrangements, work experience and retirement pension. Living arrangements, satisfaction with living arrangements, retirement pension and work satisfaction were shown to have a positive relationship with social support. The F ratios and P values are distributed as $F = 5.126$, $p < .0000$, $F = 10.547$, $p < .0013$, $F = 4.1570$, $p < .0429$, $F = 5.957$, and $p < .0156$. These data indicate those variables that may explain away the relationship between social support and the bio-psychosocial well-being of elderly women.

The family care burden and well-being in ageing

More than one-third (33.7 per cent) of respondents experienced family care burdens. Among these respondents, 66.2 per cent had responsibility for taking care of children (grandchildren) and 33.8 per cent had the burden of caring for spouses and others.

With respect to the subjective care burden, care role strain was seen in several factors: economic pressure (25.3 per cent), time strain (47.3 per cent), recreation deprivation (28.7 per cent), emotional exhaustion (37.4 per cent), physical exhaustion (36.1 per cent), and anger (25.1 per cent).

Attitudes toward caregiving responsibilities indicated that elderly women have been socialized to play this role. Of the sample, 93.6 per cent reported family care as being a woman's natural duty; 92.5 per cent stated that women's care role was due to women's inherent nurturing characteristics; 87.3 per cent claimed that caregiving is part of elderly women's self-identity; and 74.2 per cent stated that family care was their duty in helping the younger generation. Clearly, gender roles in elderly women are significantly stereotyped.

The demographic variables of age, education, marriage, living arrangements, satisfaction with living arrangements, work experience, and retirement pension are not significantly related to the family care attitudes of elderly women.

The relationship between the family caregiving burdens and the physical, psychological and social well-being of elderly women is not significantly correlated. This lack of correlation might be explained away by the attitude toward family care of elderly women, i.e. that most of them have a strong identification with the family caregiving role, as described above.

Discussion and conclusion

Economic security is particularly related to well-being in women's ageing

Elderly women's economic adequacy is significantly correlated with psychological well-being, but not related to physical and social well-being. This finding is similar to Atchley's (1989) suggestion that economic circumstances are powerful factors influencing life satisfaction. This research result also corresponds to Thompson's findings that income is a significant factor in explaining the lower morale of the retired (Thompson, 1992). However, our data do not show that there is a significant relationship between economic adequacy and physical well-being and social well-being in Taiwanese elderly women. Cultural factors such as habits of hard work and an inherent tendency to associate age with hardship may explain away the lack of relationship between economic security and physical health and social well-being (including age identity). These social values come to play a central role in women's well-being in physical and social life.

Social support is not significantly related to bio-psychosocial well-being

The findings of this study indicate that the association between social support and well-being is not significant, which is in contrast to what activity theory and life-cycle theory suggest. However, other data in our research indicate that economic sufficiency is correlated to social support. Social support is also correlated to age, and is further related to education, retirement pensions, work satisfaction, spouse care demand, and grandchildren care demand. It is clear that older women are the subject of more accommodation care, health care, and outgoing care. The higher the education of the women, the more support they receive. Social support (including relatives living together, not living together and others) does not come to affect Taiwanese women's bio-psychosocial adjustment significantly, according to the data collected. The reason for this may be related to the use of resources by elderly women. These may not turn to social support as a mechanism for resolving their difficulties in life, but may instead rely solely on themselves. Therefore, the effect of social support on the well-being of elderly women is not clear or significant.

The family care burden is not significantly related to elderly women's bio-psychosocial well-being

About one third of the elderly women in our survey still continue their family care role in their family. Among them, one third have care responsibilities for a spouse and two thirds for grandchildren. However, the family care burden does not show a significant influence on their bio-psychosocial adjustment. Cultural values such as women's 'natural duty', 'inherent role', and 'care role self-identity' may explain away the relationship between family care responsibility and elderly women's bio-psychosocial adjustment.

Age, education and work experience are significant predictors of functional health or physical well-being

In the sample, younger women who are more highly educated and who have work experience, function more independently. Younger women in fact could be expected to have better functional health; and education may further affect functional health through the promotion of positive health practices. Work experience may also provide further economic support which would help opportunities for developing health practices.

Living arrangements, social activity/participation and economic adequacy are central to psychological well-being

In this study, women who are more satisfied with their living arrangements, who participate more in social activity, and are more satisfied with their economic resources maintain better emotional health. A close family, kinship, and community participation help foster social relationships and enrich daily life, reducing the occurrence of depression in elderly women.

These three key elements constitute a similar social context to that which is addressed by Bicher (1994). Bicher states that elderly people are easily exposed to social barriers, including inadequate retirement wages, inadequate community support, the division of labour within the family, and the high cost of housing. These socially constructive factors contribute to the general dependency of elderly people.

Education, the care burden and social activity participation are the determining factors of social well-being in elderly women

Women with higher education have more opportunities of participating in social activities and a reduced subjective burden of family care, leading to higher social well-being.

More highly educated elderly women are frequently informed about and capable of arranging more social contact, which develops a positive identity. As Antonucci (1985) states, social contact has an important mediating influence on the relationship between stress and well-being. The family caregivers' subjective feeling or attitudes toward family care burdens - rather than the objective family care burden - tends to be a significant factor affecting her social well-being. Although a caregiving role often restricts the caregiver's social and leisure activities, such as opportunities to visit or relax with friends and other community activities, social well-being is addressed or explained more by subjective feelings of care. Social exchange theory here can provide further explanation, where interaction between the caregiver and the care receiver, and an interactive environment with relatives and family support, may be the significant factors.

However, many (about two-thirds) elderly women in our sample were not family caregivers. For such people there is also a need for a structure which provides an attractive, convenient, and active social environment in order to build up a sense of comfortable ageing and functional independence.

In sum, the discussions above clearly demonstrate that social barriers such as a caring role within the family, inadequate retirement conditions, and inadequate social support contribute to the general dependency and poor health of elder women. These results correspond to feminist social constructive perspectives on ageing. However, it is the family experiences impinging on older women which determine their bio-psychosocial well-being; and it is social relationships, work experience, and the care burden which shape the ageing experiences of older women.

Having produced these results, we would hope that social policy, itself, also an important social determinant factor for ageing in women, does not negatively affect women's well-being in ageing. We would expect social policy for women (not simply for elderly women) to be woman-centred and woman-concerned rather than patriarchal and male-determinant. For instance, an employment and political structure facilitating an improvement in women's status in our society is called for, as is the creation of a resource structure such as an Older Women's Network to help older women achieve an integrated life in ageing. Some related policy issues are summed up below.

Policy implications

Designing a comprehensive policy for older women

Elderly women face social barriers when they are ageing, as a result of low education, less work experience and the lack of a retirement pension, coupled with family role burdens. The data indicate that a comprehensive social policy for elderly women, covering the disadvantages they suffer in ageing, is needed. Such a policy would demonstrate social awareness of women's ageing problems and their particular needs, such as the relieving of the family care burden, involvement in social activities and economic support.

Promoting social work to encourage activity amongst older women

The data indicate that older women's need for bio-psychosocial well-being is multi-layered. The first programme needing to be created is one designed to encourage elderly women to involve themselves more in social activities. Many elderly women stay at home without participating in social events, and this negatively affects their life adjustment. Second, network programmes for elderly women are also needed. These programmes should promote the participation of elderly women in community work in order to help them enrich their developmental and ageing life, and help them integrate their later life. Third, outreach programmes need to be developed in order to reach the women who need home care or meals-on-wheels services and others.

A programme to empower older women's economic competence

A 'second-employment programme' should be established for older women in order to help them earn a living and enrich their well-being. An employment programme for women in early life, however, could prove far more effective. Creating an equal-opportunity employment programme for women should be given priority in national policy. This would be a basic strategy for offsetting women's disadvantageous social treatment in later life.

References

Alford-Cooper, F. (1993), 'Women as family care-givers: an American social problem', *Journal of Women and Aging*, 5 (1), pp.43-57.
Antonucci, T. (1985), 'Personal characteristics, social support and social behavior', in R. Binstock and E. Shanas (eds), *Handbook of Aging and the Social Sciences*, Van Nostrand Reinhold, New York:, pp.94-128.
Arling, G. (1987), 'Strain, social support, and distress in old age', *Journal of Gerontology*, 42, pp.107-113.
Aronson, J. (1985), 'Family care of the elderly: underlying assumptions and their consequences', *Canadian Journal of Aging*, 4 (3), pp.115-125.
Aronson, J. (1990), 'Old women's experiences of needing care: choice or compulsion', *Canadian Journal of Aging*, 9 (3), pp.234-47.

Arson, J. (1994), 'Old woman and care: choice or compulsion?' in P. Leonard and B. Nichols (eds), *Gender, Aging and the State*, Black Rose Books, Montreal, pp.17-45.

Atchley, R.C. (1976), 'Selected social and psychological differences between men and women in later life', *Journal of Gerontology*, 31, pp.204-11.

Atchley, R.C. (1989), 'A continuity theory of normal ageing', *Gerontologist*, 29 (1), pp.183-90.

Bicher, M. (1994), 'The dependency relationship between daughters and mothers', in P. Leonard and B. Nichols (eds), *Gender, Aging and the State*, Black Rose Books, Montreal, pp.45-88.

Biegel, D., Sales, E. and Schulz, R. (1994), *Family Caregiving in Chronic Illness*, Sage, Newbury Park, CA.

Burnside, I. (1993), Healthy older women. *Journal of Women and Aging*, 5b (3/4), pp.9-24.

Collins, J.M. and Paul, P.B. (1994), 'Functional health, social support, and morale of older women living alone in Appalachia', *Journal of Women and Aging*, 6 (3), pp.39-52.

Coyne, J.C. and Delongis, A. (1986), 'Going beyond social support: The role of social relationship in adaptations', *Journal of Consulting and Clinical Psychology*, 54, pp.454-60.

De Viney, S. and Solomon, J.C. (1995), 'Gender differences in retirement income: comparison of theoretical explanations', *Journal of Women and Aging*, 7 (4), pp.83-99.

Dwyer, J.M. and Coward, R.T. (eds) (1992), *Gender, Families, and Elder Care*, Sage, Newbury Park CA.

Elwell, F and Maltbie-Crannell, A.D. (1994), 'The impact of role loss upon coping resources and life satisfaction of the elderly', *Journal of Gerontology*, 36 (2), pp.223-32.

Gale B.J. (1994), 'Functional health of older women: three dimensions', *Journal of Women and Aging*, 6 (1/2), pp.165-85.

Graham, H. (1983), 'Caring: a labour of love', in J. Finch and D. Groves (eds), *A Labour of Love: Women, Work and Caring*, Routledge and Kegan Paul, London, pp.130-25.

Haley, W.E., Levine, E.G., Brown, S.L., Berry, J.W., and Hughes, G.H. (1987), 'Psychological, social and health consequences of caring for a relative with senile dementia', *Journal of the American Geriatric Society*, 35, pp.405-11.

Hobfoll, S.E. (1986), *The Ecology of Stress*. Hemisphere, Washington, DC.

Hobfoll, S.E. (1988), 'Conservation of resources: A new attempt at conceptualization stress', *American Psychologist*, 44, pp.513-24.

Hooyman, N.R. and Gonyea, J. (1995), *Feminist Perspectives on Family Care: Policies for Gender Justice*, Sage, London.

Horowitz, A. (1994), 'Sons and daughters as caregivers to older parents: Differences in role performance and consequences', *Gerontologist*, 25 (6), pp.612-17.

Hu, Y.H. (1990), *The Role of Women in Elder Care - A Comparative Study between Taiwan and the U.S.*

Hu, Y.H. (1995), *Three Generations' Living Arrangement.* Ci-Liu publication, Taipei.

Korczyk, S.M. (1993), 'Gender issues in employers' pension plans', in R. V. Gurkhauser and D.L. Salisbury (eds), *Pensions in a Changing Economy*, Employee Benefit Research Institute, Washington, DC, pp.59-66.

Lawton, M.P. (1975), 'The Philadelphia Geriatric Center Morale Scale: a revision', *Journal of Gerontology*, 30, pp.85-9.

Lee, A. (1995a), *A Review of Traditional Poverty Research: A Feminism Perspective.* Paper presented at seminar on family and family household, Taipei.

Lee, A. (1995b), *Gender Difference in the Social Security System - An Example of Labour Insurance in Taiwan.* Paper presented at The Symposium on Demographic Change, National Health and Social Security, Academia Sinica, Taipei.

Lee, M.L. (1996), *Economic Reality and Security of Elderly Women in Taiwan.* Paper presented at Ageing and Elderly Care Symposium, National Demographic Association, Taipei.

Leonard, P. and Nichols, B. (1994), *Gender, Ageing and the State*, Black Rose Books, Montreal.

Liu, B.C. (1992), *Welfare Policy Reconstruction: From the Point of Female Family Caregivers' Reality.* Paper presented at the 2nd Seminar of National Women's Issues, Taipei.

Moen, P., Demmpster-McClain, D. and Williams, R.M. (1992). 'Successful ageing: a life-course perspective on women's multiple roles and health, *AJS*, 97 (6), pp.1612-38.

Osgood, N.J. (ed) (1982), *Life After Work: Retirement, Leisure, Recreation and the Elderly,* Praeger, New York.

Peace, S. (1986), 'The forgotten female: social policy and older women', in C. Phillipson, *Ageing and Social Policy: a Critical Assessment*, Gower, London, pp.61-86.

Perkins, K. (1992), 'Psychosocial implications of women and retirement', *Social Work*, 37 (6), pp.526-31.

Phillipson, C. (1982), *Capitalism and the Construction of Old Age.* Macmillan, London.

Reeves, J.B. and Darville, R.L. (1994), 'Social contact patterns and satisfaction with retirement of women in dual-care/earner families', *International Journal of Aging and Human Development*, 39 (2), pp.163-175.

Smith, R. (1984), 'The structured dependency of the elderly as a recent development: some special historical thoughts', *Aging and Society*, 4 (4), pp.409-28.

Stoller, E.P. (1984), 'Self-assessments of health by the elderly; the impact of informal assistance', *Journal of Health and Social Behavior*, 25, pp.260-70.

Thompson, P. (1992), 'I don't feel old: Subjective ageing and the search for meaning in later life', *Ageing and Society*, 12, pp.23-47.

Townsend, P. (1981), 'The structural dependency of the elderly: A creation of social policy in the twentieth century', *Ageing and Society*, 1 (1), pp.18-29.

Walker, A. (1982), *Community Care: The Family, the State and Social Policy*, Blackwell/Martin, Oxford.

Walker, A. (1983), 'Care for elderly people: a conflict between women and the state', in J. Finch and D. Groves (eds) *A Labour of Love: Women, Work and Caring*, Routledge and Kegan Paul, London, pp.106-28.

Walker, A (1985), 'From welfare state to caring society? The promise of informal support networks', in J. Jonker, R. Leaper, and J. Yoder (eds), *Support Networks in a Caring Community*, Martins, Lancaster, pp.14-49.

Walker, A. (1991), 'The relationship between the family and state in the care of older people', *Canadian Journal of Aging*, 10, pp.94-113.

Walker, A. (1992), 'Conceptual perspectives on gender and family caregiving', in J. Dwyer and R. Coward (eds), *Gender, Families, and Older Care*, Sage, Newbury Park, CA, pp.34-49.

Wang, L.R. (1997), *Elderly Women's Biological, Psychological and Social Adjustment*, Technical Research Report. Unpublished.

Witt, J.L. (1994), 'The gendered division of labour in parental caretaking: Biology or socialization?' *Journal of Women and Ageing*, 6 (1/2), pp.68-85.

13 Enhancing independence in old age

NICK LE MESURIER

Introduction

Older and disabled people are significant 'consumers' of long-term care, but can find themselves caught between the pressure on healthcare trusts to reduce length of stay, and local authorities to avoid admission to institutional care. The Audit Commission identified a 'vicious circle' resulting from increasing pressure on hospital beds as admissions rise and lengths of stay shorten, and a lack of services to facilitate recovery once the patient has returned home. The result is that, in the absence of sufficient alternatives to admission to institutional care, expenditure on residential and nursing home beds has gone up, often at the expense of funding for preventative services (Audit Commission, 1997).

Part of the problem lies with the ambiguous position which rehabilitation occupies in the continuum of care from acute intervention to maintenance provision. Evidence provided by a recent Kings Fund working paper based upon a series of focus group interviews found little consensus as to what actually constituted rehabilitation, though its role was widely perceived as facilitating discharge from hospital (Robinson and Batstone, 1996). Perceptions of rehabilitation were often coloured by professional allegiances. Medical models focus upon restoring the passive individual to normal levels of functioning, while social models emphasise the person's right to achieve a preferred lifestyle and the professional's role in tackling social and environmental barriers which might hinder that achievement (ibid).

This ambiguity may be compounded by an assumption that rehabilitation is a function of other services rather than a service in its own right. At a policy level, rehabilitation is not always mentioned in health service contracts and community care plans (Nocon and Baldwin, 1998). The Audit Commission found that rehabilitation for older people with hip fracture was frequently unavailable on discharge from hospital (Audit Commission, 1996). The multidisciplinary nature of rehabilitation leaves it vulnerable to reductions in funding when acute services are under threat. Disputes over service responsibilities, particularly between health and social services, can undermine otherwise promising opportunities for collaboration, especially when the outcomes of a service provided by one agency are perceived to benefit another. Yet there can be no doubt that rehabilitation requires collaboration. A review by Stuck et al (1993), highlighted in a Kings Fund/Audit Commission report on systematic reviews of effective practice in rehabilitation (Sinclair and Dickinson, 1998), outlined the importance of comprehensive geriatric assessment in identifying impairments and disabilities in relation to common risks such as falls, immobility and cognitive impairment.

Simply attaching a rehabilitation service to the existing system of discharge and assessment will not, however, address the discontinuity which exists between hospital and community services. If rehabilitation is to work it should be an integral part of the process, but this requires not only the resources and service mechanisms to facilitate effective transfer, but also a revised conceptual framework in which the promotion of independence is seen as a primary goal in its own right.

To this end, the White Paper, *Modernising Social Services* (Department of Health, 1998), directly addressed the need for more emphasis to be placed upon services which promote independence in clients. The Social Services Modernisation Fund provided two specific grants over three years from 1999 to help the NHS and local authorities develop rehabilitation and other services to reduce unnecessary admissions to institutional care, improve hospital discharge arrangements, and improve rehabilitation services. The Promoting Independence: Partnership Grant provides £650 million (or approximately £4.3 million per local authority in England) to help joint working between health and social services agencies. Local authorities are obliged to provide Joint Investment Plans with the NHS to identify spending plans. In addition, the Promoting Independence: Prevention Grant provides funds to enable local authorities to target resources to people requiring low-level support, for whom access to higher levels of care might be prevented or delayed by the application of improved risk assessment. These people frequently had been excluded from care as many local authorities sought to control expenditure by tightening eligibility criteria. The failure to apply low-level interventions in many cases resulted in a concentration on crisis intervention, with few alternatives to admission to hospital, residential, or intensive home care available (DoH, 1998).

At the time of writing, many local authorities are responding to the opportunities presented by the Social Services Modernisation Fund by seeking to develop rehabilitation services of one kind or another. There is as yet no clear pattern to this development, and for many authorities the challenges are of an unprecedented kind. The obligation to cooperate with local NHS trusts in this way raises many questions. For example, should eligibility be determined solely on a clinical basis, as is generally the case of persons applying for treatment from the NHS, or should access to a rehabilitation service which is 'led' by a local authority take into consideration actual or potential financial implications for that authority if the applicant were not to receive rehabilitation?

Moreover, there is a likelihood that where gaps in service provision exist in a locality, the introduction of a new rehabilitation service may be welcomed by providers, but may have to face 'competition' from other services for funding. Though rehabilitation has a certain prominence, it is not one of the Health of the Nation targets. There is a risk that some NHS providers will be happy to support development of a further rehabilitation service in principle, but lack the means or the will to make a substantial commitment.

If interdisciplinary collaboration is challenging across health and social services divides, intraprofessional conflicts within the local authority can also arise when attempts are made to integrate rehabilitation into existing services. The confidence and knowledge of referrers is crucial, both within the local authority and without, but there are obstacles to overcome in introducing a form of provision which operates to a different ethos and to different working methods from those which have become established over many years. Should a rehabilitation service 'stand alone' as a separate service with its own staff and line management within the local authority, or should it attempt to integrate with other local authority services, particularly home care, by using existing staff and 'fitting in' with established rotas? These are the sort of questions which service managers are addressing in the changeover to a form of provision with a clear focus on time-limited interventions and the promotion of independence for service users.

In order to illustrate the way in which this can work, the remainder of this paper will describe a community rehabilitation, or 'Re-ablement' service developed by Worcestershire Social Services Department.

The re-ablement service in South Worcestershire

The development of the Re-ablement Service by Worcestershire Community NHS trust and Worcestershire social services department was driven by a combination of budget deficits, poor co-ordination between hospital and community services in the county, a culture of high dependency on residential and nursing home provision, and limited resources for reviewing existing placements. From the point of view of social services, these negative factors were offset by a tradition of successful, if limited, health and social services collaborations, particularly GP attached social workers (Cumella et al, 1996). Within the social services department there was an awareness that the existing system of access to social services care, in particular domiciliary care, served to dis-able service users by its failure to incorporate any form of therapeutic assessment. In short, clients were assessed on the basis of what they were perceived as unable to do, not on their potential for recovery.

The Re-ablement Service was created in June 1996. It works by providing a comprehensive multidisciplinary therapeutic assessment and time-limited programmes of rehabilitation in the client's own home. The service was originally joint-funded, but has lately been funded wholly by the social services department.

How does re-ablement work?

The Re-ablement Service is currently a single team including:
- 1 whole time equivalent (WTE) state registered physiotherapist and 1 WTE occupational therapist, contracted from Worcestershire Community NHS trust and responsible for assessing referrals and for implementing, supervising and reviewing programmes;
- 1 WTE full-time social worker manager;
- 1 WTE therapy assistant, who manages rotas, supervises re-ablement assistants;
- a full-time secretary;
- six 're-ablement assistants' contracted on a block purchase agreement from two care agencies in the county and trained by the therapists to undertake the majority of 'hands-on' work.

Eligibility criteria for the service are not precisely defined. In general, people not likely to benefit from re-ablement are:

- those with dementia;
- those with a terminal illness likely to result in death within approximately three months;
- those in an advanced stage of a progressive neurological disorder;
- those under 18 years of age.

Referrals receive a multidisciplinary assessment, first on paper then, if eligible, face to face. In many cases assessment and intervention are led by one therapist, according to the nature of the problem. Clients and carers are always fully involved in face to face assessments. Goals are identified and agreed, and plans drawn up to specify the best way to achieve them. The small size of the team and the shared office facilities provide many opportunities for informal discussion, and staff develop an understanding of each other's knowledge and skills. Professional boundaries thus become blurred. Weekly team meetings allow both new referrals and ongoing cases to be discussed, and there is a constant process of feedback and review.

Programmes generally consist of a series of planned contacts between the re-ablement assistant and the client in which specific activities will be undertaken in the location where they will be practised once re-ablement has withdrawn. The activities undertaken will depend on the needs of the client. Some clients are helped to walk a certain distance each day, others to prepare a meal, or to use a particular piece of exercise equipment, or to access local facilities. Frequently, programmes consist of a number of specified goals. In most cases clients have lost confidence in their abilities, and it is this factor at least as much as their actual illness or impairment which hinders their return to independence.

Usually the most intensive interventions are at the start of programmes, and a client can receive three or four calls a day, each up to an hour if necessary. Gradually the rate of contact will tail off, until the client is just receiving a few check calls. But in all cases, the re-ablement assistant will not 'do for' the client, but will often simply stand beside them while they do it themselves. Clients often find this somewhat disconcerting, but it is regarded by staff as the key to successful re-ablement. All clients who complete a programme are reviewed three months after completion. The service normally carries an active caseload of about 18 cases.

The service operates a charging policy based on that for normal home care services and taking account of the amount of state benefits the client is receiving. No charge is made for assessment or contact with therapists. Capital assets are disregarded in the assessment process for re-ablement. Financial assessment is undertaken by the re-ablement team. No charge is made to the client's GP. In addition, the normal charges are applied for use of aids and equipment, though the Re-ablement Service owns a small stock of assessment aids which can be loaned to the client free of charge.

Evaluation

The Service has been evaluated and a report is available (Le Mesurier and Cumella, 1998). Analysis of case records indicated that:
- referrals had come from a wide range of sources within health and social services, though the majority were from within the social services system;
- the majority of clients were elderly (age range 26-95);
- almost half of all clients referred commenced a re-ablement programme; and almost all of these (88%) completed successfully;
- assessments of functional ability before and after the programme showed statistically significant levels of improvement.

A further analysis based upon follow-up calls to 100 clients who had been in receipt of home care services found that 76 were independent of those services up to four months after completion.

The costs of re-ablement provision were compared with home care services provided by Worcestershire Social Services. Using estimates provided by the Personal Social Services Research Unit (Netten and Dennett, 1997), an estimated unit cost of £16.88 per contact hour was calculated. This compared with a unit cost of £10.50 per contact hour for home care services calculated by Worcestershire Social Services Department.

In order to illustrate cost effectiveness, case details of each of the clients in the cohort were analysed to identify level of intervention and outcome, and estimated annualised costs of service provision before and after intervention. As an example, case 1 (see table 13.1) outlines the costs of a case in which a client who had been receiving home care for some time prior to admission to hospital undertook a re-ablement programme on discharge with the aim of improving her skills in mobility indoors, meals preparation and personal care. Not only were these aims achieved in this case, but she regained the confidence and ability to walk outside as well. She did not take up home care again on discharge. The estimated annualised costs of continuing to provide home care to her had re-ablement not been available are presented as Option 1, and the estimated cost of her re-ablement programme presented as Option 2. The total estimated net savings are presented in the final row.

Table 13.1 Case 1 - estimated net saving of re-ablement over home care

Service Option	Cost
Option 1 - 8 hours/week home care (estimated annualised cost @ £10.50 per contact hour)	£4368.00
Option 2 - Re-ablement programme 35.5 contact hours over 8 weeks (calculated @ £16.88 per contact hour)	£599.76
Total Estimated Net Saving	£3768.76

Not all interventions were so straightforward, however. Case 2 (see table 13.2) describes the costs of a case in which a client who had been receiving a home care service was admitted to residential care following discharge from hospital. The re-ablement service worked with this client in the residential home with the aim of improving her mobility, transfers and use of stairs sufficiently to enable her to return home. In the event, after a fairly short intervention, she made sufficient progress to return home, but not as much as the therapists thought she could make. She did not want to give up her home care service, and so retained it at the same level. At the time of referral, however, this client was likely to have remained in residential care. Option 1 therefore presents an estimated annualised cost of residential care. Option 2 presents estimated costs of re-ablement, with the cost of the residential care she received and an estimated annualised cost of home care provision. Even though this lady did not return to full independence, a brief intervention by the re-ablement service enabled her to return home and avoided substantially higher residential care costs.

Table 13.2 Case 2 - estimated net saving of re-ablement over residential care

Service Option	Cost
Option 1	
Residential care (annualised cost @ £247 per week	£12,844.00
Option 2	
Re-ablement programme (9 hours contact time @ £16.88 per contact hour	£151.92
Residential care for 3 weeks @ £247 per week	£741.00
4.5 hours / week home care (estimated annualised cost @ £10.50 per contact hour)	£2457.00
Total Estimated Net Saving	£9494.08

From the management perspective, the re-ablement service was seen as offering a 'best value' option in the provision of services to people at risk of losing their independence. Effectiveness was achieved as a consequence of a multidisciplinary structure supporting an ongoing process of assessment and review, dedicated to the development of a client's abilities and confidence within a clearly planned and time-limited programme.

Re-ablement was seen as exemplifying important aims, attitudes and issues, including:

- a commitment to solutions, particularly assessment strategies, which promote choice and independence for clients;
- a commitment to multidisciplinary and inter-agency working;
- a desire to avoid duplicated or delayed assessments;
- a commitment to joint planning strategies based upon open discussion of resource issues.

In practical terms, the key to successful rehabilitation is to find something that the client particularly wants to do and which, for them, is meaningful within the context of their daily life. Team members felt they had to be aware of and willing to overcome personal and professional prejudices which could influence their judgement and attitudes towards the client. In one case a client's main desire was to achieve sufficient mobility out of doors to go to the betting shop. The re-ablement service incorporated that aim into his programme and found ways of enabling him to achieve his ambitions safely.

The future of re-ablement

The current process of accessing social services care has traditionally imposed a restricted set of choices on clients. Assessments have been carried out in the context of the local authority's own eligibility criteria, which have more to do with the services they have available at the time and the range of services available elsewhere in the locality, than with each clients' needs and wishes. Local authorities have effectively decided what constitutes need, and indeed, what constitutes a disabled person (Meredith, 1996).

Re-ablement offers obvious advantages over this system by providing a mechanism in which applicants for services can receive a comprehensive multidisciplinary assessment at a significant point in the pathway into care. The key features would be a single point of access and a form of therapeutic assessment based upon a triage, in which the client's potential for improvement and rehabilitation are foregrounded. Figure 13.1 illustrates this basic process.

Re-ablement is ideally suited to respond to those clients who require less intensive interventions - usually in the community - for whom opportunities exist to prevent or delay further dependency on institutional care. The concept of intermediate care provides a framework in which levels of intervention outside the acute setting are established and the responsibilities of health and social services providers defined. Properly resourced, re-ablement can occupy a key position at a level at which genuine preventative work can be done. Table 13.3 illustrates this framework as a continuum proposed by Worcestershire Social Services and Worcestershire Community NHS Trust. If the benefits of re-ablement are to be fully realised this is likely to be the sort of structure in which it will have to work.

Figure 13.1 The process of multi-disciplinary assessment

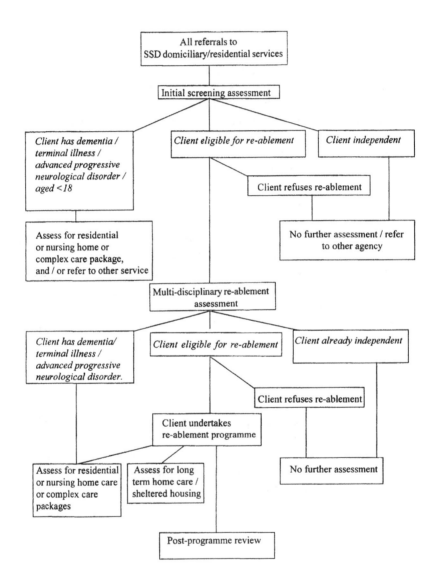

Table 13.3 Proposed continuum of intermediate care

Level	Care Definition	Care environment	Agency	Patient Category
1	Intensive, multi-disciplinary care required - led by primary care with some consultant support when necessary	Community Hospital	Health	Intensive rehab' Wide range of medical and surgical conditions General rehab' Specialist stroke rehab' Orthogeriatric rehab' Antibiotic therapy COAD, Asthmatics, Diabetes, Parkinson's Palliative/Terminal Care
2	Acute Chronic	Patient's home 24 hour service DN/Hospital at Home Service	Health	Blood Transfusions IV therapy Selected orthopaedic/ surgical Patient not requiring extensive rehab' therapy Management of chronic conditions, wound care, diabetes, terminal care.
3	Ongoing care requiring less intensive interventions - mainly therapy/ social care led	Re-ablement scheme (inpatient or outpatient) Intensive home support	Health and Social Services	Requiring ongoing therapy Elderly frail patient 'off legs' Ongoing rehab' following CVA, orthopaedic surgery, etc.
4	Continuing care required	Home, residential home, nursing home, sheltered housing.	Health and Social Category	People requiring continuing care

NOTE Patients/clients may access any level of care
at any time depending on the individual needs.
Source: Worcestershire County Intermediate Care Steering Group (1998).

References

Audit Commission (1996), *United They Stand: Co-ordinating Care for Elderly Patients with Hip Fracture*, Audit Commission, London.

Audit Commission (1997), *The Coming of Age: Improving Care Services for Older People*, Audit Commission, London.

Cumella, S., Le Mesurier, N. and Tomlin, H. (1996), *Social Work in Practice: An Evaluation of the Care Management Received by Elderly People from Social Workers based in GP Practices in South Worcestershire*, The Martley Press, Martley, Worcestershire.

Department of Health (1998), *Modernising Social Services*, HMSO, London.

Le Mesurier, N. and Cumella, S. (1998), *Enhancing Independence: An Evaluation of the Effectiveness of Re-ablement Provision in South Worcestershire*, Worcestershire County Council, Worcester.

Meredith, B. (1996), *The Community Care Handbook : The Reformed System Explained*, Age Concern England, London.

Netten, A. and Dennett, J. (1997), *Unit Costs of Health and Social Care 1997*, Personal Social Services Research Unit, University of Kent, Canterbury.

Nocon, A. and Baldwin, S. (1998) *Trends in Rehabilitation Policy: A Review of the Literature*, Kings Fund, London.

Robinson, J. and Batstone, G. (1996), *Rehabilitation, a Development Challenge: a Kings Fund Working Paper*, Kings Fund, London.

Sinclair, A. and Dickinson, A. (1998), *Effective Practice in Rehabilitation, the Evidence of Systematic Reviews*, Kings Fund. London.

Stuck, A.E., Siu, A.L, Wieland, G.D., Adams, J. and Rubenstein, L.Z. (1993), 'Comprehensive geriatric assessment: a meta-analysis of controlled trials', *Lancet*, 342, pp.1032-1036.

Worcestershire County Intermediate Care Steering Group (1998), *Intermediate Care: Information and Guidance for Locality Planning Groups*, Worcestershire County Council, Worcester.

14 Community care for elderly people in Taiwan: illusion, vision or reality?

YUAN-SHIE HWANG

Introduction

Community care has become a live issue in the last two decades all over the developed world and is now becoming a matter of great concern in Taiwan as well. However, there has been no concrete policy to guide its development. The term 'community care' first formally appeared in official documents in 1996 in a quite concise way (Interior, 1996). But this is not to say the concept had never existed before its formal introduction. Since the 1960s the community had already been regarded as an important base for carrying out welfare services under the guideline of the 'Present-stage Social Policy of Ming-Shen Principle 1965' (Executive Yuan, 1965). But this amounted to no more than a political slogan. Not until the mid-1980s did the community, as an important unit of providing care for the elderly, really receive attention from the government. Even so, little real effort was made to put such an idea into practice. What the elderly had was just some piecemeal welfare services. Until recently, projects approximating to community care have merely been put into operation in a pilot way.

The increase in the elderly population has put enormous pressure on government to pay more attention. A recent survey has also shown that elderly welfare services have been the objects of most concern and, therefore, could expect to be given the highest priority among various welfare provisions (Interior, 1997a). Strategies for coping with the needs of elderly care have, in short, become a matter of considerable concern for society. In response, community care has been thought of as one possible approach to meet such needs and has, therefore, given rise to much debate.

This chapter aims to discuss and review the development of community care policy and its practice in Taiwan. Four main points will be raised and discussed. First, the meaning of community care in the Taiwanese context will be discussed. Second, the development of community care policy and practice up to the present day will be reviewed. Third, myths about community care in Taiwan will be analysed. Finally, this chapter will end with a discussion of whither community care - is it an illusion, vision or reality?

Before entering these debates, the social contexts and the needs for care of the elderly will be delineated.

Social contexts and the needs for care

The economic transformation of Taiwan has involved, first, a dramatic shift from an agricultural to an industrial economy and then, more recently, a shift from simpler industrial processes (textile manufacturing, etc.) to new high-technology industry. There is no doubt that the transformation has contributed to the improvement of living standards and, as a result, people tend to live much longer than in previous generations. The life expectancy for males and females at birth was respectively 71.96 and 77.90 years in 1998. People aged 65 and over as a percentage of total population increased from 5.5 per cent in 1987 to 8.1 per cent in 1997 (see table 14.1). It is expected that the figure will increase to 14 per cent in 2012.

Table 14.1 Population aged 65 and over (1960-1997)

	1960	1970	1980	1987	1990	1993	1997
People aged 65 and over (thousand)	268	429	762	1,089	1,264	1,557	1,745
Percentage of total population	2.5	3.0	4.3	5.5	6.2	7.1	8.1

Source: Council for Economic Planning and Development (1998).

The economic transformation has also had a considerable impact upon the general fertility rate, family structure, agricultural population, and female labour participation rate. The general fertility rate decreased from 112 in 1971 to 54 in 1996. The average persons per household declined from 5.6 in 1971 to 3.5 in 1997. The non-agricultural population as a percentage of the total increased from 60.3 per cent in 1971 to 82.8

per cent in 1997. The increase in the elderly population, coupled with a reduction in the child population, has boosted the so-called elderly dependency ratio (number of people aged 65⁺ per 1,000 people aged 15-64), which increased from 8.4 per cent in 1987 to 11.6 per cent in 1997 (see tables 14.2 and 14.3).

Table 14.2 Family size and non-agricultural population (1971-1997)

Year	General fertility rate	Average persons per household	Non-agricultural population as percentage of total population
1971	112	5.6	60.3
1976	105	5.2	66.3
1981	89	4.7	71.9
1986	60	4.3	77.9
1991	58	3.9	79.5
1996	54	3.6	82.7
1997	n.a	3.5	82.8

Source: DGBAS (1997).

Table 14.3 Population by dependent and working age group

	1960	1965	1970	1975	1980	1987	1993	1997
Child dependency ratio	87.3	85.5	69.1	57.7	50.4	42.9	37.1	32.6
Elderly dependency ratio	4.8	5.1	5.1	5.7	6.7	8.4	10.5	11.6
Total dependency ratio	92.0	90.6	74.2	63.4	57.2	51.3	47.6	44.2

Source: CEPD (1998).

Traditionally, the emphasis on filial piety has been seen as a guarantee for one's later life. Familist ideologies have been of primary importance, being deeply embedded in people's minds, particularly in the case of elderly people. Nevertheless, the decline in family size means that the predominant family structure has gradually transformed from stem family to nuclear family. According to a recent survey of elderly people's living conditions, 72.53 per cent of elderly people thought the best mode of housing for them in the future would be to live with, or next door to their children (Interior, 1997b). However, another survey has shown only 40.4 per cent of interviewees were actually living with their parents (Interior, 1997a). In addition, women have for long been expected to play a bigger part in providing care for their own or their husband's dependants. However, the female labour participation rate has increased from 39.13 per cent in 1978 to 45.64 per cent in 1997 (DGBAS, 1998). Although this rate of increase is not so high, it can be expected to have an impact upon the supply of main carers. All these demographic trends and facts suggest that it is getting more difficult to expect the family to continue functioning as the main provider of care for elderly people.

It is clear now that caring for elderly people has been and will continue to be a matter of great concern for society. It is impossible that the government can avoid the subject under these changing circumstances. Therefore, a new forward-looking policy for coping with the problems caused by an ageing population inevitably has to be taken into serious consideration.

The meaning of community care in the Taiwanese context

The meaning of community care is still vague and arguable, even though many authors have done their best to define it (Higgins, 1989). In England, the 1989 White Paper *Caring for People* started by saying that

> ...Community care means providing the services and support which people who are affected by problems of ageing, mental illness, mental handicap and physical or sensory disability need to be able to live in their own homes, or in homely settings in the community. The Government is firmly committed to a policy of community care which will enable such people to achieve their full potential (DoH, 1989).

Whereas Bulmer (1997, p.45) considers that

> ...'Community care' is concerned with the resources available outside institutional structures, particular in the informal relationships of the family, friends and neighbours, as a means of providing.

The first definition seems to focus on stressing that people who need to be cared for will be better off living in 'homes' or 'homely settings' in the community. The 'homely' settings 'in the community' may embrace all care except that provided by hospitals. Therefore, it seems to imply that community care means home care and homely institutional care. The help may sometimes come from social and health sectors, but it is difficult to determine where the boundary is. Conversely, the second definition puts more emphasis on informal care, while the role of government seems to be much less prominent. People may think that from institutional to informal care can be seen as a 'continuum' or 'spectrum', but this is questionable because people's various needs for care may cross social and health divides.

It is not easy to understand what is meant by community care in the Taiwanese context without explaining a similar but rather confused and controversial term, 'Social Welfare Communitisation' (SWC), which signifies community-oriented welfare services. At the National Conference for Community Development 1995, SWC was proposed and defined as 'a concrete measure and working method which sufficiently incorporates social welfare systems and community development'. It was argued that SWC included three dimensions (Interior, 1995):

1. informal community care services: including supportive, consultative, instrumental services and collaborative activities;
2. institutional community welfare activities: one or more community welfare programmes provided by public or private agencies or groups in the public interest, and the advancing of community collaboration and autonomy by using community work methods;
3. integrated community service network: providing referrals for community residents in need of various services.

Further, SWC can be divided into broad and narrow definitions. In the broad sense, it means providing all sorts of welfare services for vulnerable residents, including children, adolescents, women, the elderly, and the disabled, by creating a resources network in the community. By contrast, in a narrow sense, it means providing welfare services for those who need to be cared for most, such as the elderly and disabled, in their own homes or in a homely setting, with help from informal or formal service networks in the community. Thus may the need for institutional care be reduced and people be enabled to live with dignity and independence at home. In general, the state, informal networks and non-government agencies are expected to share responsibility for providing care for those who need medical, nursing or social care in the community. Obviously, the narrow sense of SWC is equivalent to so-called 'community care'. In the words of Hsieh and Liu (1995):

> Community care involves two categories: medical and nursing interventions, and social services. In the medical and nursing field, community care means

providing preventive, medical and long-term services by local health centres, clinics, day care, short-term care, and hospice centres. In the social service field, community care means providing statutory services by government, and taking advantage of private sectors, families, kin or volunteers to provide care. Therefore, community care means a range of supporting services providing care for those who need medical, nursing and social services.

According to the above arguments, the meaning of community care in the Taiwanese context may include the following four elements:

1. Community care is a part of social welfare communitization.
2. Community care provides medical, nursing and social care for those who need to be cared for or for carers at home or in the community.
3. The providers of community care may include government, informal networks and non-profit organizations.
4. Community care stresses the capacity of communities for self-help and autonomy as its final goal.

In sum, social welfare communitisation is a working method and target which joins part of the social welfare system (personal social services) and part of community work models, such as community development and community organisation. Community care is an important part of social welfare communitisation. The relationship between these terms may be structured as in figure 14.1.

Figure 14.1 Relationship between social welfare, community development, social welfare communitisation and community care

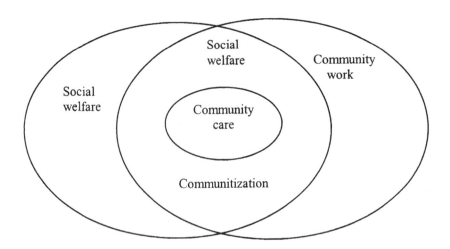

Compared to the definitions suggested by the 1989 UK White Paper and Bulmer, the meaning of community care in the Taiwanese context is rather confused. Unlike the White Paper's definition, there is no direct way to define what community care is by the official document in Taiwan. In addition, even though SWC stresses the importance of partnership between formal and informal sectors, it places more emphasis on informal care in order to reach the goal of replacing 'care in the community' with 'care by the community'. This is similar to the definition provided by Bulmer.

The development of community care policy

As already explained, the community has since the 1960s been regarded as an important base for carrying out welfare services under the guideline of the 'Present-stage Social Policy of Ming-Shen Principle 1965' (Executive Yuan, 1965). But there was no further official document putting forward ideas relating to community care until 1981. The 1981 official document, *Establishment Criteria for the Senior Welfare Agency* (Taiwan Provincial Government, 1981), prescribed that social welfare agencies should provide 'in-home care services'. This is the first mention of a measure relating to community care. Later, the 1986 document - the Five-year Plan for the Second Stage of the Programme for Community Development, Taiwan Province' - stressed the importance of building an integrated community social welfare system so as to provide various services for children, adolescents, the elderly, the disabled, mental patients, low-income households, etc. Many tangible measures for caring for elderly people in the community were introduced, such as an in-home (nursing) service, day care, lunch clubs, etc.

Since this time, community-oriented welfare services have attracted much government attention and been included in a higher level of government policy documents - the '1991 Outline of Community Development Work' promulgated by the Ministry of the Interior, and the *1992 Contemporary Implementation Project for Community Development Work* proclaimed by the Government of Taiwan Province (Taiwan Provincial Government, 1992). These two documents both suggested creating a community-oriented welfare service system. In the sphere of elderly services, the Projects point to setting up senior citizen clubs and providing in-home care services.

At the 1994 National Conference for Social Welfare, the Department of Social Affairs proposed that future strategies of caring for elderly people should include 'linking community resources to strengthen family functioning and social responsibility, to build a supportive community system, and to reinforce community care' (Interior, 1994). This may be the first time that the idea and concept of community care was clearly used on a formal occasion by central government. The 1994 Outline of Social Welfare Policy promulgated by the Executive Yuan (Cabinet) promised to 'reinforce community care and nursing facilities for the senior citizen' and to 'build in-home service networks by integrating community resources'. In addition, its Guidelines set out to 'integrate aged welfare agencies within particular areas, so as to provide services such as in-home care, an in-home nursing service, day care and recreation, etc.'. The Guidelines also mentioned building a community-oriented service network for in-home care. However, the actual term 'community care' still did not appear in the Outline or the Guidelines.

Nevertheless, community care had already become a policy focus for elderly welfare provision by the first half of the 1990s. Two official documents, according to suggestions of the National Conference for Community Development 1995, were published by the Ministry of the Interior: 'Practical Key Points for Promoting Social Welfare Communitization' (PKPPSWC) in 1996 and 'Practical Key Points for Promoting Social Welfare Privatization' (PKPPSWP) in 1997. The term 'community care' appears for the first time in the former official central government document (the PKPPSWC) which lists the aims of community care as follows:

1. To enhance organized and planned welfare delivery so as to take care of children, adolescents, women, the elderly, the disabled and low-income households within the community quickly and effectively;
2. To improve the quality of life of those who need to be cared for, by strengthening family and community functioning and the availability of the social welfare system;
3. To make sure that welfare services can be fulfilled at grass-roots level by incorporating the social welfare system and community development work, by integrating resources inside and outside the community, and by building up a community welfare service network.

The guiding principles of the PKPPSWC contain the following five key elements:

1. Prioritization of welfare needs: to push the implementation of welfare services item by item according to the nature of local circumstances and community priorities;

2. Unified welfare planning: to combine and make the best possible use of resources inside and outside the community so as to plan welfare activities by way of unification;
3. Promoting the efficiency of welfare resources: to take advantage of social welfare resources sufficiently and to pursue more efficiency by avoiding repeated wastage in resource usage;
4. Universalizing welfare participation: to encourage residents and organizations inside and outside the community to join in community welfare work voluntarily and spontaneously;
5. Team action to encourage welfare work: to encourage community welfare work collectively by integrating related administrative units, welfare agencies, groups, schools, temples, churches, etc.

Community care, according to the PKPPSWC, will be carried out by way of the miniaturisation and communitization of welfare agencies, developing the outreach services of welfare agencies, and making the best use of community resources. The PKPPSWC also stresses the importance of identifying residents' problems and needs, and building a community welfare service network.

Even though the PKPPSWC does not have 'community care' in its title, the character of community care has undoubtedly influenced its content. In addition, the publication of the PKPPSWP in early 1997 has shown the government's intention regarding the privatisation of welfare provisions. Its aim is 'to promote social welfare service provision collectively by coordinating social resources and commissioning from the private sector'. Commission can be of two types: 'publicly owned, privately run' and 'contracted out' service provision. The former involves the government in providing land, buildings, facilities and equipment for the private sector to run service provisions. The latter involves the government in contracting with the non-profit sector for service provision without providing land or buildings.

The 1997 amendatory 'Senior Citizen Welfare Law' prescribes that local governments should provide or coordinate private resources to offer in-home services for elderly people suffering from physical or mental distress and loss of daily normal functioning so that they can obtain the continuing care they need at home. These services include home (nursing) care, home services, friendly visiting, paying regards through telephone, meal service, improvements to the home environment, etc. The Law also requires that welfare service agencies should provide day care, respite care, voluntary services, occasional protection and temporary settlement, retirement preparation services, counselling services, and comprehensive services for elderly people.

In May 1998 the Executive Yuan passed the 'Project for Strengthening Services geared to Caring for Elderly People' (PSSCEP). Various government departments involved in issues of caring for elderly people, including the Department of Health (DoH), Ministry of the Interior, Council for Veterans' Affairs, Council for Labour Affairs, Provincial and County governments, have been required to provide services collaboratively. Many tangible measures relating to community care have been proposed, including:

1. To provide services such as day care, recreation, social intercourse, psychological counselling, rehabilitation, etc. for elderly people by integrating registered social welfare agencies, local elderly centres, community activities centres, religious loci, etc.

2. To provide accessible and appropriate care arrangements for patients who need long-term care after professional assessment by conducting demonstration projects on 'resource management centres for long-term care'.

3. To check up on elderly people who live completely alone and to incorporate various resources so as to provide services, according to their needs, such as paying regards through telephone, friendly visiting, training for self-care, home help, escort services, transport services, etc.

4. To provide home services by setting up 'community support centres for home services' at each town.

5. To provide labour supportive projects such as a respite service, occasional or short-term care.

6. To clarify the functions and establishment criteria of various long-term care resources such as nursing homes, day nursing care, day care, caring agencies, etc., and then, according to actual needs and each unit's rights and obligations, to compile a systematic plan to integrate the various agencies.

7. To check up and repair abandoned or unused public buildings, and then contract with the non-profit sector in order to have them set up and managed as community-style elderly care or nursing homes.

8. To encourage public and private hospitals to transfer spare beds into nursing homes, according to the principle of miniaturization and communitization.

In the health field, long-term care for the elderly is also one of the salient issues for the Department of Health (DoH). At the National Conference for Social Welfare 1998, the DoH promised to investigate

'Preferred Projects for Executing Community Care' and to propose a 'Three-year Plan for the Long-term Care of the Elderly'. The DoH intends to integrate and build a continuous and comprehensive long-term care system through intensive coordination and collaboration between health and social sectors. This will be implemented via two approaches: institutional care and community care. The former involves three measures: (1) encouraging public hospitals to transfer some of their beds into nursing homes; (2) encouraging the private sector to set up nursing homes; and (3) fostering models of multi-level care services such as day nursing care and day care. This last involves measures such as encouraging and developing in-home nursing care, in-home services, respite care, etc., and encouraging religious and charity organizations to set up 'support groups for carers'. In addition, in-home nursing care is already covered by National Health Insurance. Clearly, in Taiwan, community care policy for elderly people has demonstrably advanced within the last few years.

Community care in practice

Policies and legislation relating to community care for elderly people are rather new. Yet some of the items referred to have existed and been in effect since the 1980s. The provision of community care in practice can be divided into two parts: social and health sectors. In the social field, the main provisions for the aged include in-home care and day care. The Taiwan Provincial Government started to provide in-home care in 1987 and this has since been implemented throughout its 21 counties. Meanwhile Taipei City started from 1984 and Kaohsiung from 1982. The providers are various, including paid full-time and part-time in-home carers, and unpaid volunteers supervised by social workers. The provision, either day-care or in-home care, has increasingly been shifted from the public sector to the voluntary sector through contracting out in recent years. It is worth noting that those cared for overwhelmingly are elderly people with middle/low or low incomes. Table 14.4 provides a brief illustration of the volume of day care and in-home care over recent years.

Meanwhile in the health field, there are two kinds of in-home care services provided by the NHI: hospital-based and independent nursing agencies contracted to the hospitals. Discharged patients who need to be cared for continuously - on doctor's advice or orders - will be looked after. At the time of writing, there are 173 in-home nursing agencies and

47 nursing homes having contracts with the Bureau of the NHI for providing in-home nursing care.

Table 14.4 Day care and in-home care for aged (number of cases)

	Day-care	In-home care
1993	118,316	n.a
1994	119,912	161,496
1995	184,513	152,541
1996	197,086	165,297
1997	256,132	163,221

Source: DGBAS (1997).

Day care and day nursing care for elderly people have been provided by the social and health sectors respectively. In the social service sphere, the department of social affairs of the Ministry of the Interior has subsidized county governments to provide day care services since 1989. In the health service sphere, there are 13 hospitals and 1 local health centre providing day care service. These services include health counselling, nursing, rehabilitation, recreation, meals, transport, emergency treatment, escort, etc. Recently, the number of day care centres has been expanding at an increasing rate and governments have been trying to provide more through contracting out. Such centres are not only for those who are healthy or, at least, who are able to take care of themselves with a little help, but for the disabled as well.

In 1994, four community care pilot projects were introduced in Taipei City – two for elderly people and two for the disabled. This might be the first time that the term 'community care' was formally used in Taiwan. These provided comprehensive nursing care, in-home services, case visiting and case services in four districts of Taipei City. Meanwhile, to promote the policy of so-called 'social welfare communitization', the department the Ministry of the Interior chose five towns as pilot areas in 1998. Those items of service included which were clearly close to the scope of community care are shown in table 14.5. These services were either provided by local government or contracted out to voluntary agencies. It is expected that this community-oriented service style will increasingly become the predominant style of caring for elderly people in Taiwan.

Table 14.5 Items of community care in five pilot projects of the 'social welfare communitisation' 1998

Suaw, Ilan	Wen-shan,Taipei	Lu-kang, Changhaw	An-ping, Tainan	Feng-shan, Kaohsiung
1 Meals service	1 Meals service	1 Meals service	1 Meals service	1 Meals service
2 Day-care	2 In-home service	2 In-home service	2 Day-care	2 Greetings sending
3 In-home service.	3 Visiting and concern for elderly who live alone.	3 Respite care	3 Visiting and concern for elderly who live alone.	3 Respite care.
		4 Greetings sending and line concern.		

Discussion: myths and dilemmas of community care

Community care is a new term for the Taiwanese. Even though the concept had been proposed in the 1980s, there was no tangible measure putting it into operation until recent years. The following discussion highlights myths and dilemmas faced in this recent development.

Is community care a good alternative form of caring for elderly people in Taiwan?

The family structure, as shown earlier, has increasingly been shifting from extended to nuclear style. Its traditional function of caring for elderly people has, by the same token, been in *de facto* decline. An alternative approach to 'replacing', 'supplementing' or 'supporting' the traditional role of family as caregivers is necessary. According to the survey conducted by the Ministry of the Interior (Interior, 1997b), those people aged over 50 who choose caring or nursing institutions and homes for the elderly as their ideal housing arrangement for the future are only 2.09 per cent and 1.09 per cent respectively. The majority prefer to live in their own homes, in particular with or next door to the next generations of their family (73.93 per cent). Furthermore, according to the estimate of the DoH, those who need institutional care total about 31,863, whereas the current capacity is only 14,691beds, i.e. only 46 per cent of the total beds needed. Nevertheless, the current residence rates of public and private elderly homes in Taiwan Province are only 64 per cent and 75 per cent of their maximum capacities respectively.

These trends indicate that the family is still thought of as the best housing choice for the elderly. However, there is the problem of who will take care of the elderly if the family is unable or losing its capacity to provide care, especially for those who are disabled. For most elderly people, institutional care substitutes for family care remain a last resort. However, a sound community care system, which enables people either to live as normal a life as possible in their own homes or in a homely environment in the local community, with little or some help from outside the family, could be a more acceptable alternative.

The 1994 Outline of Social Welfare Policy claimed 'to construct a family-centred social welfare policy, to promote family ethics, to develop family relationships, and to preserve members' welfare through family ethics' on the one hand, and 'to strengthen caring and nursing facilities for the elderly in the community, to build in-home care service networks by integrating community resources...' on the other. The 1996 PKPPSWC, as mentioned earlier, also asserted the importance of family and community in providing care for the elderly. In addition, at the National Conference of Social Welfare 1998, Premier Vincent C. Siew in his closing address asserted:

> Family is the pillar of our society. The specific role of the family is impossible to replace fully, even if more social welfare systems are provided. I want to appeal specifically to our people to have more affection and concern for their family. The departments of social welfare should design a family-centred service model which integrates social assistance, social welfare and community mutual help to support the family as a basic unit of social welfare provision. In doing so, people who need to be cared for will be able to obtain support and warmth (21 July 1998).

Obviously, the family is still expected to play a major role in caring for elderly people. What differs from previous situations is that the government has started to get involved in mobilising help from communities. This may be regarded as an appropriate supplementary or supporting approach to caring for elderly people in a changing social context. But it has raised another problem: namely, that community care may (once again) merely mean family care, and especially care by female kin. As Dalley (1996) pointed out, women are expected to provide care not only for their immediate dependants (their children and their ageing parents), but also frequently for their husbands' ageing dependants (that is, their parents-in-law). To demonstrate that community care is not merely equivalent to family care or female care, we need to know how community care is to make its contribution. The question is quite strongly related to existing community resources, to which I now turn.

Are community resources sufficient for implementing community care in the present situation?

This issue can be discussed under two headings: do we have sufficient resources? Are present resources well distributed? If community care is not equivalent to family care, we should have available resources outside the family to provide. As Higgins (1989) suggests, elderly people in receipt of domiciliary care may, for example, also make use of institutional care on an irregular basis. There is no doubt, therefore, that an institutional outreach service is one of the most important resources for providing care for the elderly in the community. In Taiwan, there exist 114 registered homes for the elderly; 61 public and 53 private. The capacities of most registered residential homes are extensive but they are isolated from the communities in which they are located. So far as the communities are concerned, the resources available from such institutions are extremely limited. In addition, there are about 600 unregistered homes for disabled elderly people. Most of these are relatively small and dispersed around various communities. However, the motivation for setting up these institutions has been rather profit-centred. Their qualities have already become a source of great concern to society. It is unrealistic to expect such homes to be suitable for playing a big part in community care provision at present.

Another potential source is the home care services provided by county governments through paid workers or volunteers. But the scale of these services is quite small, the number of full-time paid workers being only 107 and volunteers 1,400 in 1998. Recently, governments have commissioned non-profit voluntary sector organizations to provide care through subsidy or contracting-out. But again the scale of this activity has been small and centred on urban areas.

In addition, contracting-out has increasingly been expanded as a style of service provision. Although the innovation of partnership between public and private sectors may have contributed to the improvement of efficiency and effectiveness in welfare provision, many potential problems need to be taken into consideration before further expansion is envisaged. First, whether these voluntary agencies or groups are sufficiently well structured to undertake such a commission? Second, whether the money spent represents 'value for money'? (Chan and Hwang, 1999). Finally, whether or not the qualities they provide have been supervised appropriately (Lin and Chen, 1997)? Such concerns may be of varying urgency between different groups and agencies, but most of the answers veer towards the negative.

Does the voluntary sector have the ability to share the responsibility of caring for elderly people in the community?

Influenced by the idea of 'welfare pluralism' and the strategy of 'the mixed economy of welfare' the voluntary sector has been regarded as a feasible means of providing care for elderly people. The publication of the PKPPSWP may be seen as one of the responses to this trend. Even prior to its publication, contracting-out of social welfare services had already been in operation. Governments have since made every effort to privatise welfare services in many fields, in particular with regard to buildings and facilities, yet the outcomes have been varied. In addition, some well-founded voluntary sector organizations also provide in-home care by contract with governments, but the scale of such operations is small and most of the services are in urban areas. Indeed, many problems have already occurred in the provision of services under the banner of welfare privatisation, including (Chen, 1997):

1. Voluntary sectors suitable to contract with are not easy to find and their qualities are uneven. The competitive mechanism which 'privatization' expects does not exist and thus a few sectors can secure a near-monopoly of all contracts.
2. Regulations over rights and obligations for purchasers and providers are still ambiguous. This has caused difficulties for subsequent monitoring and performance assessment.
3. Cream-skimming is characteristic of many privatised authorities and results in services being unavailable for those people whose need is greatest.
4. The experience of coordination and collaboration between governments and voluntary sectors is insufficient. There is no established model to follow concerning interaction between both sides.

Voluntary or non-profit agencies as service providers may be a good alternative in caring for elderly people. However, because of such deficiencies as those mentioned above, it remains uncertain whether they are yet able to play their roles appropriately and to share responsibility as expected.

Has Taiwan an integrated network of services for the elderly to underpin coordination and collaboration between the sectors?

Researches have clearly pointed out the absence of coordination between government departments in providing care for the elderly, in particular between the social and health sectors (Chan & Hwang, 1999). Both sectors share responsibilities for providing care for the elderly people who are affected by health and other problems. But the line between them is blurred and interaction between the sides is extremely limited. Of course, rigid categorization is often unhelpful and bears little relationship to real life (Higgins, 1989). People who need care may usually be travelling in the 'continuum' or 'spectrum' of a range of settings in which care can be delivered. Lack of interaction between health and social sectors may mean a discontinuity in service provision, and thus may impact on service delivery.

For elderly patients without sufficient family or other carers, who need to be cared for, discharge from hospital may imply different consequences for different patients. For low-income patients free nursing or caring homes may be available, subject to a mean test. For others, however, discharge may spell an enormous economic burden for their families, if patients need to be placed in public or private nursing or caring homes. As a result, patients or their families may prefer staying in hospital with cost-sharing under the National Health Insurance to a placement in nursing or caring homes at enormous financial cost. For elderly people who are disabled and need in-home (nursing) care, appropriate help from social and health sectors will be necessary. But a recent survey has shown the gap which exists between the two sides at the local level (Hwang, 1998b). In brief, the service network for delivering care for elderly people is still far from complete. This deficiency may cause either overlap or interruption in service provision: a situation not only detrimental to patients and their families, but also to the containment of medical expenditure.

Is a bottom-up community-based service model possible?

In traditional community work, the bottom-up service approach to personal independence and participation has been emphasized as a demonstration of community ability. According to the 1996 PKPPSWC, communities are expected to provide care for their residents by building a community service network. Self-sufficiency and independence are encouraged. However, the problem remains as to whether actual communities have the ability to realize this goal.

For the past 30 years, governments have made an effort to foster community independence. But the stereotype of thinking that public funds will materialize once the government asks the community to do something seems to have become deep-rooted in the mind of the public. Furthermore, community residents appear to think that what they have done has been for governments rather than for themselves. Ironically, the intention to emphasize independence has turned into a means of creating dependence. This constitutes a dilemma for bringing community care into effect. Indeed, it is doubtful whether such communities have the ability or wherewithal to coordinate or integrate their own resources without help from others.

In addition, even where there exist some voluntary agencies, communities normally expect the government to provide the money for any activities which are required by government. As a result, even those communities able to play a role in community care, have as their first priority getting public funds rather than self-funding. This being so, the role of the state in community care is likely to remain heavy, at least in financial terms. Therefore, the way forward to community autonomy via a bottom-up approach to service provision could be a long one.

How is community care to be managed?

Care management has been seen as an essential element in realizing community care in England. Thus Hsieh (1995) has argued that, while community care is essential to caring for the disabled elderly, case management is essential to community care. Lu (1997) and Hwang (1998c) have also made similar suggestions. In legislation, the term 'case management' has been introduced in the Law for the Disabled of 1997. At the level of practice, a recent survey has shown that social workers have regarded care management as an effective measure for providing services (Hwang, 1998b). But the development of care management is still at an embryonic stage in Taiwan. Although a few voluntary agencies assert that they have provided services by way of case management, the scale of such operations has been quite limited and, strictly speaking, methods are still rooted in traditional casework.

Case management is important and necessary in Taiwan for various reasons. First of all, client problems are always complex and need to be sorted out via the collaboration of multidisciplinary or cross-agency teams. Second, in the current social work context, available resources are insufficient, yet are being used repeatedly and inefficiently. Third, because the importance of needs-led services has increasingly been emphasized in the provision of care, clients should have the right to be involved in the planning of their own care. Fourth, as mentioned earlier, the interaction between public and private sectors being vague, there needs to be some kind of mechanism for coordinating the two sides. Fifth, the introduction of contracted-out services means there is a need for someone to design and purchase services for clients (Hwang, 1998b).

To work out such problems, care management seems to be a solution waiting to be developed. Unfortunately, there are only 686 social workers employed in government departments in Taiwan at the time of writing. It is clear that the workload of such social workers is set to be heavy if their number does not increase. Yet it could be very difficult to add to the number of government employees under current circumstances of government re-engineering. In addition, most of the social work staff do not have much idea, in any case, about what care management is (Hwang, 1998b). How to persuade or encourage them to learn more about and acquire more skills in care management constitutes another challenge facing the cause of community care.

Whither community care: illusion, vision or reality?

In terms of both policy and practice it is clear that the expression 'community care' is rather new. But in terms of various policies and practices providing services for elderly people, we may conclude, at least, that community care has long been regarded as one of the main strategies for caring for senior citizens. Nevertheless, the above discussion has clearly shown community care in Taiwan to be still in its infancy. It is too weak to say that a basic community care system already exists. But how might community care develop in the future? Will it turn out to be an illusion, vision or reality?

Obviously, the increase in the elderly population and the decline in traditional family functioning have already focused the government's attention upon looking for alternative approaches to caring for elderly people. Before 1995, although there had been many welfare services for the elderly, most of them had been fragmented and inadequate. Taiwan had certainly never experienced the era of the expansion of the welfare state, as occurred in the England of the 1950s and 1960s, when the state invested substantial resources in welfare services, with the result that the fundamentals for carrying out community care had been developed to a significant extent. By contrast, the prerequisites for carrying out community care in Taiwan remain relatively insufficient and thus more efforts need to be made in various respects. Without this kind of awareness, the fundamentals for implementing community care will not easily be established.

Traditionally, it has been informal sectors, in particular the family, which have played the bigger part in providing care. But in Taiwan, rates of women's social and labour-force participation have been increasing. This suggests that traditional caregiving may be in decline. The situation is further exacerbated by the growth in the elderly population. Pressures on carers, in particular female carers, have for long been neglected and thus a potential conflict may have come to exist between carers and the cared-for. Thus it is that a progressive community care policy should try its best to reduce the burdens placed on informal carers. For example, strategies such as an allowance for carers, and the provision of respite care, could be implemented so as to provide an incentive for informal carers to maintain their caring tasks. If governments just think they can put caring responsibilities back on the family, or on females, under the guise of community care, the problems will remain, or even worsen.

The advocacy of community care by government means, to a certain degree, that informal or voluntary sectors are being expected to bear more responsibility for caring for elderly people. Indeed, the government has never played a main role in this regard. However, following changes in the socio-economic context and increasing awareness of the idea of civilian rights, government has been forced to involve itself more in welfare provision. At this initial stage, it would be wrong for government to position itself as if in no more than an 'enabling' role.

In general, the implementation of community care requires close collaboration and integration between social and health sectors, together with the cautious arrangement of considerable resources. As mentioned earlier, however, mechanisms for coordination between health and social sectors and the different levels of government remain inadequate and their division of labour is blurred. This situation results not only in a waste of resources but also in a reduction in convenience for users. To make good such deficiencies, it will be necessary to build a multidisciplinary and cross-sectoral team. In addition, partnership between the public and private sectors, or formal and informal sectors, might be another route to this. Of course, care management will be essential for creating a seamless service through integration, collaboration and coordination between the different sectors.

The atmosphere of 'social welfare communitisation' is vibrant in Taiwan, yet it is no more than a slogan at present, given the dilemmas already refered to. There is no doubt that government intends to emphasize community care as the focus for delivering care to elderly people. However, there are as yet no clear policy guidelines. The 1996 PKPPSWC has given some brief statements, but offered no further detailed plans to say how the policy will be implemented. The first-stage pilot project of 1998 was introduced in rather an irrational way, with no careful planning in advance. It was very difficult to draw substantial criteria for assessment and the process was full of uncertainty. In addition, the duration of these projects was just one year. It is doubtful how far the goals of the PKPPSWC can be realized under such weak circumstances.

Many preconditions for fulfilling the idea of community care have been discussed throughout this chapter. Obviously, these conditions have been extremely insufficient and weak in Taiwan. If the government merely intends to encourage self-sufficiency or autonomy without giving substantial support, in particular funds, its prospects will be poor. In short, it will be an illusion for government to think it can realize the idea of community care without recognizing and tackling the difficulties involved.

Although there is no clear and specific policy for community care, many measures are in existance or 'projected', and these would seem to have already provided part of the essential basis for its implementation. These measures or projects, such as the PKPPSWC, the PSSCEP, the 'Three-year Planning of Long-term Care for the Elderly', and the various efforts government has made in recent years, have provided a good guideline for the development of community care. Whether these efforts will contribute to the realization of the idea of community care will much depend on the continuing quality of the government's determination. If this remains positive, the prospects for community care will be optimistic and it should be possible to shift from vision to reality.

References

Bulmer, M. (1997), 'The social basis of community care', in J. Bornat et al. (eds), *Community Care - A Reader,* OUP, London, pp.45-52.

CEPD (Council for Economic Planning and Development) (1998), *Taiwan Statistical Data Book 1998,* CEPD, Taiwan.

Chan, Y. and Hwang, Y.S. (1999), *A Study on Propelling Social Welfare Communitisation: Case of Lu-Kang, Changhaw,* Ministry of the Interior, Taiwan.

Chen, W.H. (1997), 'The practical method and policy development of privitisation, *Community Development Journal,* 80, Ministry of the Interior, Taiwan, pp.4-9.

Dalley, G. (1996), *Ideologies of Caring,* Macmillan, London.

DGBAS (Directorate-General of Budget, Accounting and Statistics) (1997), *Social Indicators, the Republic of China,* DGBAS, Executive Yuan, Taiwan.

DGBAS (1998), *Yearbook of Manpower Survey Statistics, Taiwan Area, Republic of China, 1997,* DGBAS, Executive Yuan, Taiwan.

DoH (1989), *Caring for People: Community Care in the Next Decade and Beyond,* HMSO, London.

Executive Yuan (1965), *The Guideline of the Present-stage Social Policy of Ming-Shen Principle,* Executive Yuan, Taiwan.

Higgins, J. (1989). Defining Community Care: Realities and Myths, *Social Policy and Administration,* 23 (1), pp.3-15.

Hsieh , M.O. and Liu, S.C. (1995), *A Study on Creating a Community Care Network for the Elderly People in Taipei City,* Taipei City Government, Taiwan.

Hsieh, M.O. (1997), 'Community care needs of the disabled elderly and the establishment of a service network, *Journal of Sociology,* National Chengchi University, Taipei.

Hwang, Y.S. (1998a), *A Study on Community Care for Elderly People in Traditional Urban Areas,* Taiwan Provincial Government, Nantou.

Hwang, Y.S. (1998b), *A Study on Working Skills of Community Care,* Taiwan Provincial Government, Nantou.

Hwang, Y.S. (1998c), 'Community care under the mixed economy of welfare: British experience, lessons for Taiwan', *Social Policy and Social Work,* 2 (1), pp.39-85.

Interior (1994), 'Brief conclusion of the National Conference for Social Welfare 1994', *Community Development Journal,* Special Issue for the National Conference for Social Welfare, Ministry of the Interior, Taiwan.

Interior (1995), 'Conclusion of the National Conference for Community Development 1995', *Community Development Journal,* 71, pp.158-60, Ministry of the Interior, Taiwan.

Interior (1995), Group Discussion Conclusion of the National Conference for Community Development 1995, *Community Development Journal*, 71, pp.158-60, Ministry of the Interior, Taiwan.

Interior (1996), *Operation Handbook of Subsidy for Enhancing Social Welfare*, Ministry of the Interior, Taiwan.

Interior (1997a), *Report of Survey for National Living Conditions*, Ministry of the Interior, Taiwan.

Interior (1997b), *Report of Survey for Elderly Condition*, Ministry of the Interior, Taiwan.

Lin, W.I and Chen, I.W. (1997), *A Study on Model and Legal System for 'Publicly Owned, Privately Run' of Social Welfare*, Ministry of the Interior, Taiwan.

Lu, P.C. (1997), *A Study on Community Care Model for Elderly People*, Ministry of the Interior, Taiwan.

Taiwan Provincial Government (1981), *Establishment Criteria for the Senior Welfare Agency*, Taiwan Provincial Government, Nantou.

Taiwan Provincial Government (1992), *The 1992 Contemporary Implementation Project for Community Development Work*, Taiwan Provincial Government, Nantou.

15 Crime, punishment and community in England and Wales

SUSAN HANLEY
MIKE NELLIS

Introduction

In May 1997, a decisive election victory for the Labour Party, led by Tony Blair, brought eighteen years of Conservative Party rule in Great Britain to an end. Although there had been no formal attempt to change the name of the party, it had presented itself, in its later years of opposition, as 'New Labour', to distinguish itself ideologically from the earlier traditions of the Labour Party (which in Blair's, and others', view had rendered it unelectable) and to signal its concern with modernising political and economic life in Britain, in preparation for the challenges of the new millennium. Modernisation has been the keynote of New Labour's tougher stance on crime (Gould, 1998), and despite its essentially contested nature (Lacey and Zedner, 1995), the concept of 'community' has been central to its approach.

Traditionally, the Labour Party had subsumed concern about crime into concern about inequality and poverty; it had tended to believe that if the latter were addressed directly, the former would decline as a result. Between 1960 and 1975 a strong political alliance emerged between the expanding social work professions and the Labour Party, but rising rates of crime and opposition to this 'welfare' approach from the police and the magistrates eventually brought the strategy into disrepute. The Conservative government that came to power in 1979 (under Margaret Thatcher) drew in part on strong working-class support for her much tougher law and order policies. For the next decade, the tone of criminal justice policy was set entirely by the Conservative government, although actual practice, as we shall see, was not always consistent with the tough talk. The Labour Opposition nonetheless had no purchase on law and order issues during the Thatcher years. It was only after Tony Blair became Shadow Home Secretary in 1991 that this began to change.

Before examining New Labour's approach, the complexity and inconsistency of initiatives in criminal justice under the previous Conservative administrations needs to be acknowledged, because of their continuing symbolic significance at the present time. For, despite the tough law and order rhetoric with which the Thatcher government began, and the extreme punitiveness which characterised the later years of John Major's premiership, there were in the intervening period (approximately the mid-1980s to the early 1990s) two developments which came to be seen, and in some quarters are still seen, as the acme of progressive penal policy and practice, and as the yardstick by which New Labour's achievements might be measured.

The first of these concerned juvenile justice (10-17-year-olds), a sphere of policy that at the time, was administered at local level by social services departments and at central government level by the Department of Health (not, as now, the Home Office). Ministers emphasised the need to punish young offenders, placing considerable store on the re-introduction of military-style detention centres, and on a toughening-up of supervision in the community. A proactive network of academics, practitioners and managers (in the voluntary sector as well as the social services), however, brought about an unexpected 'revolution' in the response to juveniles, simultaneously persuading the police to make greater use of diversion from court, and magistrates to use new, more intensive forms of non-custodial supervision (Jones, 1989; Nellis, 1991). The network was strongly influenced by labelling theory (which suggests that interventions by criminal justice agencies can be stigmatising, and should therefore be kept to a minimum, and by the empirically-based belief that the majority of young offenders grow out of crime in their late teens and early twenties, if they are not unduly criminalised by the agencies). They effectively distanced themselves from the liberal rhetoric of social work, endorsed a multi-agency approach (especially police-social worker cooperation) emphasised the demanding, re-educational nature of the intensive supervision projects and, against the grain of the times, successfully reduced the use of custody. Although the network's commitment to 'penal reductionism' (Rutherford, 1992) was far from what the Thatcher government had had in mind, they eventually took political credit for its achievements, and claimed them as policy.

The second progressive development was influenced by the first, but originated in central government, and owed most to the relatively liberal vision of the then Home Secretary, Douglas Hurd (Rutherford, 1996). By the mid-1980s the Home Office was keenly aware of the problems associated with overcrowding in the adult penal system, and despite its own law and order rhetoric, was openly questioning the cost-effectiveness of imprisonment. The strategy that emerged from this was dubbed 'punishment in the community', and entailed a deliberate attempt to toughen up the penalties administered by the Probation Service, down-playing the social work ethos, and thereby persuading magistrates and judges to use imprisonment less. The focus was particularly on the 18-25 age group, the group above the juveniles for whom this approach was so obviously working. However, unlike the local authority and voluntary sector social workers, probation officers resisted the toughening of community penalties, despite the promise of reduced use of custody. It was only in 1993 that, under pressure, the Service began to embrace change (Cavadino et al, 2000).

By 1993, however, internal ideological changes within the Conservative government had wrought changes of policy and personnel in the Home Office which could hardly have been greater than if there had been a complete change of government. None of Douglas Hurd's three very short-lived successors as Home Secretary quite shared his liberal vision. Michael Howard, who succeeded them in 1993, consciously repudiated it, openly encouraging an increase in prison use, a belief that 'prison works' (as containment rather than rehabilitation), and dis-regarding the potential of the Probation Service. He still insisted on tougher community penalties, but not with a view to their being used instead of prison. It was during Howard's period as Home Secretary that New Labour in opposition had to develop and promote its own distinctive criminal justice policy, and it was his legacy - a record prison population of 62,000 - that they inherited.

New Labour and criminal justice

New Labour's subsequent outlook on law and order was formed by Tony Blair while he was still Shadow Home Secretary. He promoted a shift away from the Party's traditional stance based, first, on strong Christian-based convictions that responsibilities, duties and obligations mattered as much as the rights of individuals, and, second, on accounts by his respectable working-class constituents' of the devastating effects that crime and fear of crime had on community life. In response to these, Blair coined a catchphrase which continues to encapsulate New Labour thinking on law and order: 'tough on crime, tough on the causes of crime'.

It implies that while traditional Labour concern with deprivation and disadvantage would not be neglected, a new pugnacity - a readiness to punish firmly and swiftly - could be expected towards criminals themselves. The murder of a 2-year-old child by two disturbed 10-year-old boys in February 1993 - an event which prompted a great deal of national soul-searching - gave Blair the opportunity to elaborate his moral vision:

> The news bulletins of the last week have been like hammer blows struck against the sleeping conscience of the country, urging us to wake up and look unflinchingly at what we are. We hear of crimes so horrific they provoke anger and disbelief in equal proportions...These are the ugly manifestations of a society that is becoming unworthy of that name. A solution to this disintegration doesn't simply lie in legislation. It must come from the rediscovery of a sense of direction as a country, and most of all from being unafraid to start talking again about the values and principles we believe in, and what they mean for us, not just as individuals but as a community. We cannot exist in a moral vacuum. If we do not learn and then teach the value of what is right and wrong, then the result is simply moral chaos which engulfs us all. (Blair, quoted in Sopel, 1995, pp.155-6; emphasis added).

Blair became leader of the Labour Party in 1994; Jack Straw replaced him as Shadow Home Secretary and had the somewhat more difficult task of turning Blair's moral vision into viable and appealing policies before the anticipated election in 1997. It fell to Straw to outmanoeuvre Michael Howard in debates on penal policy, to avoid ever appearing soft on crime, and to convincingly reclaim law and order as the preserve of Labour. Insofar as recorded crime had almost doubled since the Conservatives had come to power, and prosecutions were actually falling, Straw's task was by no means an impossible one (Rose, 1997). Both politicians vied with each other to appeal to 'middle England', a symbolic construction denoting the affluent middle classes of England and Wales, whose electoral support was crucial to electoral victory (Gould, 1998). Howard appealed to their punitive instincts with 'prison works'. More subtly, Straw appealed to their felt need for safe communities, which translated into something rather more complex than just increased use of imprisonment. Nonetheless, Straw consistently backed Conservative proposals that inevitably increased the prison population, and whatever his personal inclinations may have been when he finally became Home Secretary, there were a number of Conservative policies - privatising prisons, increased use of electronic monitoring of offenders ('tagging'), and the development of new 'secure training centres' for 12-

14-year-olds - from which he chose not to distance himself.

As New Labour's criminal justice policy evolved, before and after coming to power, it was subject to three further intellectual influences, to all of which the idea of 'community' was fairly central. The first was the ideology of communitarianism, a political ideology that has emerged in the USA as a reaction to the excesses of neo-liberal individualism and against what it sees as the erosion of informal social control - the moralising and exemplary influence of kin, neighbours and workmates: 'the community' - on the behaviour of individuals. Its clearly articulated notion of a citizen's duties and responsibilities was particularly commended to New Labour (partly with crime control in mind) by a left-of-centre think-tank, Demos, which ensured considerable publicity in Britain for its leading American exponent, Amitai Etzioni (1995; see also Hughes, 1998, pp.104-129).

Second, Straw in particular was influenced by the 'broken windows' thesis of Wilson and Kelling (1992; see also Kelling and Coles, 1998), which argued, in essence, that the long-term prevention of community breakdown, and the emergence of intractable forms of crime and disorder, was best effected by early and decisive action against even minor crime and 'incivilities' (anti-social behaviour, such as children breaking windows, which may not itself be illegal). In America, this thesis gave rise to the concept of 'zero tolerance policing', and some British police forces had already adopted elements of it before New Labour recognised its electoral potential (see Young, 1998, for a critique).

The most recent influence on New Labour has been the ongoing debate on 'the third way', Anthony Giddens' (1998, 2000) term for the attempt to reinvigorate social democracy in a radically changed global economic environment. Although explicitly hostile to communitarianism (whose idealised small-scale communities he believes it impossible to recreate in late modern conditions) and to the moral conservatism with which it is tainted, such limited comments as Giddens has made on crime control tend in the direction of tough, localised forms of crime prevention. They acknowledge that the traditional left's explanations of, and responses to, crime were inadequate and now allow for something akin to zero tolerance: 'surveillance and saturation policing [to] create public spaces in which people could associate with each other' (Giddens, 2000, p.49).

It is not our intention at this point to take issue with these ideas, merely to register their influence on the New Labour government. A critical literature exists in relation to them all, and from it a critique of government policy could easily be distilled, aspects of which will be alluded to later in this chapter. For present purposes, however, it is sufficient to indicate that the intellectual influences on New Labour were somewhat different from those prevailing in the Conservative Party, and to describe the milieu in which thinking about its flagship law and order legislation, the Crime and Disorder Act 1998, developed. This legislation was a mix of provisions built around the core idea of making communities safer. Over and above this core concern, it created some new court orders for both juvenile and adult offenders, running alongside existing ones.

Although this chapter concentrates primarily on the measures in the new Act, this legislation does not exhaust all that can be said about New Labour, crime, punishment and the community. Key developments have also occurred outside this framework. New Labour has pressed, for example, to transform the Probation Service from a 'social work' to a 'law enforcement' agency, to centralise control over it, and to link it more closely to the Prison Service in ways that exceed even what the previous Conservative government had envisaged (Nellis, 1999). The concept of supervising offenders in the community is already being transformed by an expansion of electronic tagging that stands to make England and Wales, proportionately, the world's most prolific user of this measure (Whitfield, 1998; Nellis, 2000a). The development of closed circuit television (CCTV) as a form of community crime prevention has advanced further in England and Wales than in any other European country (Norris and Armstrong, 2000). New Labour is actively promoting these developments. In assessing the significance of the new government's crime policy, they also need to be taken into account.

New responses to youth crime

High levels of crime committed by the young dominated New Labour's agenda, and in regard to them the Audit Commission (1996) (a national body established to scrutinise the cost-effectiveness of public services, especially local authorities) provided the Party with the starting points of its youth justice policy, even while the Conservatives were still in office. The Commission's survey of existing provision found much to criticise but its proposals, far from endorsing the then government's emphasis on punishment, emphasised the long-term value of prevention. It advocated a graded response to juvenile offending, acknowledging that while most young offenders do grow out of crime, some persistent offenders do not, and that any legal and administrative system should deal effectively with both. Its emphasis on preventive measures outside the criminal justice system - support for families, improved schooling - its anxiety about the premature labelling of less serious offenders and its belief that intensive supervision programmes should be targeted on more serious offenders had obvious affinities with features of the 'successful revolution' in the 1980s, which did not endear it to the then government.

New Labour, however, built many of the Audit Commission's proposals into its own White Paper, *No More Excuses* (Home Office, 1997), packaging them in more punitive language, with less sensitivity to the dangers of labelling, and with greater emphasis on coercion than the Commission had envisaged. The White Paper proposed a statutory aim for the youth justice system, namely to prevent children and young people from becoming offenders (but dealing with them promptly and firmly if they do offend) and outlined the specific measures that were eventually to be included in the Crime and Disorder Bill, and later in the Act itself.

An early sign of New Labour's new pugnacity was its resolution of a long-standing legal debate on doli incapax, the presumption that a child between 10 and 14 has to be proven to know right from wrong, as well as to have committed an offence, before they can be found guilty in court. The presumption had hitherto been integral to all welfare approaches to young offenders, but New Labour abolished it, thereby making it easier to prosecute under-14s (deferring, for the foreseeable future, the likelihood of the age of prosecutability being raised to 14, which would bring England and Wales in line with most mainland European countries).

Diverting young people from prosecution - through the use of police cautioning - had been a key feature of the 'successful revolution' in youth justice in the 1980s, but the practice of multiple cautioning in some parts of the country was too readily perceived as leniency, and brought the idea into disrepute. New Labour's Final Warning System was intended to tighten and simplify procedures for diversion, allowing, at most, two chances, first a reprimand, second, a final warning. The latter may include referral to a Youth Offending Team, for assessment and possible rehabilitative assistance. Any offences committed after a warning will normally result in prosecution. There is clearly less flexibility in the new system of diversion, and the overall effect is likely to be the earlier prosecution of young offenders, with all the attendant risks of labelling. For those facing their first prosecution, however, a later piece of legislation, the Youth Justice and Criminal Evidence Act 1999, has introduced a 'youth offending panel' which aims to involve offenders, their families, and victims (if they consent) in drawing up a contract that will facilitate both reparation and rehabilitation.

The Crime and Disorder Act added an array of new community measures to complement the basic supervision order, including two that were quite without precedent: Parenting Orders for adults, and Child Safety Orders for youngsters under the age of prosecutability. The question of how best to make parents accountable for the crimes and misdemeanours of their children taxed British policy makers throughout the twentieth century, and usually voluntary guidance from social workers was the preferred option. This may have included parental attendance at childcare classes. The new Parenting Orders actually impose requirements on parents and guardians to address their child's anti-social or offending behaviour, either by attending classes of this kind, and/or by insisting upon the exercise of greater control over a child, e.g. attending school regularly or avoiding certain places and people. Non-compliance results in a fine. Child Safety Orders were introduced in the face of mounting evidence that future delinquent behaviour can be predicted from the behaviour of under-10-year-olds (Rutter et al, 1999), and were intended to prevent such youngsters from becoming involved in criminal or anti-social behaviour. Predicting is one thing, however; intervening without premature labelling is another, and as Cavadino et al (2000) point out there is no evidence that either Parenting Orders or Child Safety Orders will work in the ways intended. Both orders can be overseen by a probation officer, social worker, or member of a Youth Offender Team, although any parental counselling is likely to be done by voluntary organisations, working in 'partnership' with statutory services.

Two short, and partially overlapping, measures were introduced by the Act, enabling magistrates to specify requirements that may once have been arranged at the discretion of social workers themselves, within the general framework of a supervision order. Reparation Orders, a tokenistic nod towards the more general idea of 'restorative justice' (Marshall, 1999; Mediation UK, 1999), require the young offender to make reparation to the victim of the offence or to the community at large. The reparation must be commensurate with the seriousness of the offence(s), may not exceed a total of 24 hours, and must be undertaken within the first three months of the order. Action Plan Orders are specifically tailored to address the causes of the child's or young person's offending behaviour. The Order will require the offender to comply with a three month action plan, meeting requirements specified by the court, which may include school attendance or reparation.

Anti-Social Behaviour Orders attracted much adverse comment in the Crime and Disorder Bill's passage through Parliament, even though they built on civil-law remedies which had already been used by several local authority housing departments to deal with difficult or violent neighbours. They can be applied for by either the police or local authority in consultation with each other against an individual or several individuals (adults or juveniles) whose behaviour causes alarm, distress or harassment to those living nearby. The order, which has effect for a minimum of two years, imposes prohibitions which a court considers necessary to prevent any further anti-social acts. Breaching it is a criminal offence punishable by imprisonment, even if the incident which precipitated the making of the original order was not itself imprisonable.

Lastly, the Crime and Disorder Act attempts to streamline custodial sentencing for young offenders, in ways that pay no regard whatsoever to the reductionist ideals of the 'successful revolution'. The new Detention and Training Order merges the existing sentence of 'detention in a young offender institution' (for 15-17 year olds) and 'secure training orders' (for 12-14-year-olds) into a single sentence, (with the future possibility, at the Home Secretary's discretion, that 10-11 year old persistent offenders might also be subjected to them). The new Order is distinctive because it blurs the traditional division between custody and the community, insofar as the latter half of the sentence is to be served in the community, under supervision, with a view to continuing whatever work has begun with the offender in the custodial part of the sentence. While this in one sense extends the long-established idea of 'aftercare' it is also a significant step closer to what New Labour has recently begun to refer to as a 'seamless sentence' which deliberately blends elements of custodial and community control. The introduction of electronic tagging as a means of facilitating early release from prison for selected prisoners (both juvenile and adults) in January 1999 clearly aids this blending process, and could, in future, be used much more extensively than at present.

The statutory establishment of Youth Offending Teams in each local authority, whose staff will largely be responsible for the supervision of both old and new community penalties, is the Crime and Disorder Act's most innovative organisational feature. As with other aspects of the Act, the idea for the teams evolved from some pre-existing initiatives in particular local authorities with which central government had been particularly impressed (e.g. multi-agency cooperation in Northampton-shire, see also Loewenstein, 2000). The profile and authority of the new teams is, however, raised to a level that multi-agency initiatives in the youth justice field have not formally had before. Each local authority must now bring representatives, and enable funding, from a range of specified agencies - social services, Probation, police, education services and health authorities - into a single team to develop and deliver youth justice services, based on an annual 'Youth Justice Plan'. This plan must be submitted to, and approved by, the centrally established Youth Justice Board, which, under the new legislation, is responsible for overseeing the national development of youth justice policy, advising government, and identifying and promoting good practice.

Responses to adult offenders

There were within the Crime and Disorder Act a series of measures that, though available for juveniles, were primarily a reflection of growing public and official concern about certain categories of adult offender. These relate to sex offenders, drug-using offenders and offenders motivated by racial hatred. Although it is easy to specify the detail of the legislative provision, it is difficult to understand the true significance of the measures without also understanding the nature of the debates which led to them being included. Space, however, permits only brief attention to these.

Sex offenders, especially those who offend against children, are relatively easy to demonise, and local neighbourhoods have proved notoriously, if understandably, reluctant to have them living in their midst. The mid-1990s saw a degree of moral outrage develop around the resettlement of several high-profile sex offenders released from prison, in whose rehabilitation local communities had no real reason to feel confident. An attempt to create a sex offender's register, which aimed to enable police, social services and probation to keep track of all such offenders in the community, failed to reassure. Several instances of concerted community action by neighbours and parents fearful for their children's safety, objecting to the presence of sex offenders in private accommodation and probation hostels, and determined to drive them out, merely intensified the moral panic (Hebenton and Thomas, 1996). Against this volatile backcloth, it is uncertain whether the new Sex Offender Orders will be seen by local communities as an adequate form of protection. These permit the police to ask a court to make an order against any convicted sex offender whose present behaviour in the community gives reasonable cause to believe that only such an order will protect the public from serious harm, even if no new offence is committed. The order may run for a minimum of five years, requires the offender to register regularly with the police and may contain prohibitions (e.g. to avoid visiting children's playgrounds, swimming pools, etc.) necessary to ensure public safety. Breach of such an order without reasonable excuse is a criminal offence punishable by imprisonment.

There is within England and Wales an elaborate and sophisticated drugs policy, based largely on an influential White Paper (Home Office, 1998), which, strictly speaking, is beyond the scope of this chapter. It relies on a complex multi-agency structure at local and national level that addresses both the criminal justice and public health aspects of drug abuse (see Wilson and Ashton, 1998). The new Act's Drug Treatment and Testing Orders are simply an addition to the existing strategy, a community penalty (supervised by a probation officer) aimed at drug users aged 16 and over who commit crimes to fund their drug habit and who show a willingness to cooperate with treatment (residential or non-residential).

Over the 1980s and 1990s there has been a progressive intensification of public debate on race and crime in England and Wales. This initially took the form of concern about police over-reaction to crime allegedly committed by African-Caribbean young people, based on unfounded racist beliefs about their greater criminality. The debate grew into a concern about demonstrable discrimination against black people in the criminal justice system more generally, and after 1993, into a concern about police under-reaction when black people were victims of serious crime. The murder of a black teenager by a gang of white racist youths, and the campaign for justice initiated by his parents highlighted the long-standing issue of racial harassment and violence to which Britain's ethnic minority populations are often subject (Bowling, 1999). The original Crime and Disorder Bill only proposed the creation of the offence of racially aggravated assault, which would have increased the severity of penalties above and beyond the usual penalty for assault, but in the course of parliamentary debate the possibility of racial aggravation, and attendant increased penalties, was introduced for a wider range of offences, including burglary and criminal damage.

Community safety initiatives

The theory and practice of crime prevention at the local level had been growing in prominence for a number of years before New Labour came to power, and the Conservative government initiated a number of projects to develop this during the 1980s and 1990s (Crawford, 1998). All were premised on the idea of multi-agency working, but there was nonetheless confusion as to who should be the local lead agency. The Home Office appointed the Morgan committee to give guidance on this, but its resulting report (Home Office, 1991), sensibly recommending that local authorities should take the lead, did not square with broader Conservative efforts to restrict the powers of local government. The report was shelved, despite strong support in local authorities themselves (with the caveat that proper resources should be provided for implementation). In opposition, however, New Labour championed the Morgan Report, and incorporated its central recommendation into the Crime and Disorder Act, albeit with the police as co-leaders with local authorities.

Henceforth, local authorities and police forces are to work with other key agencies at a district level to develop and implement three-year rolling strategies for reducing crime and disorder. The expectation is that agencies will be prepared not only to develop common strategies, but to pool resources in order to achieve their implementation. In addition, agencies should seek to ensure that their policies and practices do not conflict with one another in terms of impact and desired outcomes, an idea encapsulated in the moderniser's idea of 'joined-up government', which has become commonplace across a range of new Labour policies. The starting point of these local crime reduction strategies is to be crime audits, detailed studies of patterns of crime and issues of concern, including anti-social behaviour, based on consultation with interest groups representing the many different types of community in a given local authority area. The results of these annual audits are to be incorporated in a community safety strategy devised jointly by each local authority and police force, albeit with the statutory assistance of probation and health services.

In addition to this strategic approach to community safety, the Crime and Disorder Act also introduces an entirely new measure, the Local Child Curfew. This originated in America, via two British police force areas that had experimented with it in the mid-1990s. They involve imposing a ban in a specified public place, on unsupervised children under 10 years, between the hours of 8 p.m. and 6 a.m., for a period of up to 90 days. Police and social services are required by the Act to investigate any breaches of the Curfew Notice, empowered to take children under 10 home (or into police protection) if they violate the curfew, and to make enquiries as to whether further action is required to safeguard a specific child's welfare.

The crime reduction programme

The grand ambitions of the Crime and Disorder Act could not be achieved by legislation alone and the Act is slowly being underpinned by a wide-ranging Crime Reduction Programme, which is in turn linked to other New Labour policies which aim to reduce 'social exclusion' (Jones Finer, 1998). In launching this programme, the Home Office has continued to emphasise the need for individuals to accept responsibility for their criminal behaviour, but has also acknowledged that crime is often grounded in social exclusion, inter-generational cycles of deprivation and family breakdown. The Crime Reduction Programme (Home Office, 1999) ostensibly contributes to the fulfilment of New Labour's promise to get 'tough on the causes of crime'.

The programme draws upon available evidence of 'good practice' in crime prevention (on which the Home Office has produced a great deal of research; see Goldblatt and Lewis, 1998) and is supported by an allocation of £250 million of government money. It reinforces previous encouragement of more coordinated effort across government departments, working with the police, local government, the voluntary sector and local communities. At its heart is a recognition of the need to work with families, children and schools to prevent a new generation of young people from becoming the offenders of the future. It commits the government to tackling existing crime in local communities, particularly high-volume crime such as domestic burglary, and to working with the private sector to develop products and systems which are more resistant to crime (e.g. better security of retail premises, thief-proof cars). It promotes the development of more effective sentencing practices and work with offenders, and envisages that the £250 million will fund initiatives with a quick and clear impact on crime, on improving the quality of life, and on projects which enhance the cost-effectiveness of the criminal justice system itself.

Although the future development of the Crime Reduction Programme will to some extent be shaped by the findings of the local 'crime and disorder' surveys, certain priorities have already been set. The current one is to reduce domestic burglary. Future foci will include domestic violence, resettlement of short-term prisoners, tackling school exclusions, improving fine enforcement, restorative justice and improving the information made available to sentencers.

The Crime Reduction Programme wisely recognises that neat boundaries cannot be drawn around the phenomenon of crime - any attempt to reduce it necessarily touches on other aspects of social life and other policy initiatives, not all of which are specifically focused on crime. Thus New Labour's policy on family breakdown, requiring couples contemplating divorce to attend information/counselling sessions, and give careful consideration to the needs of their children before embarking on the legal process of separation, can be seen, over and above its intrinsic merits, as a contribution to the reduction of delinquency. Similarly, their various efforts to improve educational attainment (a major theme in the May 1997 election) can be seen as a way of equipping young people with the intellectual and personal skills necessary to occupational advancement, which in turn can reduce the likelihood of criminal involvement.

Government plans to improve access to training and employment opportunities are central to their overall strategy of social inclusion and are assumed to have a crime-reducing effect in the longer term. The influence of communitarianism and American-style workfare strategies are much in evidence here. The England and Wales 'New Deal' scheme offers the unemployed access to assessment and guidance, and a supported pathway into education and training, work experience, and/or employment, but at the same time threatens those who fail to take advantage of the opportunities which the Scheme offers with a reduction in, or loss of, their benefits.

Employment policies are related in turn to larger schemes for the regeneration of economically and socially disadvantaged communities. This has involved establishing Regional Development Agencies, and introducing initiatives such as the 'New Deal for Communities' (Social Exclusion Unit, 1999) which encourage partnerships between the local private, statutory, and voluntary sectors to develop strategies and bid for funding to regenerate local communities in which there are high levels of unemployment, social disadvantage and crime. A two-way process operates here. The government recognises that legitimate employment opportunities must be opened up if young people in particular are to be given hope and incentives to law-abiding behaviour, but it also recognises that in some areas crime must be dealt with decisively before business can even be attracted there.

A critique of Government policy

Thus far, this chapter has focused on the philosophical influences that have shaped New Labour's response to crime, and on the legislation, policy initiatives and practical measures that have constituted that response. A notion of 'community' has been and remains central to these developments. This is not itself new in England and Wales - 'community' has long been understood as a site in which crime can and should be prevented, and as a place where punishment, or treatment, can be administered. What is new under New Labour - although there are clear continuities with some aspects of previous Conservative criminal justice policies - is the intensification of control and regulation in the community, both in the name of crime prevention and in the name of punishment. Many commentators who welcomed the shift from the somewhat simplistic 'prison works' policies of the Conservative's to the slightly more sophisticated 'tough on crime, tough on the causes of crime' have nonetheless been alarmed at what they see as an unduly authoritarian strain in New Labour's approach to crime (Dunbar and Langdon, 1998). Despite the availability of sound research (Goldblatt and Lewis, 1998) it is not always open to the Home Office to claim, despite rhetoric to the contrary, that its policies are all equally evidence-led. Some, patently, contradict empirical evidence and hard-won professional experience (Wilson and Ashton, 1998).

There is, nonetheless, a prima facie coherence to New Labour's wide-ranging approach to crime, and to the general ethos of the Crime and Disorder Act, which has guaranteed its appeal both to traditional Conservative voters ('middle England') and to working-class people in socially deprived and crime-blighted areas. New Labour has in any case unprecedented expertise in packaging and presenting its policies to the public, tailoring them to particular constituencies, via different media outlets, in ways that heighten their plausibility (Fairclough, 2000). But few of its proposals on crime are in fact beyond rational criticism; the precise forms of 'getting tough' may well have undesirable consequences and, because at least some of them are based on questionable premises, the measures in the Crime and Disorder Act may not always achieve the desired results. Quite apart from the Act's rather cavalier disregard of the insights of labelling theory (see Muncie, 1999), it raises legal, technical and moral issues which will probably affect its fortunes in the longer term.

Legal critics have been quick to point out that, paradoxically, despite notional government commitment to 'joined up-ness', certain measures in the Crime and Disorder Act many not in fact be compatible with the Human Rights Act 1998 (due for implementation in October 2000) which honours a long-standing Labour promise to make the principles and rulings of the European Convention on Human Rights available in British courts. Whether the legality of the Anti-Social Behaviour Order, the Child Curfew Order and the Sex Offender Order is tested in court (as possible infringements of the Convention's 'no punishment without lawful authority' clause) remains to be seen, but the Human Rights Act is almost certain to restore some emphasis to debate on offender's civil liberties, albeit not, as pertained in the past, without balanced reference to the civil rights of crime victims. Critical comment has already been made on some aspects of youth justice provision in England and Wales by the United Nation's Committee on the Rights of the Child, which has found they fall short of the Beijing Rules - the UN's Standard Minimum Rules for Juvenile Justice (see Bell, 1999, for details).

On a different tack, the Act may fall prey to a number of long recognised difficulties with the multi-agency approach (Gilling, 1997; Crawford, 1998). Different structures and value-bases, budget arrangements, and operational priorities can make inter-agency collaboration at local level complicated, and time-consuming to achieve. The local child curfews represent a more specific technical difficulty. Although promoted by the government as a major way of getting tough on youth crime, not one of the first set of local community safety plans sent to the Home Office proposed the use of such a measure. This may reflect ideological opposition to curfews in local government, and/or a possible fear of a future legal challenge, but it is as likely to reflect the simple practical difficulties faced by police offices in ascertaining the age of particular young people who are found out 'after hours', coupled with a reluctance to alienate whole cohorts of young people in particular neighbourhoods.

There has also been strong moral criticism of the Crime and Disorder Act for not returning to a philosophy of 'penal reductionism', as some observers, rather forlornly, had expected a New Labour government to do. This criticism tends to have come from the generation of practitioners, penal reformers and academic commentators who regard the 'successful revolution' in youth justice in the 1980s and the 'punishment in the community' strategy (for probation) in the 1990s as touchstones of good practice, which should have been celebrated and built upon, rather than being forgotten (Smith, 1999). To these critics, the present strategy, which seeks to toughen community penalties without any corresponding commitment to reduced prison use (and has eschewed 'penal reductionism' as a policy aim in the same way as the United States has done), seems unnecessarily draconian. But, even if one allows for an element of nostalgia in these criticisms (generational shifts do affect attitudes to criminal justice policy) the cogency of their overall analysis, as expressed say, in the Home Office's (1990) White Paper *Crime, Justice and Protecting the Public* needs to be acknowledged. Neither the 'successful revolution' nor the 'punishment in the community' strategy actually failed. The former simply lost political and professional momentum as key personnel moved into different careers, while the latter had barely been implemented before a media backlash began (portraying it as a 'criminal's charter' because it sought to reduce prison use). Finally, it was sidelined by an ideological volte face in the Conservative Party. Penal reductionism is indeed a difficult strategy to 'sell' to the electorate, but given that Britain has the highest rate of custodial sentencing in Europe (Barclay and Tavares, 2000), and a particularly tough approach to women offenders (Carlen, 1999), it is hard to portray it honestly as a country which has been going 'soft on crime'.

What seems to lie at the heart of many of the liberal anxieties about New Labour's approach to crime and punishment is its apparent lack of compassion. The tough talk is arguably being taken to extremes and 'the community' - once understood as a more hopeful place to effect rehabilitation than prison - is now being infused with forms of discipline and surveillance akin to those used in prison itself (Brownlee, 1998). The official portrayal of offending as a matter of individual moral choice, regardless of the offender's circumstances and opportunities, finds clear practical expression in measures which restrict the discretion of professionals towards offenders, limiting the time and attention that can be shown to them as people, insisting, quite inflexibly, on the strict enforcement of community penalties (which can now include the withdrawal of welfare benefits from unemployed offenders). In such small, cumulative ways the decency and humanity of practitioners can be devalued and eroded despite their own best intentions, and those in the youth justice and probation services who have traditionally subscribed to 'social work values' in work with offenders, emphasising care as much as control, are feeling this loss keenly.

The pugnacity of government rhetoric (which, at its worst, lends support and legitimacy to the routinely punitive tone of comment on crime in Britain's more downmarket newspapers - see Kidd-Hewitt and Osborne, 1995) also serves to create a climate which diminishes public tolerance of convicted offenders under supervision in the community, and makes it harder for rehabilitative and reintegrative practices to flourish. This has been demonstrated most dramatically in respect of sex offenders, particularly paedophiles, but even less serious offenders (and some who are merely social nuisances, such as beggars) have been 'demonised' by government rhetoric and media stereotyping, in ways that call their fundamental humanity into question, and which imply they can never change for the better.

Conclusion: what next?

The Crime and Disorder Act 1998 may have been New Labour's flagship legislation, representing the fulfilment of its immediate election promises, but the government's modernisation project in respect of criminal justice is by no means at an end. At the time of writing (March 2000), the Criminal Justice and Court Services Bill has just been laid before Parliament. It contains provisions for reforming the Probation Service in order to enhance the credibility of community penalties, increasing central government control over its operations. Although the Service will not itself be renamed (as had once been mooted; Nellis, 2000b) the two orders with which it is most closely associated, probation and community service will be renamed 'community rehabilitation order' and 'community punishment order' respectively. There will be a further expansion of electronic monitoring as both a whole or a part of a community sentence, as well as a condition of release on licence from prison, including, by 2003, the use of tags to track the movements of convicted offenders such as sex offenders, rather than as now, simply to restrict them to particular places. In order to break the link between criminal activity and the financing of drug habits, the police will be given powers to perform compulsory drug tests on all arrestees, and the courts will be enabled to make 'drug abstinence orders' for between six months and three years, monitored by regular testing. All court orders will henceforth be enforced more rigorously, even though it is understood that this may add a further 15,000 people to the already high prison population, at a cost of £60m.

The detailed provisions of this Bill may be altered in the course of its passage through parliament, but the thrust of it will not. It augments New Labour's determination to be 'tough on crime' in a way that, as yet, has no parallel in any other European country. There are undoubtedly positive elements within the government's overall strategy - e.g. the commitment to sound, evidence-led ways of challenging offender's behaviour in prison and on probation, the effort to cleanse the criminal justice system of racism, the tentative interest in restorative justice - but these are hardly its hallmark. Far more significant, in terms of the departure from postwar tradition that it represents, is the readiness to see the prison population increase (with all new prisons being built and run by the private sector) and the development of electronic monitoring (also in private sector hands) on a scale which, proportionately, surpasses even the United States. Coupled with the huge expansion of surveillance by CCTV, all this suggests that England is undergoing a sea-change in its approach to crime control. Worryingly, the tenor of these changes, and the level of financial investment in them, suggests that the government itself is putting very little faith in its policies for being 'tough on the causes of crime'- reducing poverty and disadvantage, increasing social inclusion through education and training - and accepting that for the foreseeable future the management of crime and disorder will require much greater levels of coercion and control.

References

Audit Commission (1996), *Misspent Youth*, Audit Commission, London.

Barclay, G. and Tavares, C. (2000), *International Comparisons of Criminal Justice Statistics 1998*, Home Office Statistical Bulletin 04/00, Home Office, London.

Bell, C. (1999), 'Appealing for justice for children and young people: a critical analysis of the Crime and Disorder Bill 1998', in B. Goldson (ed), *Youth Justice: Contemporary Policy and Practice*, Ashgate, Aldershot.

Bowling, B. (1999*), Violent Racism: Victimisation, Policing and Social Context*, Oxford University Press, Oxford.

Brownlee, I. (1998,) *Community Punishment: A Critical introduction*, Longman, Harlow.

Carlen, P. (1998), *Sledgehammer: Women's Imprisonment at the Millenium*, MacMillan, Basingstoke.

Cavadino, M., Crow, I. and Dignan, J. (2000), *Criminal Justice 2000: Strategies for A New Century*, Waterside Press, Winchester.

Crawford, A. (1998), *Crime Prevention and Community Safety*, Longman, Harlow.

Dunbar, I. and Langdon, A. (1998), *Tough Justice: Sentencing and Penal Policies in the 1990s*, Blackstone Press, London.

Etzioni, A. (1995), *The Spirit of Community: Rights, Responsibilities and the Communitarian Agenda*, Fontana, London.

Fairclough, N. (2000), *New Labour, New Language*, Routledge, London.

Giddens, A. (1998), *The Third Way*, Polity Press, Cambridge.

Giddens, A. (2000), *The Third Way and its Critics*, Polity Press, Cambridge.

Gilling, D. (1997), *Crime Prevention: Theory, Policy and Politics*, UCL Press, London.

Goldblatt, P. and Lewis, C. (eds) (1998), *Reducing Offending: An Assessment of Research Evidence on Ways of Dealing with Offending Behaviour*, Home Office research study 187, Home Office, London.

Gould, P. (1998), *The Unfinished Revolution: How the Modernisers Saved the Labour Party*, Little Brown and Company, London.

Hebenton, B. and Thomas, T. (1996), '"Tracking" sex offenders', *Howard Journal*, 35 (2) pp. 97-112.

Home Office (1990), *Crime, Justice and Protecting the Public*, Cm 965, HMSO, London.

Home Office (1991), *Safer Communities: The Local Delivery of Crime Prevention Through the Partnership Approach* (The Morgan Report), Home Office, London.

Home Office (1996), *No More Excuses: A New Approach to Tackling Youth Crime in England and Wales*, Cm 3809, HMSO, London.

Home Office (1998), *Tackling Drugs to Build a Better Britain: A National Strategy*, HMSO, London.

Home Office (1999), *The Government's Crime Reduction Strategy*, Home Office, London.

Hughes, G. (1998), *Understanding Crime Prevention: Social Control, Risk and Late Modernity*, Open University Press, Buckingham.

Jones, D. (1989), 'The successful revolution', *Community Care* (Inside Supplement), 30th March, pp. i-ii.

Jones-Finer, C. (1998), 'The new social policy in Britain', in C. Jones Finer and M. Nellis (eds), *Crime and Social Exclusion*, Blackwell, Oxford.

Kelling, G. and Coles, C. (1998), *Fixing Broken Windows - Restoring Order and Reducing Crime in our Communities*, The Free Press, New York.

Kidd-Hewitt, D. and Osborne, R. (eds) (1995), *Crime and the Media*, Pluto Press, London.

Lacey, N. and Zedner, L. (1995), 'Discourses of community in criminal justice', *Journal of Law and Society*, 22 (3), pp. 301-325.

Loewenstein, P. (2000), *Modern Youth Work and Youth Crime Prevention*, National Youth Agency, Leicester.

Marshall, T. (1999), *Restorative Justice: An Overview*, Home Office, London.

Mediation UK (1999), *Restorative Justice: Does it Work? Digest of Current Research on Victim Offender-mediation and Conferencing*, Mediation UK, Bristol.

Muncie, J. (1999), 'Institutionalised intolerance: youth justice and the 1998 Crime and Disorder Act', *Critical Social Policy*, 19 (2) pp. 147-175.

Norris, C. and Armstrong, G. (2000), *The Maximum Surveillance Society: The Rise of CCTV*, Berg, Oxford.

Nellis, M. (1991), 'The last days of "juvenile" justice?' in P. Carter, T. Jeffs and M. Smith, *Social Work and Social Welfare Yearbook 3*, Open University Press, Milton Keynes.

Nellis, M. (1999), 'Towards the Field of Corrections': Modernising the Probation Service in the 1990s', *Social Policy and Administration*, 33 (3) pp. 302-323.

Nellis, M. (2000a), 'Law and Order: The Electronic Monitoring of Offenders', in D. Dolowitz (ed), *Policy Transfer and British Social Policy*, Open University Press, Buckingham.

Nellis, M. (2000b), 'Renaming probation', *Probation Journal*, 47 (1) pp. 39-44.

Rutherford, A. (1992), *Growing Out of Crime The New Era*, Waterside Press, Winchester.

Rutherford, A. (1996), *Transforming Criminal Policy*, Waterside Press, Winchester.

Rutter, M., Giller, H. and Hagell, A. (1999), *Anti-Social Behaviour in Young People*, Blackwell, Oxford.

Smith, D. (1999), 'Social work with young people in trouble. Memory and prospect', in B. Goldson (ed), *Youth Justice: Contemporary Policy and Practice*, Ashgate, Aldershot.

Social Exclusion Unit (1999), *Bringing Britain Together: A National Strategy for Neighbourhood Renewal*, HMSO, London.

Sopel, J. (1995), *Tony Blair: The Moderniser*, Bantam Books, London.

Whitfield, D. (1998), *Tackling The Tag: The Electronic Monitoring of Offenders*, Waterside Press, Winchester.

Wilson, D. and Ashton, J. (1998), *What Everyone in Britain Should Know About Crime and Punishment*, Blackstone Press, London.

Wilson, J. and Kelling, G. (1982), 'Broken windows: the police and neighbourhood safety', *The Atlantic Monthly*, March, pp. 29-37.

Young, J. (1998), 'Zero tolerance: back to the future', in A. Marlow and J. Pitts (eds), *Planning Safer Communities*, Russell House Publications, Lyme Regis.

PART V
EAST-WEST IDEAS ON
WELFARE AND GROWTH

16 Looking East, looking West: trends in orientalism and occidentalism amongst applied social scientists

JOHN DOLING

CATHERINE JONES FINER

Introduction

In the world of international social policy relations, mutual perceptions, misunderstandings and prejudices can count for at least as much as the actuality of policies in operation from one place to another. This has demonstrably been true of East-West social policy relations over the past half-century, where prevailing patterns of opinion, both East-West and West-East, have evinced recurrent swings of emphasis.

This chapter identifies and comments on three such episodes in mutual social policy relations, as set out in table 16.1, from the point of view both of trends in Orientalism and trends in Occidentalism. The authors are themselves both western, which obviously detracts from the symmetry of the exercise. Nevertheless, the topic is one worth developing as a stimulus for discussion.

We note the underlying mutual suspicions and hostility characteristic of the entire period, and consider the extent to which this has undermined prospects for the development of genuine, longer-term 'positive' social policy relations. The chapter concludes with a review of the current situation and, in the context of globalisation and mutual uncertainty, identifies specific topics as possible 'bridge-builders' for the future of social policy relations between East and West.

Table 16.1 Recent episodes in orientalism and occidentalism

Period	Orientalism (West on East)	Occidentalism (East on West)
1950s-1960s	Negative	Reluctant positive
1970s-1980s	Doubtful positive	Negative
1990s	Positive-negative	Negative-positive

Source: Adapted in part from White and Goodman (1998) pp.5–13.

First period: 1950s-1960s

Negative orientalism on the part of the West

The interest from western nations in South and East Asian countries in the 1950s and 1960s had little to do with the desire to learn lessons directly in relation to their own internal agendas. Development economics - more broadly development studies - was concerned with questions of whether and under what conditions Asian, and other underdeveloped countries would achieve rapid economic growth and industrialisation. The pioneers in the field saw the problem of underdevelopment as one arising from the failure of private markets to invest sufficiently to generate increased demand (Choudhury and Islam, 1993). Such analyses led to policy proposals aimed at underdeveloped countries, for example in the form of government investment in strategic sectors and the planned development of import substitution industries. Whilst such interpretations were greatly contested throughout this period, the point is that the impetus for debate lay not in learning lessons for the western nations to adopt, but in attempts to increase the economic wealth of underdeveloped countries. Moreover, even though they might lead to more welfare for some people in the underdeveloped world, these were *economic* lessons being propounded.

Reluctant positive occidentalism on the part of the East

The USA and Britain were the two western countries exercising most direct influence on the shaping of emergent and recovering societies in post-World War II Asia Pacific: the USA as a result of its military presence (in respect of Japan, Taiwan and South Korea especially) and Britain as a result of legacies of colonialism still operational (albeit with some post-war shame and embarrassment) in respect of Hong Kong and Singapore.

In both cases, this western governmental impact had been prefaced and reinforced by legacies of western missionary effort. This was especially telling in respect of charitable institutions such as schools, hospitals and homes for the destitute/disabled/elderly. Moreover it was a legacy massively - albeit chaotically - supplemented by influxes of international aid to Hong Kong, *par excellence*, in the wake of the Chinese Communist Revolution of 1949 and the flight of millions from the mainland. Conditions of such disruption, mass migration and deprivation were precisely the sorts of conditions indigenous, traditional styles of social welfare could not be expected to cope with. Continuity of village-kin networks, family status and locality had been essential to the old ways of running a good society.

The 1950s and 1960s saw the old and especially the new tigers of Asia Pacific variously adapting to and building upon such legacies and impositions in respect of what was thought to be 'useful' western social policy. They were encouraged to do this not least by the hefty presence of western social policy 'experts', supplemented by western-trained assistants, not least in the teaching departments of leading Asia Pacific universities. Naturally such a presence (on distinctly preferential terms) was to provoke mounting local resentment in the long run. For the time being, however, it was accepted that westernisation was the key to modernisation, which was the necessity for the future. Confucianism, by contrast, signified 'living in the past'.

This was not therefore an occidentalism based on positive respect for The West. The same Asian societies were swift to dismiss western 'developed' societies *per se* as effete; lacking in socio-economic discipline and above all in family virtue. Conceivably this distaste functioned as Asia Pacific's best defence against being patronised by outsiders recognised, for the time being, as being richer and more powerful than themselves. Furthermore, it did not take long for western imports and implants (notably in respect of specialist social services and professional social work) to be indigenised in accordance with local taste and scruple.

Second period: 1970s-1980s, crisis of the western welfare states

Positive orientalism on the part of the West

The interest in social policies in other countries, particularly the search for policy lessons, has been far from geographically random. The relevance of policy elsewhere to the situation at home appears to have been greatly influenced by the level of economic development in the countries under scrutiny. From the West, therefore, the focus of the 1970s-1980s was primarily on Japan as the most successful (in GDP terms) of the Asian economies, followed by the four little tigers. Interest in the next wave, the ASEAN four of Malaysia, Thailand, Indonesia and the Philippines, as well as in China, was considerably more muted. Not only did their social policies not yet come with the credential of advanced economic position, but highly publicised poor human rights records undermined their claim to offer welfare models relevant to a less authoritarian West.

Economic policies. The beginnings of the interest in the NICs of Asia Pacific as a source of policy lessons can be traced to the post-1970s period in which the earlier, post-war models of economic and welfare organisation were crumbling. The NICs were now of interest in the West, to both politicians and social scientists, because they seemed to constitute a model based on liberal principles - free markets, minimal state intervention, low social overheads - that was also increasingly becoming ideologically dominant in the West.

According to this interpretation the success of the Asian economies could - in contrast to some of the earlier development studies literature - be located firmly in the free rein given to market processes. As Henderson (1993, p.201) was later (somewhat over-statedly) to put it:

> We were told, in effect, that the reason why Japan had become the world's most successful economy and why the other four [Hong Kong, Korea, Singapore, Taiwan], almost alone among the societies of the developed world, had moved decisively in the direction of high productivity - high wage economies, was because they had been relatively free of distortions in capital, labour, technology and other markets. In particular, it was suggested that, unlike many other developing - and developed - economies, their respective states either had not intervened to distort markets, or if they had, had done so to correct pre-existing distortions...Having got relative prices 'right', the positive influence of 'market forces' could be maximized, and the stunning double digit growth rates typical of the last three decades could be achieved.

However this neo-liberal interpretation came increasingly under attack, as the work of a number of social scientists, from the USA in particular, began to suggest that the perception of liberal systems based on minimal government was largely mistaken. Thus, Chalmers Johnson

(1982) introduced the concept of the 'developmental state' applied to Japan, but by extension to some other Asian countries. Following on from this, Wade's now-familiar argument (1990) was that the secret of the success of at least two of the Asian economies (Taiwan and Korea) lay in the 'governed market' in which their states took dominant roles to ensure that specific industrial sectors developed in ways consistent with the former's perception of the national interest (Wade, 1990). Likewise, Alice Amsden (Amsden, 1989), in her study of Taiwan, saw the approach as 'deliberately getting prices wrong' involving subsidies, tax concessions and high levels of lending which gave governments leverage over the actions of individual companies. In these ways states influenced investment decisions, pushing industrial companies into adopting new technologies, new practices and so on which would ensure the rapid transfer of new technologies into key industries by developing their international competitiveness and establishing a comparative advantage which enabled them to take on and beat the industries of the old industrialised countries.

Social policies. This interpretation of the governance of the Tiger economies could be applied equally to their governance of welfare. The combination of an unchallenged, national objective of economic growth, and a belief in the responsibility of the family and community to care for its members, meant that free-standing social welfare services, established on humanitarian or equity grounds had never been given high priority. In general the role of social policies as with all other parts of the corporate plan, was perceived as being (merely) to further the economic goals of the nation:

> Most Asian social policy has been more strongly shaped by the develop-
> mental priorities of politically insulated states than by extra-bureaucratic
> political forces (Deyo, 1992, p.304).

Here, too, the model was not therefore one of a liberal, free market. Indeed, there are, as Catherine Jones (1993) has argued, important contrasts between the welfare systems or models characterising the Tiger states and those of the older industrialised countries. Thus, by comparison with Esping-Andersen's ideal types, the Tiger states clearly did not conform to his category of liberal regimes, being possessed of too much central direction and too little sense of individual rights. Neither could they be described as social democratic or even conservative corporatist, since they did not formally accommodate the interests of the working class. Rather they seemed to represent another regime type, one characterised by conservative corporatism without worker participation, laissez faire but not liberal, and having solidarity without equality.

In both content and in emphasis, then, the welfare systems of the Tiger economies were reckoned distinctive. Restricting 'social expenditure, in order to pour national resources into the primary goal of national policy' (Ku, 1995, p.360) had meant that social services, social security systems, health care programmes and so on had had to be limited in their development. Overall, social welfare expenditure, in terms of GDP per capita, remained small by comparison with that of the European industrialised countries. Data on expenditure on social protection - unemployment benefit, work injuries, family allowances, sickness benefit, etc. - indicate that such measures (to the extent they were present at all) were less well developed than in most western countries. Nevertheless, by the 1970s, the little Tigers had begun to shift their national economic strategies toward the 'promotion of higher value-added manufacturing [which, in turn] prompted greater investment in "human capital" along with new strategies to enhance labour force stability and productivity' (Deyo, 1992, p.291). Consequently, the sectors of education and training were increasing in importance, taking a greater proportion of national GDP per capita.

Expenditure on welfare programmes thus varied from patterns typical in the West. But there were also large within-group variations. For example there were large differences in the scale of state housing provision, this being particularly high (even by western, let alone Asian standards) in Singapore and Hong Kong:

> in one of the most striking paradoxes of urban policy in the world, the two market economies with the highest rates of economic growth in the last twenty-five years are also those with the largest public housing programmes in the capitalist world, in terms of the proportion of the population directly housed by the government (Castells et al, 1990, p.1).

So, in this respect again, the systems of welfare seemed to bear limited resemblance to the stereotype of minimal government and liberal free market provision. Nevertheless, throughout the 1980s and first half of the 1990s, Asian Pacific economies continued to be held up as models of free enterprise from which the West could and should learn:

> A bewildering array of positive images became projected on to East Asia that

have told us as much about those doing the projecting as about the societies themselves. Their arguments have tended to run thus. East Asia has the most dynamic economies in the world. They have managed to combine this dynamism with social cohesion, an apparent 'health miracle' and very low crime rates, while keeping their welfare expenditures low. From the perspective of societies with low growth rates, escalating social problems and high welfare expenditures, we need to seek out the secret of East Asian success and where possible reproduce it (White and Goodman, 1998).

It was on this basis that a succession of senior British politicians were given to report, with enthusiasm, on social policy ideas from Asia Pacific: on the virtues of small or minimal government; on minimal worker protection as a key to the creation of flexible labour markets; on revamped, revitalised education systems as a key to economic growth; on the importance of cultivating a sense of personal and family responsibility amongst ordinary people; and of the virtues of social insurance based on individual saving (e.g. Blair, 1996, pp.57-62 especially; Finer, 1999, pp.304-325).

Negative occidentalism on the part of the East

The impact of the oil crises upon the resources-starved NICs of Asia Pacific was undoubtedly profound. Nevertheless it seemed nothing like so profound as was the effect of the much-publicised difficulties being experienced by western welfare states, notably Britain, on key Asia Pacific perceptions. Indeed it was over this period that Japan, Hong Kong, Singapore, South Korea and Taiwan were each working to establish (inter alia) specifically indigenous social welfare identities of their own; in response to both local and global pressures. The example of the welfare state West, in this context, stood as an awful warning of the enfeebling path down which no self-respecting government should consider taking its people. By contrast, 'Confucian values' (in all their latter-day variety) were being re-appreciated and publicised as a vital key to social stability and good order.

Thus it was that the 1970s and 1980s witnessed the beginnings of a Japanese drive to launch its own 'welfare society' (wherein the functioning, three-generational family would play a key sustaining role); the beginnings of popular democracy in South Korea and Taiwan, and even the beginnings, in Hong Kong (in the wake of the Cultural Revolution riots of the latter 1960s), of a top-down drive to transform this increasingly anachronistic colony into a 'society' that cared for its people (e.g. Jones, 1990, p.210); not merely by revamping the accumulation of social services in a more populist direction, but by educating families in the ways of Family Life and the inhabitants of whole housing blocks in the ways of Mutual Aid (Jones, 1990, pp.221-222). 'Western individualism' - perceived overwhelmingly as 'licensed selfishness', as indicated by varieties of secular liberalism rather than by any reading of Judeo-Christian tradition - was the bogey Asia Pacific societies were being instructed to shun at all costs.

Third period: 1990s

Positive-negative orientalism on the part of the West

The Asian crisis of the late 1990s brought about another sea change in western perceptions. The prolonged recession in Japan, combined with currency depreciations (particularly in Thailand, Malaysia, the Philippines, Indonesia and Korea), financial market crises, and the IMF-imposed monetary and fiscal austerity measures (Malaysia has adopted the approach but not the actuality of the IMF), all served to undermine the previous positive image. Seen as the result of failures of their respective governments to pursue appropriate levels of probity in their policies, the Asian crisis shattered the image of states that, because they were deemed to have got the main things right, had been reckoned appropriate models for the West.

In so far as this has been the case, it was some ways as ill founded as earlier perceptions. Not all the Asian economies faltered; Taiwan having notably escaped for the time being. Economic cycles and recessionary periods have not been exactly unknown in western economies. The economic fundamentals remain basically sound (particularly in Malaysia and Korea) and full recovery seems likely to be apparent soon. Most of all, it was not welfare policies that were the root cause of the crisis and, with the major exception of Korea, it was not the Little Tigers who suffered most. Once again, nevertheless, the West has seen itself as the teacher, instructing for the good of the pupils.

Negative-positive occidentalism on the part of the East

By the early 1990s, Japan and the 'Little Tigers' had seemingly written off 'the West' as serious competition, let alone as a residual source of models for emulation - political, economic or social. Witness the shock, therefore, of the Asian Financial Crisis and the significance of its portrayal, in South Korea and again in Malaysia, *par excellence,* as being in part a Western contrivance, compounded thereafter by IMF/World Bank impositions. Certainly the much reported willingness of Korean families to pledge their savings in support of national economic recovery was testimony as much to the bottom-up strength of 'Asian Values' - so long dismissed as mere authoritarianism in the West - as it was to the financial naivety of the families concerned. Of greater significance and wider regional implication for longer-term, however, were to be the repercussions arising from the realisation that not even modern, go ahead Asia Pacific governments could necessarily, invariably, deliver the goods to the very people they had instructed to count on them.

The key social values of deference to superior authority and of subordination of the individual to the interests of the group (be this the family, the corporation and/or the state), have always been predicated on an assumption that the group in question is going to continue to be functionally effective. Not for nothing has the hugeness of China been described as a country alternating throughout its recorded history between periods of more or less effective governance and intervening eras of - more or less - turbulence and riot (e.g. Finer, S.E., 1997, Volume 1, Book II, Chapters 5 and 6; Volume 2, Book III, Part 2, Chapters 3 and 4; Volume 3, Book IV, Chapter 2). The same could be said of the much smaller Japan and, more recently and specifically, in relation to the Little Tigers of Hong Kong, Singapore, South Korea and Taiwan. To the extent that democracy has since taken root in the various states concerned, their ability to deliver on the socio-economic front could yet prove a decisive test for the political structures now in operation. To the extent democracy has *not* yet 'taken root', the possibility of riot presumably remains. In the words of the World Bank:

> Economic stresses are leading to social and political problems. The rapid development which brought rising incomes to most East Asian households in the past decades has also led to rapid social change, urbanization, migration and expansion of education. The sudden stop to this rapid growth is expected to disturb the social equilibrium (World Bank, 1998, p.82).

But once again this is Western talk, based on western perceptions and assumptions, albeit ostensibly on Easterners' behalf. The prospects for a genuine dialogue between East and West depend not merely on there being a greater measure of mutual understanding but a greater measure of mutual humility and respect, above all a respect for differences.

Prospects for the future

No one 'knows' about the future, least of all now. But it is in conditions of such mutual uncertainty, coupled with the seeming inevitability of mutual repercussions as a consequence of any actions undertaken or with-held, that the time - paradoxically - could be ripe for the incremental, pragmatic build-up of mutually positive social policy relations. We suggest two sample areas for enhanced future exchange, the first (West-East) seeming more obvious in global terms than the second (East-West).

Social security. Bezanson and Griffith-Jones (1999) argue that the Little Tigers' success story was not simply about GDP growth but also about the substantial reduction in the incidence of poverty, brought about because of their ability to create jobs with steady and growing incomes. Against this background, the Asian financial crisis has had a number of impacts. Rising unemployment has been the most direct, but significant too has been the resulting move into informal-sector participation where earnings are generally lower, combined with increases in food prices, interest rates and the cost of imported drugs, leading to decreasing levels of health care. One outcome has been the setting of a new agenda. 'The design of affordable social protection nets is both essential and difficult for countries undergoing financial and currency crisis...[they] must be developed in forms that are consistent with, and encourage, economic recovery' (ibid, 1999, p12). Arguably, this is a western forte, given that the west has been struggling with this agenda for the last 30 years.

Hitherto, the leading economies of Asia Pacific have shown themselves expert at 'indigenising' social/public policies inherited from abroad, as well as at themselves drawing lessons from abroad, on a needs-be, pragmatic basis. But such efforts were geared, above all, to mobilising and motivating the employable with promises of ever better standards of living and of educational/career opportunities for their children. Manifestly there was no 'need' in such a context to consider western practices with regard to the able-bodied unemployed, since there was no officially registered unemployment to speak of and no concept, therefore, of such a category as the 'respectable unemployed'. Even those not fit for work - such as the elderly or disabled - could find the terms of any backstop assistance on offer so minimalist and deliberately shaming for themselves and their families as to be literally not worth asking for (e.g. Chan, 1998).

Hitherto, in other words, significant rates of unemployment have been presumed a western problem; even a product of western welfare statehood and its generosity with regard to unemployment benefits. The NICs of Asia Pacific, with their 'growth or bust' philosophy had seemingly assumed that unemployment would/could never be a matter for their own governmental concern, since there would/could never be a problem of unemployment which was beyond the personal power of families to cope with. There were not usually even standardised mechanisms for recording the numbers of 'the unemployed' since, without there being benefits to register for - let alone benefits fit for men to claim - it could be difficult for governments even to begin to estimate the numbers of 'genuinely unemployed' under their authority.

It is in such circumstances that governments in Asia Pacific have, some of them, been thinking again, with a view to borrowing (again) from western experience, this time explicitly on a needs-be basis, as best suits them. As before, the borrowing is unlikely to be of entire models of approach so much as of specific programmes or techniques of intervention, precisely because these are capable of being taken 'out of context' and utilized differently in a different environment, to possible pathbreaking effect.

Given prevailing condemnatory public attitudes to the unemployed in leading Asian Pacific societies, as so long encouraged and reinforced by the governments concerned, striking the right balance between morality and political practicality is not going to be easy for any of them. Yet, by the same token, any measures or combinations of measures they do come up with could, in turn, prove of significance for the western countries from which they may have borrowed in the meantime. The UK - given the present government's declared predilection for at least some Asian Pacific ways of socio-economic management (e.g. Blair, 1996; Finer, C.J., 1997) - constitutes an obvious case in point.

Housing and urban development. The East Asian economies have demonstrated an ability to build housing at a rate sufficient to cope with rapid urbanisation, a product of high rates of natural increase, large-scale rural-urban migration and sometimes the arrival of foreign workers and their families. In a matter of just a decade or two - sometimes three - urban landscapes have been transformed from mainly low rise housing and squatter settlements with all their attendant deficiencies in sanitation, water supply and other facilities to modern, well equipped, high rise blocks. Whereas it might be thought unlikely that western countries will ever again be challenged to build at this rate, there are potential lessons from the East Asian experience. Their success has perhaps been most marked where government controlled and planned. Through national five and ten year development plans, governments set targets for housing production by house type (including size) and location and specified the resource input needs. Moreover they were able to exert effective influence on those resources - land, labour and capital - so that the targets could be met (Doling, 1999). Their achievements indicate that forms of state planning may be as effective in achieving infrastructural development as, in the case of the East Asian economies, it has in economic development. But more than that, the cases of Singapore and Hong Kong in particular show that public provision, and not just public regulation, can be effective. So, in housing production, just as in economic growth, they demonstrate that the state does provide an effective alternative to laissez-faire speculation and development.

Conclusion

It is interesting that neither of the above fields was singled out for discussion earlier in this volume, or at the conference which gave rise to it (above p.3). They have not been part of the established substance of social policy discourse between East and West; unemployment because - in modern terms - it is new to the East; housing because it would be novel for the West to think of learning about anything so 'concrete' from the East.

This is not to suggest that the only prospects for more balanced social policy relations in the future will be via the avoidance of territory already well trodden in the past. However, it is to suggest that novel subjects discussed in novel directions may offer a useful pointer towards a less 'loaded' and hence more useful pattern of social policy discourse to come.

References

Amsden, A. (1989), *Asia's Next Giant: South Korea and Late Industrialisation*, Oxford University Press, New York and Oxford.

Besanzon, K. and Griffith-Jones, S. (1999), 'The East Asian crisis: A global problem requiring global solutions', *IDS Bulletin*, 30, (1), pp.1-12.

Blair, T. (1996), *New Britain: My Vision of a Young Country*, Fourth Estate, London.

Castells, M., Goh, I. and Kwok, R. (1990), *The Shek Kip Mei Syndrome: Economic Development and Public Housing in Hong Kong and Singapore*, Pion, London.

Chan, Chak-Kwan (1998), 'Welfare Policies and the Construction of Welfare Relations: The Case of Hong Kong', *Social Policy and Administration*, Vol. 32, No. 3, pp.278-291.

Choudhury, A. and Islam, I. (1993), *The Newly Industrialising Economies of East Asia*, Routledge, London.

Deyo, F. (1992), 'The political economy of social policy formation: East Asia's newly industrialized countries', in R. Appelbaum and J. Henderson J (eds), *States and Development in the Asian Pacific Rim*, Sage, London.

Doling, J. (1999), 'Housing policy and the Little Tigers. How do they compare with other industrialised countries?', *Housing Studies*, 14, (2), pp.229-250.

Finer, C.J. (1997), 'Social policy' in P.Dunleavy, A.Gamble, I.Holliday and G.Peele (eds) *Developments in British Politics (5)*, MacMillan, Basingstoke.

Finer, S.E. (1997), *The History of Government from the Earliest Times*, OUP, Oxford.

Goodman, R., White, G. and Kwon, H-j, (1998), *The East Asian Welfare Model: Welfare Orientalism and the State*, Routledge, London.

Henderson, J. (1993b) 'The role of the state in the economic transformation of East Asia', in Dixon and Drakakis-Smith (eds), *Economic and Social Development in Pacific Asia*, Routledge, London.

Johnson, C. (1982), *MITI and the Japanese Miracle: The Growth of Industrial Policy*, Stanford University Press, Stanford.

Jones, C.J. (1990), *Promoting Prosperity: The Hong Kong Way of Social Policy*, The Chinese University Press, Hong Kong.

Ku, Y-W. (1995), 'The development of state welfare in the Asian NICs with special reference to Taiwan', *Social Policy and Administration*, 29, (4), pp.345-364.

Wade, R. (1990), *Governing the Market: Economic Theory and the Role of Government in East Asian Industrialization*, Princeton University Press, Princeton.

World Bank (1998), *East Asia: The Road to Recovery*, The World Bank, Washington D.C.

17 Elite political-cultural projects, economic growth and the achievement of social welfare in East Asia[1]

PETER W. PRESTON

Introduction

This paper considers the relationship between economic development and social welfare in East Asia. The paper will adopt an hermeneutic-critical approach, assuming that social science comprises a variety of context-dependent ways of making arguments, each of which will construe any particular issue differently. The author's work is located within the classical European tradition of social theorizing which is centrally concerned with the emancipatory elucidation of the dynamics of complex change in the ongoing shift to the modern world (Preston, 1996).

The paper will comprise three areas of reflection: (i) a discussion of the various ways in which the issue of growth and welfare can be handled within Western disciplines of social science; (ii) a discussion of two exercises in analysis made by Western authors dealing with particular issues relating to East Asian development; and (iii) the presentation of three 'case studies' of East Asian experiences (characterized from the author's position).

In the first place, therefore, the paper will consider the ways in which five areas of (Western) social scientific reflection have construed the question of the relationship of economic development and social welfare. In each of these five areas the issue of economic development will be primary and social welfare, and its relationship to economic development dealt with thereafter. Then secondly, these theoretical reflections will lead into two areas of substantive discussion: (i) the World Bank's analysis of the East Asian Economic Miracle; and (ii) the sociology of economics presented by Ron Dore. And in the third section of the paper three 'case studies' will be noted: (i) Singapore; (ii) Japan; and Taiwan.

307

The conclusions should be as follows:
(i)   the idea of 'economic development' is inevitably contested;
(ii)   the idea of 'social welfare' is inevitably contested;
(iii) their relationship in practice is shaped by the political-cultural projects of local elites;
(iv) the grasp that Western analysts manage to obtain on these ideas will be context-dependent; and
(v) consequently, any claims or recommendations which we social scientists might want to make about growth and welfare had best be seen to be tentative, provisional and dialogic (that is, open to revision in conversation with other thinkers and actors).

Lines of theoretical reflection

It is clear that the countries of East Asia have undergone extensive change in the years following the end of the Pacific War. The countries of East Asia have recorded consistently high economic growth rates. A variety of discipline-based analyses have been offered (from international relations, political science, economics, anthropology, and history) and a variety of key factors have been suggested, including the role of the cold war, the activity of the state, the nature of socio-economic life and the peculiarities of local cultures and histories. An inter-disciplinary approach can also be noted, international political economy, which would point to the slow movement towards a distinctive regional integration around a Japanese core.

International relations arguments

International relations specialists have pointed to the role of the USA within the region:
(i) as the country which militarily defeated the Imperial Japanese armed forces and played an influential role in establishing post-war patterns of economy and society;
(ii) as the country which adopted the role of bulwark against perceived communist expansion in the region and which played a further important role in shaping the post-war patterns of economy and society;
(iii) as the country which in the light of (i) and (ii) made very great expenditures within the region in connection with its military posture;
(iv) as the country which in the light of (i) and (ii) facilitated the membership of countries within the region in the key international bodies

of the post-war period (UN, IBRD, IMF etcetera); and
(v) as the country which in the light of (i) and (ii) allowed exporters in the region relatively easy access to its markets.

International relations specialists have thus characterized the USA as the regionally hegemonic power. The general prosperity of countries of the region is explained, therefore, in terms of a largely fortuitous external interest in ordering the region.

It might be thought that the relationship between social welfare and economic growth would not be addressed in these international relations analyses but that is not the case. A standard US position in respect of left-wing political action was summed up by the idea that 'communism was a disease of the transition from the traditional to the modern world'. This implied that economic and social reform could alleviate the poverty which was taken to be the breeding ground of left-wing action. Hence, for example, land reform in Taiwan and Japan.

Political scientific arguments

Political-scientists have debated the role of the state in economic growth and a series of (often disparate) points have been made:
(i) liberal theorists have argued that the state has worked in a 'market conforming' manner and has therefore assisted development in an essentially passive or enabling fashion;
(ii) revisionsist (political-economy) theorists have argued that the state has worked in an extensive fashion to mobilize society in pursuit of economic growth.
In both cases the successful record of economic growth in the region is granted.
The relationship of economic growth and social welfare is construed somewhat differently in these two lines of commentary:
(i) liberal theorists have argued that economic growth provides wealth which trickles down through the various social strata and thereby raises the level of living of all members of society;
(ii) revisionist theorists have argued that the elite has mobilized the mass of the population in pursuit of economic growth and that an element of this mobilization has been the promise (and provision) of material wealth, in other words, the linkage is intrinsic to a process of political mobilization.

Economics arguments

Economists have debated the logic of the marketplace in East Asia and a series of (often disparate) points have been made:
(i) market-liberal theorists[2] are committed apriori to a particular model of humankind as an rational-calculative consumption maximizer and have looked to read the post-war development experience of East Asia in these terms, for example, modernization (or catch-up);
(ii) political-economists are concerned with analysing shifting structural patterns and have looked to read the post-war development experience of East Asia in these terms, for example, as sequences of productive activity variously located in space.

The political-economists have granted that the region has recorded significant long-term economic growth. The market-liberal economists have been more uncomfortable theorizing the development experience of the region; thus, Krugman's (1994) notion of 'catch-up' is essentially dismissive.

The relationship of growth and welfare has been construed somewhat differently in these two lines of commentary:
(i) market-liberal theorists are wedded to the idea of trickle-down and point to generally increasing levels of living and growing welfare provision (although this is an awkward issue for them to handle);
(ii) political-economists point to the ways in which established social practices and cultural traditions, which have served welfare functions in the past, have been modified in the post-war period of economic growth - the picture is patchy and has to be uncovered piecemeal.

Cultural/historical arguments

Cultural and historical analysts point to the particularity and detail of the development experiences of the countries of the region:
(i) to the diversity and prosperity of the indigenous empires within the region;
(ii) to the displacement of established patterns in the process of the irruption within the region of industrial-capitalism;
(iii) to the reconstitution of patterns-of-life within the context of colonial (or quasi-colonial rule);
(iv) to the diversity of post-war pursuits of locally determined political-cultural projects.

The post-war period is read, therefore, not simply in terms of economic growth, but much more in terms of extensive and intensive patterns of economic, social and cultural change. Thereafter, the matter of social welfare is read in terms of changing patterns of provision amongst different communities (for example, the provisions made by the people of a city-state such as Hong Kong are going to be rather different to those made by migrant peasant farmers in Kalimantan).

International political economy arguments

The work of international political economy recalls the classical European tradition of social theorizing, with its key concern for the emancipatory elucidation of the dynamics of complex change, and points to the historical development experience of region which is grasped as a series of phases whereby the indigenous civilizations of the area are remade in the process of being drawn into the industrial-capitalist system which experience provides the basis for later autonomous national action within an increasingly regionalized and internationalized economic space (Strange, 1988; Preston, 1998).

The historical particularity of the route to the modern world undertaken by the countries of East Asia is noted; as is the historical particularity of the patterns of social welfare deployed within the societies of the countries of East Asia.

(Related) political philosophical and epistemological arguments

The arguments lodged within the boundaries of particular disciplines affirm complex sets of assumptions as they pursue their several areas of concern. A further set of assumptions are involved in all and any enquiry and these relate to the purposes and procedures of analysis.

In terms of classical European political philosophy we can distinguish, broadly, liberalism, which takes the world to be comprised of discrete individuals whose aggregate actions constitute society via the invisible hand of the market place plus the moral imperatives of tradition, and which may be understood only to a very limited extent (Locke, Smith, Spencer (Held, 1987), and democracy, which insists on the inevitably social nature of human life and on the necessity of collective well-being for individual well-being, such well-being being secured via the collective political actions of actors knowledgeable about an extensively intelligible social world (Rousseau, left-Ricardianism, Marx [Held, 1987]).

In turn these two could be distinguished from liberal-democracy, which attempts to compromise between these two positions such that the state, the agent which deploys the extensive but imperfect knowledge available, secures both a minimum collective provision and the framework for individual actions (J.S. Mill [Held, 1987]), and social-democracy which acknowledges the social nature of human life, insists that social life can be understood extensively, and proposes that a technically competent elite should secure and deploy such understanding (Saint-Simon, Hobhouse, Fabians [Held, 1987]).

The statements here represent abstract versions of complex sets of ideas that have found their routine expression in real-world political and social conflicts, and disentangling the philosophical elements of, say, the delimited-formal ideology of a political party is going to be quite tricky. In particular, it must be acknowledged that the distinctions between democracy and social-democracy, in abstract theory and real-world practice, are none too clear and probably are not fixed.

The crucial distinction, so far as I can see, is in regard to the nature of the knowledge of the social world that is in principle obtainable and the extent of its spread in society, and relatedly the possible manner of its deployment. In brief, do we rely upon experts deploying hard won technical knowledge on behalf of the majority, or do we suppose that the requisite dialogically recoverable knowledge is widely distributed through society. It would seem that both liberalism and democracy grant (differently) that agents are knowledgeable whereas liberal-democracy and social-democracy in Europe have tended to look to technical expert knowledge.

In respect of economic development and social welfare a range of positions are possible: (i) (market) liberals look to autonomous individuals knowledgeable about their own desires, which are secured in the marketplace, thus social order is spontaneous and welfare follows on behind economic advance; (ii) democrats look to social-individuals with extensive knowledge coming to rational agreement about economic development and social welfare, which are collectively secured; (iii) liberal-democrats and social-democrats look to the elite in control of the state which thereafter corrects for either market or social failures in order to achieve development and social welfare.

In brief, underlying the arguments of disciplines and, in a different sphere of activity, political policies, there are complex sets of culture-bound assumptions about both (a) what ought and ought not to be pursued, and (b) what can and cannot be effectively secured in society.

Conclusion on lines of theoretical reflection

The hermeneutic-critical line of work within the social sciences stresses the role played by the context-dependent theoretical machineries deployed by the theorist to make sense of the world.

In which case, it is clear that there are a number of ways of construing the issue of economic growth and social welfare in East Asia. (This approach can be contrasted with more familiar empiricist strategies of enquiry which either seek to describe/explain the world as it is given in routine understanding, or seek to describe/explain/model the world as it is given in routine understanding in order to inform the policy making of states).

If we turn to consider particular debates we can see how various strands of argument are woven together in order to make substantive claims.

Particular debates (grasping the system)

The line of disciplines based argument noted above are the bases for substantive analyses. The materials are run together in a variety of ways in order to produce a variety of argument (or, to put the matter more familiarly, to address a variety of issues). We can briefly consider two contrasting debates: (i) the World Bank's treatment of the 'East Asian Miracle'; and (ii) Ron Dore's sociology of economics.

The World Bank's East Asian Miracle

The World Bank is one of the institutional locations of the market-liberal project. The intellectual claims of the Bank in respect of the development experience of East Asia found recent expression in a report entitled The East Asian Miracle. (World Bank, 1993). The Bank's report deals with the four tigers of Hong Kong, Taiwan, South Korea and Singapore, plus Indonesia, Malaysia and Thailand, and Japan. After a review of their performance the document acknowledges that something different has happened in East Asia whilst continuing to insist on the priority of markets.

In the Bank's analysis, at the outset, these countries are taken out of their historical context and represented in technical language as members of a descriptive economic category, the high performing Asian economies (HPAEs). Thereafter a comparative review of the standard agency data in pursuit of general and technical lessons is possible. The descriptive factors mentioned include high growth rates, a measure of equality in growth and sharply improved human welfare.

The Bank offers an explanation for this successful record in terms of 'getting the basics right' (1993, p.5) and this is taken to include: (i) private domestic investment and human capital growth; (ii) sound development policy; and (iii) government intervention. The first two factors cited are anodyne (although, clearly states can get these things wrong). It is with the final point that we meet the omni-present theme of the report, how to deal with the ideologically unpalatable record of state-directed success. The Bank makes two moves: (i) methodology is invoked, thus whilst success has occurred it is difficult to be precise about the role of government intervention (maybe success happened for other reasons); (ii) the HPAEs are disaggregated and the role of intervention played down, thus there seems to have been some successful interventions in Northeast Asia, but fewer in Southeast Asia, and the later may have more lessons outside the region than the former. Finally, the policy record of the governments of the HPAEs is summarised, in an exercise in theoretical persuasive definition, as 'market-friendly' (1993, p.10).

The report is interesting in that the Bank systematically misreads descriptive material in the light of its apriori commitment to a market-liberal policy stance. The HPAEs become merely a somewhat eccentric and unreplicable variant of the standard liberal-market model espoused by the Bank.

The material of the World Bank report can be treated as political rhetoric, but the contestedness of the lessons of the historical development experience of East Asian countries within the present spread of international financial institutions must be noted. The assertion of the novelty of the East Asian experience is a matter of interest for the Japanese, a matter of celebration for leaders such as Malaysia's Mahathir and Singapore's Lee Kuan Yew, and it is quite clear that the denial of these claims is a matter of anxious concern for the USA (Wade, 1996; Higgot, 1998).

Ron Dore's sociology of economics

The tradition of institutional economic analysis argues that all economic systems are necessarily lodged within social systems, in turn located within cultures, which are thereafter shaped and understood by agents with reference to distinct moral and intellectual traditions (Streeten, 1972;

Hodgson, 1988; Preston, 1996). The patterns of economic life of peoples are diverse and each has its own logic. The proponents of institutional economics regard the claims of market-liberal theorists to the universal relevance of their model of rational-calculative economic behaviour in juridically regulated market systems as ideological (in the pejorative sense [Gray, 1998]). In Gudeman's (1986) terms their purported universal model is simply one more local model. The institutional line of economic analysis is itself diverse, but it is the concern for the detail of patterns of social life which is important.

An influential contribution to the debates about the nature of the Japanese economy which does access the detail of social relationships has been made by Ronald Dore. It is clear from Dore's work that there is a distinctive notion of social welfare lodged within their distinctive economic system.

Dore (1986) has analysed the corporatist political-economy of Japan and shown how it contrasts with the regulated competitive liberal-market system of the USA. Dore (1986, pp.20-25) describes the sectors of the Japanese economy and notes that the core manufacturing sector is both ordered (with cross shareholdings, industry organisations, supportive banking, and various networks of suppliers and customers) and has strong links to the politico-bureaucratic establishment. Dore (1986, p.25) calls it a 'developmental' industrial-capitalist political-economy. It is this character which allows the Japanese state-regime to respond to patterns of change within the global system effectively, creatively and prospectively (thus change is not mere reaction), and this subtlety of response is the key to its success. Dore pursues this argument in three main areas: (i) the enterprise; (ii) the workers; and (iii) the government.

The enterprise works as a community. There is an internal commitment towards those who run the firm. And the firm itself works within an ordered-market environment. This allows both long-termism and confidence builds amongst the various players (employees, managers, customers, suppliers, bankers, and ministries). At the level of individual firms there is ferocious competition but thereafter there is an acknowledgement of the collectivity of producers - the system manages to combine both competition and cooperation. Dore (1986) speaks of 'relational contracting' whereby links with customers and suppliers are read as broader than orthodox market-liberal ideas of 'spot-contracting' allow.

The workers are employed within a firm understood as a family, which responds to trading conditions collectively. In adverse conditions the firm as family attempts to accommodate and sacking people is a rare and last resort. With this management commitment employees are able to be flexible about their work and wages.

The government offers a spread of encouragements and services to retrain, redeploy and reassure employees in the matter of change. Plus, of course, through most of the post-war period the economy has been expanding, and this makes things easier. As regards the enterprise the government has a role via industry associations, Ministry of International Trade and Industry, available high savings and the long established links of administrative guidance. In sum, a way of intervening extensively, cooperatively and subtly in the overall character and direction of the economy and society.

Dore (1986) insists that Japan is to be regarded as a corporatist system and that orthodox market-liberal economics has no intellectual purchase or relevance. And Dore can see no reason why a successful corporatist economy should change. In a developmental political-economy, productive efficiency is more important than allocative efficiency (the concern of market-liberal economic theory), and it depends upon an idea of society being fair (that is having an ethical base), and in turn this requires corporatist arrangements in regard to consensus building within society about collective social goals.

These arguments have been influential and notwithstanding further reflection (which illuminates, for example, the contribution of political/managerial repression of militant trade unionism in the early post-war years [Henshall, 1999, pp.158-159]) the system is routinely characterized as 'corporatist' (Appelbaum and Henderson, 1992; Sheridan, 1993, 1998; Tsuru, 1993). Indeed, Clammer (1997) argues that the fundamental social relations constituting the system (concerns for harmony, hierarchy, tradition and emotion) reveal a profoundly ordered society which is concerned to reproduce throughout the social world the reciprocity and intimacy of personal relationships.

Conclusion on the substantive analyses

A series of points can be made.

The general analyses of the World Bank are one key vehicle of the articulation and dissemination of the 'Washington consensus'. We might offer the following comments: (i) the Washington consensus is widely influential; (ii) the institutions promulgating the consensus are very powerful; and (iii) the intellectual core of their work is best read as a (market-liberal) 'local model'.

The analysis of the East Asian Economic Miracle is interesting for three broad reasons: (i) as an intellectually interesting exercise in defensive apologetics for the Washington consensus; (ii) as a politically interesting exercise in granting that the state has had some role to play in East Asia (a line of deference to the Japanese); and thereafter (iii) for its acknowledgement of the linkage between high growth, equality and improved welfare.

The data record that the countries of the region have experienced sustained high economic growth rates along with relatively equal patterns of advance within countries. The relationship between the individual and the collectivity is specific to cultures. The market-liberal notion of an autonomous self contracting in a rational-calculative manner with similar selves in order to secure personal wants is merely another 'local model'.

The liberal route to social welfare is to see it as an individual responsibility with any collective provision offered only to ameliorate given social incompetences. The democratic route looks to collective provision of the needs of the denizens of that collectivity. The social-democratic and liberal-democratic positions insist that authoritative collective provision and personal concern are both necessary.

In Japan the situation is radically different. The individual is lodged within a network of persons to whom responsibility is owed and from whom routine support can be expected. This pattern of cultural expectations is general (it is reproduced in the economy, society and polity). The 'provision of social welfare' is thus accomplished through its wide routine distribution throughout the social world.

Case studies: Singapore, Japan and Taiwan

The classical European tradition of social theorizing (recently usefully restated as structural/critical international-political economy) points to the importance in ordering change of the key groups in any polity who are able to deploy the power of the state-machine to promulgate specific political-cultural projects, where such projects reflect not merely the interests of the ruling group, but, rather more immediately, their reading of the constraints and opportunities afforded by the global system structures within which perforce they operate (Strange, 1988). Any political-cultural project will both plot a route to the future and seek to mobilize the local population in its support. This is clear in our three case studies; which are Singapore, Japan and Taiwan. In each it can be seen that an historically distinct version of 'social welfare' serves to bind the population into the political-cultural project of the ruling elite.

Singapore - an Asian social democracy

The original ideological commitments of the People's Action Party (PAP) core-group of English educated professionals, all of whom had made what Anderson (1983) dubs colonial pilgrimages, are best regarded as social-democratic, thus their early programme embraced demands for an end to colonial rule, the formation of a unitary Malayan state and a spread of social and economic development ideas which may be summed as the pursuit of national development (Fong nd). The circumstances and future of a peripheral capitalist formation are theorized by a group of English educated professionals, and the shift to independence thus entails a very significant measure of intellectual, as well as political-economic, continuity. Subsequently, the delimited-formal ideology of the ruling core-group of the PAP undergoes a series of changes as the new nation-state, ordered by an activist state, responds to events in the wider world system.

Over the early period 1954-68 the PAP runs through a series of overlapping and cross cutting political battles: to secure independence, their power and thereafter to mobilize the population in the search of growth and welfare goals. The PAP achieved internal self-government in 1959 with their indigenized programme of social democracy.

Securing the hegemony of the PAP was a complex and drawn-out matter. In the run-up to the 1959 election the PAP fought against other pro-independence parties and they distinguished themselves by making a successful alliance with the left wing unions and Chinese students. After securing internal power there was a confused interval which involved two areas of manoeuvre: the Malaysian Federation issue and relatedly the PAP elite's struggle with its erstwhile allies, the unions/students. The battle against the left unions/students, which had taken institutional form with the establishment in 1962 of Barisan Socialis, was tilted firmly in the direction of the PAP by the expedient of Operation Cold Store, the detention of some one hundred political opponents. The union with Malaysia lasted from September 1963 to August 1965 and after separation Barisan Socialis withdrew its remaining members from parliament and the PAP hegemony was established. George (1973) identifies Israel as the PAP model, with a militarized and hierarchical state which used routine political repression.

In establishing the early mobilizing state the civil service, armed forces, community organisations, media and so on, were all used for securing PAP's economic, political and socio-cultural goals. The PAP's socio-cultural mobilization followed on this recruitment/cooption of the population in general, which latter becomes straightforward social engineering, and entailed the dissemination of PAP official ideology through many channels: media, unions, community level organisations, schools, parliament, state occasions etc. Relatedly, we have the blocking of alternative messages through control of media, and cooption or suppression of alternate centres of thinking.

The pursuit of growth and welfare was central to the political project of the PAP, and this programme was vigorously pursued through efforts to diversify the economic base of the country, to industrialize and to provide minimum welfare services in the shape of health, schooling, housing and jobs. Goh Keng Swee's growth policies involved fiscal incentives and infrastructural development, after independence there is a shift from Import Substituting Industrialization to Export Oriented Industrialization strategies so as to address the problems of withdrawal from Malaysia, Singapore's established trade area. One key strategy, for economic growth and social welfare has been the Central Provident Fund (CPF), which is an important saving and welfare mechanism with its forced saving for old age (Asher, 1985).

In Singapore one can note characteristic features of state-regime actions: the relentless promulgation of the idea of economic growth, taken as a non-ideological pragmatic course of action requiring a disciplined population; relatedly, again presented as pragmatic, the design of social institutions to express and channel this mobilization-for-growth (thus schools, urban planning, ethnic-identities, language policy, industrial planning); and similarly, the extreme care shown by the state-regime to control incoming cultural-messages which expressed itself in direct controls of the media, to exclude unwanted material and deploy desired messages, plus the typical Singapore-state campaigns (for clean streets, against long hair, against cigarettes, for politeness, etc), all designed to maintain the population's mobilization-for-growth. At this point we may ask two questions: how has this been read by the elite and how has it been read by the masses?

So, for the elite, we can see an early espousal of social democracy which becomes ever more technocratic and authoritarian. One can speculate that this has something to do not just with the inherent logic of social-democracy (thus in the absence of effective checks and balances and opposition it tends to the authoritarian-technocratic) but with the elites realization of the exposed position which their policies had lead them to vis-à-vis the world system. Here technocratic-authoritarianism might be taken as a response to realized relative weakness. On the other hand, for the masses, they have been subject to the relentless exhortation of the PAP to work hard to secure the pragmatic achievement of economic growth, and they now have: (i) a remarkable record of material prosperity; and (ii) a high cultural and political price to pay - and with the latter there is evidence that the younger generation are increasingly unhappy with the costs, arguing both that they do not need an authoritarian government, and that as Singapore moves to a high-tech knowledge-based economy the repression is inappropriate (Chua, 1995).

Overall, when we consider the polity of modern Singapore we have to begin with the achievement of many social-democratic goals in Singapore under Lee Kuan Yew. Lee took the poor legacy of the colonial power and secured employment, schools, housing and health for the people of Singapore. Subsequently, in November 1990 Goh Chok Tong took over from Lee Kuan Yew and the first statement of the new governments official ideology was published in the form of a lavishly illustrated book entitled Singapore: The Next Lap (1991) which plots a route to a future as a developed nation playing both a global role, as an Asian 'hub city', and a regional role as part of a 'growth triangle' taking in Johor and Riau. The stress throughout is on upgrading so as to meet ever more demanding global system demands. All of which seems to represent a re-packaging of extant lines of successful development.

Japan - the preference for harmony and the elite sponsored pursuit of national development

The shift to the modern world in Japan was an ordered 'revolution-from-above' which saw the long-established Tokugawa Shogunate displaced in favour of a reforming oligarchy established under the aegis of the Emperor Meiji. The Meiji elite reconstructed the form-of-life of the Japanese in their pursuit of a strategy of economic growth and regional security. This fundamental political-cultural project continues to shape the form-of-life of the contemporary Japanese (Preston, 2000).

Many commentators on Japan have suggested that there is a core to the culture of the Japanese and it can be found in the notion of 'groupism'. The standard story in respect of Japan stresses that the country has a conformist character, that Japanese people are happiest in groups. It is possible to invoke natural explanations for this groupism. Buckley (1990, p.83) offers one version which argues from an urban society with a dense population to the need to avoid excessive confrontation with other people. Buckley also offers a second version by noting a past occasion in the demands of agricultural work for cooperation. The traditional rural focus on the group has thus been passed down to the urban present and reused in school, and workplace and politics. Richie (1987, pp.36-39) offers an example: a young man gains employment as an assistant in a sushi bar and comes under pressure to make a commitment to his workplace group by having a tattoo applied to his back, and at first refuses, and is bullied, and then agrees and is made welcome as new member of this particular little family. This preference for groupism is repeated, it is suggested, at a national level in the stress on the Japanese as a uniquely homogeneous people (and thus all one big group). Buckley (1990, pp.97-99) notes that this idea is widely accepted and routinely expressed.

However, in social science terms the issue is not so clear. Eccleston (1989) argues that Japanese society does manifest conflict, which is routinely controlled, and that the ideology of groupism - which is offered at levels of individual psychologies and the national - serves as a block to critical reflection. And van Wolferen (1989), who analyses Japanese system as a series of overlapping essentially elite power networks, argues that the invocation of 'culture' is precisely an ideological cover for the actual practices of Japanese society which he takes to be routinely repressive. However, whilst it is true that social order can be explained in terms of social control mechanisms (an external and mechanical explanation) it is also the case that social order can be explained in terms of the system embracing its participants, thus Sugimoto (1997) speaks of a 'friendly authoritarianism'.

In contrast, Clammer (1995, p.103) suggests that the 'philosophical principle underlying most Japanese social thinking is not, as it is so often vulgarly supposed, groupism or its variants...but harmony'. The notion is a product of religious traditions, in particular Buddhism, and the historically generated and carefully sustained pattern of life of the Japanese. It can be said that society is prioritized in Japanese culture and the individual is derivative. The self is relational and Western style individualism is read as selfishness, the cardinal social sin.

Clammer (1995) argues that Japan is neglected in Western social theorizing. Some theorists look to political-economy and some offer culturalist explanations, but both are partial, however an adequate analysis requires changes in the epistemological underpinnings of analysis in order to grasp the essence of Japanese life. Clammer (1995, p.7) suggests that one key is '...seeing Japanese social project as a huge anti-alienation device and as such a profoundly utopian one. Ideas which seem to lie outside of social theory...(the principle of interdependence, the desire for harmony, the centrality of emotion rather than reason, the aestheticisation of life, the search for wisdom in nature and the acceptance of the body) prove to be central'. The Japanese social world is highly ordered (constructed). Clammer (1995, p.8) argues that 'the negotiated reality has to be placed squarely in the context of a society where the historical continuity of certain aspects of social structure, such as emphasis on hierarchy, is very marked'. And, he continues (1995, p.8) it 'is this that creates a dialectic between the demands of reciprocity at the personal level and the equally insistent demand for stability in social relations in general. Or, put in a slightly different way, a central requirement of Japanese social organisation is to maintain the intimacy of face to face relationships (in the workplace, school, neighbourhood and family) while extending that reciprocity from purely personal interaction to the constitution of the society as a whole'. The familiar means-end rationality of the West does not exhaust rationality in Japan. Emotion, aesthetics and demands of community also figure. The self has long been decentered in Japan.

The mix of modern industrial capitalism and tradition has caused comment and a recent attempt to grasp these matters, reports Clammer (1995, p.13), has been cast in terms of modernity and postmodernity. The contemporary form of urban life in Japan looks postmodernist. Some have argued that it is. Others have argued that it always has been. Against these debates, Clammer (1995, p.15) points out that postmodernism is a western notion. It comes in lots of varieties. And applied to Japan it looks odd: (i) yes, urban culture is full of consumerism, but it is contained within a distinctively Japanese cultural sphere (Clammer, 1997); (ii) yes, the self is decentered, but it is located in patterns of social relations not the postmodernist realm of freely chosen consumption; (iii) yes, calculative reason is not crucial, but the subjective self thereafter identified cannot be grasped in terms relating to Freud, as is case in West, rather it points to realm of emotions; and (iv) yes, public grand political metanarratives are absent, but there is a strong sense of 'Japanese-ness' in its place which finds concrete expression in formalized aesthetics such as the tea ceremony.

The Japanese decentered self is located in community and everyday life is humanistic. Clammer (1995) reports that the personal is reproduced in other spheres, school, office or club. This is not a society of expressive individualism. There has been no epochal shift, rather as socially constructed cultural practices are continually reworked, enfolding tradition is reaffirmed. In general, therefore, 'Japan has thus neither achieved...or overcome...the modern: it has by-passed it by establishing and following a project quite unlike that of the Enlightenment' (Clammer, 1995, p.23). Indeed, Japan has its own cultural logic. 'Japanese society, unlike the postmodernist image of contemporary society, remains deeply humanist' (Clammer, 1995, p.30) and it is unpacking this logic, which binds individual and community, which is key to understanding Japan.

In summary, Clammer reports that:

> The project of Japanese society is genuinely utopian: an attempt to create harmony. The theme of harmony, however much empirically contradicted in practice, remains an ideal, another indigenous metatheory of Japanese life, something to be realized as people subordinate selfish goals to collective aims, and as they perceive their dependency on others - children on parents, teachers and peers, sportspeople on their coaches, those why have trained with and on their audiences, and so on. This attitude, reproduced endlessly in daily life...makes the Japanese an interesting race of deconstructionists: in the text of the individual there is no author, but a multiplicity of formative forces. No one autonomously writes his own life: it is co-authored by those who form, accidentally or by design, the individuals social universe...Human life is accepted as transitory, difficult and often tragic and human beings as weak, confused and eternally living in an environment of moral ambiguity. But the human condition can be, if not totally transformed or transcended, at least alleviated, and this can best be done not by radical individualism or through radical liberty, but through discipline: submission to and mastery of an art, a skill and, at the highest level, of relationships themselves (Clammer, 1995, p.103).

The particular form-of-life of the Japanese is made the key to understanding state policy making (to cast matters in a more familiar form) by Sheridan (1994, p.1), who argues for new directions in Japanese life, roughly a Japanese version of European social-democracy, and she insists that such a proposal is not utopian because the history of Japan reveals a series of 'dominant purposes', which have changed from time to time, whereby the country deliberately chooses a national direction.

It is clear, notes Sheridan (1994, p.1), that there has been extensive discussion of Japan's successful industrialization and many explanations have been offered by outsiders, including, pointing to a submissive culture enabling mobilization, the role of government, and a neglect of welfare in favour of development. Some in Japan rehearse these arguments and look for a shift from state to marketplace as the economy matures. Sheridan (1994, p.3) does not agree, arguing that unaided market forces did not determine Japan's development in the past and need not in the future unless their is a political decision that they should. Sheridan argues four points: (i) that Japan's government does not intervene in the economy from the outside but is an integral part of it; (ii) that it is possible to identify deliberate changes in economic and national direction in the past; (iii) the capacity for making such choices still exist; and (iv) it is possible therefore to offers a programmatic new direction focused on increasing the welfare of the people.

The role of the government was never an addition to a functioning or developing free market economy, rather it was deeply involved in moving Japanese economic activity forwards, from agrarian feudal to industrial capitalist. Sheridan (1994, p.46) says: 'The case of Japan may be seen as one in which the government translated the greater portion of its national aims directly into economic terms, and consequently pursued economic development to the maximum extent'. In other words, this is a matter of broad mobilization, the pursuit of a political-cultural project, formulated by the elite and disseminated through the population.

The four basic aspects of Japanese government intervention identified by Sheridan (1994, p.54) include: (i) the notion of the 'state economy,' which asserts that the state must secure the general interests of the community; (ii) integrated policies for growth, equity and welfare; (iii) competent public authorities; and (iv) a cooperative relationship between planners and market. In the case of Japan national development goals are routinely translated into economic terms via this system of intervention. This is a distinctive trait of the Japanese system. Sheridan (1994, p.90) adds that the government was committed to welfare, not as a separate sphere to economic growth, as in the West, but as an integral element of development.

In respect of Japanese welfare Sheridan (1994, p.93) notes a series of familiar views: (i) growth at the cost of equity - which suggests growth was key and welfare ignored; (ii) growth without welfare - which suggests growth based on subsistence level toil for masses; (iii) growth with increasing disposable income - suggesting Japanese story is pretty much like the western one; (iv) the need for better welfare index - suggesting that western idea of welfare-as-transfer needs to be adjusted to see the welfare effects of Japanese economic activity; and (v) Japan as welfare superpower - suggesting that mis-analysis by westerners blinds them to extensive welfare provision. Yet Sheridan (1994, p.94) insists that what is crucial in Japanese case is that policy for economic growth includes welfare, the two are not opposed as they are in Western thinking. The continuing thread in Japanese policy making is the concern of state with national development (Sheridan, 1994, p.197). The concern for national development has been central to the activities of the state and it has forged a consensus amongst the population.

Sheridan (1994, pp.212-216) comments that it has been argued that a mature economy does not need the state because the market can do the coordinating job but this is not true, because the mix of state and market is always a political decision. To shift from established Japanese model to a more market centred model, as advocated by Kenichi Ohmae (1987), would be a political decision in favour of Americanisation. This would be a mistake because the Japanese system is strong and has many quality of life tasks to which it must attend. Sheridan (1994) argues that a rational route to the future would deploy Japan's ability to make policy decisions to advance long established concerns for national development by upgrading the quality of life concerns of the mass of the people, the neglected producers.

Taiwan - successive geo-political relocations and the domestic pursuit of an independent path

The history of Taiwan in the modern period is marked by a series of exercises in externally sponsored geo-political relocation as the territory has been, by turns, a peripheral part of the Qing Empire, a colonial territory of Imperial Japan, a base for the nationalist Kuomintang and most recently the home of the Taiwanese. Reviewing this long period it can be noted that the Qing dynasty migrants to Taiwan brought with them traditional Chinese culture - paternalism, authoritarianism, familialism, Han nationalism, scholar-officialdom and anti-militarism. The Japanese period saw an infusion of Japanese Meiji rational modernizing culture. However, when the Kuomintang retreated to the island they reaffirmed the traditional Chinese values in the context of their struggle with the PRC. The gradual liberalization of recent years has allowed a more Western style political culture to develop. The political-cultural project of the contemporary Taiwanese elite reads history and context and looks to economic development and deepening regional linkages as a route to an independent stable future (Chiou, 1999).

Over this long period the material form-of-life of the people of the island has shifted away from the peasant farming typical of the pre-industrial world to a variation of the familiar theme of industrial-capitalism. One aspect of this shift has been the slow movement away from family-centered production, consumption and welfare towards the rather more disaggregated pattern typical of the modern world where consumption takes place in the home but production and welfare are organised elsewhere (Worlsey, 1984). It can also be noted that the political-cultural projects of the Qing Dynasty, Imperial Japanese and Kuomintang mobilized rule did not centrally involve social welfare. It is only recently that the issue has become part of public provision and discussion.

Taiwan was a remote territory of the Chinese empire for centuries. It began to attract mainland immigration in the seventeenth century when the Dutch established a trading base for the area in the southern part of the island. The territory was absorbed within the Chinese sphere in 1683 by the Qing Dynasty but the involvement of the mainland remained slight and the island remained a backwater. The territory only became a Chinese province in 1885. As the Chinese empire declined in the nineteenth century the territory became an objective of the expanding Japanese empire and following the Sino-Japanese war of 1894-1895 the island was ceded to the Japanese.

The Japanese inaugurated a development programme in Taiwan with a view to making the island an agricultural supplier for Japan. The Japanese built infrastructure, undertook a land reform, which reduced sub-tenancy, and eliminated some absentee landlordism, and introduced agricultural extension services. In due course agricultural production for the market and export to Japan rose. A little later in the 1930s as the Japanese economy began to shift towards the production of war materials there was a significant measure of industrialization in Taiwan. The pattern of agricultural and industrial development had the effect of weakening established landed groups without allowing the emergence of independent industrial or working class groupings. The territory developed firmly within the orbit of the colonial system.

In October 1945 the Japanese handed power to the nationalist Chinese government, and Haggard (1990) argues that the nature of Taiwanese development owes much to the political project of the Kuomintang. The Kuomintang was reorganised along Leninist lines in 1923-4 but it was a weak party with factionalism and the problem of regional warlords. Power came to center on Chiang Kai-shek and the military. The Kuomintang's attitude to the Chinese manufacturing classes was parasitic and control over finance was the means to the creation of an obedient clientistic corporatism. It was justified in terms of Sun Yat Sen's three principles, democracy, nationalism and socialism. The orientation to capitalism was restrictive. In 1945 Chiang Kai-Shek appointed a nationalist governor to Taiwan. The administration took over the Japanese colonial economy and proceeded to mismanage it (much as they had done on the mainland). In February 1947 an island wide uprising was triggered. The dissent was violently suppressed. The Kuomintang became dominant.

Rigger (1996) notes that the Kuomintang ran an authoritarian system from 1950s to mid-1980s. It is clear that the Kuomintang used standard techniques of repression and control but it also won popular legitimacy. The citizens were enmeshed in the project of the vanguard. The Kuomintang ran a series of state sponsored organisations and ran local elections which drew in local elites and ambitious citizens: a system of cooption. It was a corporatist system and the space for an independent civil society and opposition was thus highly restricted.

Rigger (1996) records that after the 1947 rebellion Taiwanese political life was very subdued. In 1972 Chiang Ching-kuo became premier and Chiang Kai shek died in 1975. However, as the economy shifted from import substituting industrialization to export oriented industrialization there was significant growth and by the mid-1970s new groups were emerging who could escape the Kuomintang's cooption techniques - independent professionals, small business men and some local politicians. There was a gradual liberalization of political life as two leadership groups emerged - professionals and local politicians. In 1986 the Democratic Progressive Party (DPP) was formed. The opposition fought within the electoral sphere but the key issues were not economic; instead the opposition called for political reform and ethnic justice (as between mainlanders and locals). Mainlanders dominated the state machine and military and enforced a Chinese cultural identity that overrode the locals' identity. Locals prospered in agriculture, small business and local politics.

The 1950 outbreak of the Korean war had seen renewed US financial support for Taiwan. The advice of US experts had coincided with elite wishes and rural reform was supported alongside import substituting industrialization. Within the Taiwan state machine technocrats in the bureaucracy had significant influence. Haggard (1990) notes that there was an ongoing debate surrounding the extent of state involvement. An issue at the back of this was the relationship between mainlanders and Taiwanese. Any private sector growth would strengthen the latter who might then launch political demands for change. Haggard (1990) recalls that by the mid 1950s the economy was showing some problems typical of import substitution industrialization strategies - viz. small domestic market, corruption and balance of payments problems. In 1958 economic policy power was concentrated in the hands of a group of reformers and a spread of reforms was launched in an attempt to reduce military spending, curb state spending, reduce consumption, encourage savings and strengthen the position of private industry in pursuit of what was to become the strategy of export oriented industrialization. The pattern of industrial development revolved around small firms. Dobbs-Higginson (1995) records that in the 1970s the state provided the infrastructure which drew such small firms into a more integrated economy. At the same time the state established capital-intensive industries. And in the early 1980s the pattern of exports to the USA resulted in very rapid local economic growth. Thereafter the late 1980s saw a relative fall in the price of oil and the revaluation of the yen, offering an opportunity for new niche markets to be developed as the overall pattern of industrial production and exporting within the region reconfigured. As the economy matures the rate of growth is expected to fall somewhat; however the economy is now operating in higher value-added spheres and is exporting capital throughout the region. A developing sphere of Taiwanese investment is in the Fujian Province, across the Formosa Strait, in China.

In 1988 Chiang Ching-kuo died and Lee Teng-hui took over and proceeded to greater liberalization. Overall, in the late 1980s, a process of reform-from-above was begun in the political sphere. Lee also looked to affirm a local Taiwanese identity and political culture. In recent years attempts have been made to redirect the linkages of the economy within the global system. In this case it is a matter of winding back dependence on the USA and Japan in order to look primarily to the region and thence to the countries of the OECD. However, in the case of Taiwan a major economic linkage is developing with mainland China. This is rather problematic because, as Chiou (1999) points out, the formal relationship with the PRC is very awkward. The efforts of the Taiwanese government discretely to maintain its independence from China are (arguably) being subtly undermined by mounting cross-straits economic linkages. In terms of patterns of identity, it would seem that, as East Asia changes, it could be the link to China which dominates Taiwanese thinking for the foreseeable future.

Chu (1996) discusses the implications of the years of Taiwan's rapid economic advance. In 1962 Taiwan's per capita GNP was US$162 and in 1992 it was US$10215. It is an extensive economic change. In the late 1980s there was a surge of mass conspicuous consumption. The class composition of Taiwanese society is complex with newly affluent groups. Chu (1996) identifies an old middle class, a new middle class, white collar employees and affluent workers.

First, the old middle class in post 1949 society comprised the military, civil servants and school teachers. The bulk of these were mainlanders but there were locals in the lower levels. The jobs were desirable, privileged and permanent and 'officialism' developed. After the lifting of martial law in 1987 things did improve. In recent years the loyalty of the old middle class to the KMT has declined somewhat.

Second, the new middle classes comprise the owners of small/medium sized enterprises and professionals. The state's economic polices generated economic growth and this included SME and professional groups. They were often locals rather than mainlanders. The 1950s opposition were mainlanders and the Kuomintang defeated them. However the 1970s opposition were locals with US training. They went into local politics. Eventually the DPP was formed in 1986. Chu (1996) notes that both sub-groups of the new middle class have one thing in common - they are loyal adherents of Chinese familism. The family network acts to help individual members who owe it loyalty in return. The family can help with employment, education, welfare and so on. An effective system of Chinese familialism can explain why a weak state welfare system can be tolerated. An economic key is the habit of saving. The savings of the family are the base for its support and welfare activities.

Third, the lower white collar employees are a new group and they spend their incomes on status goods; since economic advance has priced them out of the property market at the same time as the easy money of the late 1980s encouraged their consumption oriented behaviour. The pursuit of consumption has led to a decline in saving. It may be that this will lead to pressure for state supplied welfare. There has also been a movement away from familism.

Fourth, Taiwan's affluent workers are beneficiaries of the years of economic growth. There are signs that they are anxious to keep their position. But there are also signs of a concern for welfare.

In all, argues Chu (1996), the economic growth of last thirty years has impacted differentially on Taiwanese society. Each group seems to have its own concerns, and there is no particular sign of collective action.

Conclusion

In the cases of Singapore, Japan and Taiwan it can be seen that patterns of economic development and social welfare are quite distinctive. Again, in the cases of Singapore, Japan and Taiwan it can be seen that extant patterns of economic development and social welfare have accumulated over time, being products of history. In each country the political elite has pursued a political-cultural project of national development. And in each country the pattern of welfare services has been intended to bind the population into the political-cultural project of the ruling elite.

From the outset it was clear that a series of key terms in the debate in respect of the East Asian experience of growth and welfare would need to be revisited in order to displace any disposition to read them as unproblematical. Thus, it can be safely asserted that the idea of economic development is both context-dependent and highly contested. In a similar way the idea of social welfare is context-dependent and highly contested. It is further clear that the matter of their relationship is contested. Thereafter, we can insist that the pursuit of growth and welfare is not some sort of neutral process, it is political.

At which point matters might seem to be enough complicated but, in fact, there is a further layer of difficulty which must be acknowledged because the grasp that any social scientists can obtain on these ideas is itself context-dependent. It seems clear, in other words, that any claims or recommendations which social scientists might want to make about growth and welfare had best be seen to be tentative, provisional and dialogic (that is, open to revision in conversation with other thinkers and actors).

Notes

1 An earlier version of this paper was presented at the Welfare and Growth in Asia Conference, held at The University of Birmingham, April 1999. The author is grateful for the comments received.
2 I distinguish market-liberalism (that is, sets of philosophical, political and policy ideas, where clearly there are other strands of liberal thinking), and liberal-markets (that is, economic/social systems, where clearly there are many ways of ordering markets - on this see Gudeman, 1986; Dilley, 1992).

References

Anderson, B. (1983), *Imagined Communities*, Verso, London.
Appelbaum, R. and Henderson, J. (1992), *States and Development in the Asian Pacific Rim*, Sage, London.
Asher, M.G. (1985), *Forced Saving to Finance Merit Goods*, Australian National University, Canberra.
Berger, P.L. and Hsiao, H.M. (eds) (1988), *In Search of an Asian Development Model*, Transaction Books, New Brunswick.
Buckley, R. (1990), *Japan Today*, Cambridge University Press, Cambridge.
Chalmers, I. (1992), *'Weakening State Controls and Ideological Change in Singapore'* in Asia Research Centre Working Paper, Murdoch University, Australia.
Chan Heng Chee (1971), *Singapore The Politics of Survival*, Oxford University Press, Singapore.
Chiou, C.L. (1999), 'Taiwan: A Democratizing Strategic Culture' in Ken Booth and Russel Trood (eds) *Strategic Cultures in the Asia-Pacific Region*, Macmillan, London.
Chong, A. (1991), *Goh Chok Tong: Singapore's New Premier*, Pelanduk Publications, Petaling Jaya.
Chu, J.J. (1996), 'A fragmented middle class in the making' in R. Robison and D. Goodman (eds) (1996), *The New Rich in Asia*, Routledge, London.
Chua Beng Huat (1995), *Communitarian Ideology and Democracy in Singapore*, Routledge, London.
Clammer, J. (1995), *Difference and Modernity*, Kegan Paul International, London.
Clammer, J. (1997), *Contemporary Urban Japan*, Blackwell, Oxford.
Dobbs-Higginson, M. (1995), *Pacific Asia: Its Role in the New World Disorder*, Mandarin, London.
Dore, R. (1986), *Flexible Rigidities*, Stanford University Press, Stanford C.A.
Eccleston, B. (1989), *State and Society in Post-War Japan*, Polity, Cambridge.
Fong Sip Chee no date *The PAP Story - The Pioneering Years*
George, T.L.S. (1973), *Lee Kuan Yew's Singapore*, Andre Deutsch, London.
Giddens, A. (1979), *Central Problems in Social Theory*, Macmillan, London.
Gudeman, S. (1986), *Economics as Culture*, Routledge, London.
Haggard, S. (1990), *Pathways from the Periphery: The politics of the newly industrializing countries*, Cornell University Press.
Held, D. (1987), *Models of Democracy*, Blackwell, Oxford.
Henshall, K.G. (1999), *A History of Japan*, Macmillan, London.
Higgot, R. (1998), 'The Asian Economic Crisis: A Study in the Politics of Resentment', in *New Political Economy*, Vol. 3, 3.
Hodgson, G. (1988), *Economics and Institutions*, Polity, Cambridge.
Gray, J. (1998), *False Dawn: The Delusions of Global Capitalism*, Granta, London.
Krugman, P. (1994), 'The Myth of Asia's Miracle' in *Foreign Affairs*.

Pang Eng Fong (1988), 'The distinctive features of two city states: Hong Kong and Singapore' in P.L. Berger and H.M. Hsiao (eds) *In Search of an Asian Development Model*.

Preston, P.W. (1996), *Development Theory*, Blackwell, Oxford.

Preston, P.W. (1998), *Pacific Asia in the Global System*, Blackwell, Oxford.

Review Publishing Company 1991 *Asia 1991 Yearbook*, Hong Kong.

Richie, B. (1987), *Geisha, Gangster, Neighbour, Nun*, Kodansha, Tokyo.

Rigger, S. (1996), 'Mobilisational authoritarianism and political opposition in Taiwan' in G. Rodan (ed) *Political Oppositions in Industrializing Asia*, Routledge, London.

Rodan, G. (1992), 'Singapore's Leadership Transition: Erosion or Refinement of Authoritarian Rule' in *Bulletin of Concerned Asian Scholars*.

Sheridan, K. (1993), *Governing the Japanese Economy*, Polity, Cambridge.

Sheridan, K. (1998), *Emerging Economic Systems in Asia*, Allen and Unwin, St. Leonards.

Shin Min Daily News Series (1991), *From Lee Kuan Yew to Goh Chok Tong*, Singapore.

Stanley, T.A. (1988), 'Japan as a Model for Development: the Example of Singapore' in G.L. Bernstein and H. Fuki (eds), *Japan and the World: Essays on Japanese History and Politics in Honour of Ishida Takeshi*, Macmillan, London.

Strange, S. (1988), *States and Markets*, Pinter, London.

Streeten, P. (1972), *The Frontiers of Development Studies*, Macmillan, London.

Sugimoto, Y. (1997), *An Introduction to Japanese Society*, Cambridge University Press, Cambridge.

The Government of Singapore (1991), *Singapore The Next Lap*, Singapore.

Tsuru, S. (1993), *Japan's Capitalism*, Cambridge University Press, Cambridge.

von Wolferen, K. (1989), *The Enigma of Japanese Power*, Tuttle, Tokyo.

Wade, R. (1990), *Governing the Market: Economic Theory and the Role of Government in East Asian Industrialization*, Princeton University Press.

Wade, R. (1996), 'Japan, the World Bank and the Art of Paradigm Maintenance: The East Asian Miracle in Political Perspective' in *New Left Review*, 217.

World Bank (1993), *The East Asian Miracle: Economic Growth and Public Policy*, Oxford University Press, Oxford.

Name Index

Subject Index